LEARNING THE LAW

LEARNING THE LAW

By

GLANVILLE WILLIAMS, Q.C., LL.D., F.B.A.

Honorary and Emeritus Fellow of Jesus College, Cambridge;
Honorary Bencher of the Middle Temple;
formerly Professor of Public Law and Quain
Professor of Jurisprudence in the University of London,
and Rouse Ball Professor of English Law
in the University of Cambridge.

"A man has but one youth, and considering the
consequences of employing that well, he has reason
to think himself very rich, for that gone, all the
wealth in the world will not purchase another."
Sir R. North, *On the Study of the Laws.*

ELEVENTH EDITION

INDIAN ECONOMY REPRINT 2010

Universal
Law Publishing Co. Pvt. Ltd.
NEW DELHI - INDIA

First Edition	1945	Eighth Edition	1969
Second Edition	1945	Ninth Edition	1973
Second Impression Revisd	1946	Second Impression	1974
Third Impression	1948	Tenth Edition	1978
Third Edition	1950	Eleventh Edition	1982
Fourth Edition	1953	Second Impression	1984
Fifth Edition	1954	Third Impression	1986
Sixth Edition	1957	Fourth Impression	1986
Seventh Edition	1963	Fifth Impression	1988
Second Impression	1966	Sixth Impression	1990
Third Impression	1967	Seventh Impression	1992
Fourth Impression	1968	**Indian Economy Reprint**	**2010**

Published by
UNIVERSAL LAW PUBLISHING CO. PVT. LTD.
C-FF-1A, Dilkhush Industrial Estate
(Near Azadpur Metro Station)
G.T. Karnal Road, Delhi-110 033
Tel.: 011- 42381334, 27215334, 27438103
Fax : 011-27458529
E-mail *(For sales inquiries)* : sales@unilawbooks.com
Website : www.unilawbooks.com

This reprint of Glanville Williams: Learning the Law, 11th Edition
is published by arrangement with
SWEET & MAXWELL LTD., London

British Library Cataloguing in Publication Data

Williams, Glanville
Learning the law—11th ed.
1. Law—Great Britain—Study and teaching
1. Title
340'.07 KD432

ISBN 978-81-7534-006-0

©

Stevens & Sons

Printed in India at Taj Press, New Delhi

CONTENTS

v

CHAPTER 1

THE DIVISIONS OF THE LAW

> But in these nice sharp quillets of the law,
> Good faith, I am no wiser than a daw.
>
> —Shakespeare, *King Henry the Sixth,*
> Part 1, II, iv.

THIS little book aims to help those who have decided to study law—whether in a University or Polytechnic or Technical College or as a professional qualification.

From time to time I have been told of some who have read the book before making the decision, and have been sufficiently attracted by the taste it has given them of legal studies to make up their minds to continue. I did not, however, intend to proselytise when I wrote. As you will see if you look at Chapter 13, there are quite enough people trying to enter this profession without adding to the number. If you are uncertain about your career there may be strong personal and social reasons why you should take up something else: entering the world of commerce or industry, or becoming a technologist or research scientist. In the foreseeable future there is likely be a much greater shortage of computer experts, electronic experts, good business managers and people who combine linguistic with other abilities than there will be of lawyers. I assume, however, that you have decided to study the law. Even if you have only narrowed your immediate options to obtaining higher education in one of the humanities, I would certainly wish to bring to your notice the attraction of Law as compared with the usual Arts subjects.

Law is the cement of society and also an essential medium of change. A knowledge of law increases one's understanding of public affairs. Its study promotes accuracy of expression, facility in argument and skill in interpreting the written word, as well as some understanding of social values. Unless you want to teach, it is of wider vocational relevance than most Arts subjects. Its practice does, of course, call for much routine, careful, unexciting work; and it is for you to decide whether you think you are temperamentally suited to it.

CRIMES AND CIVIL WRONGS

One of the layman's inveterate errors is to suppose that the lawyer is largely—even exclusively—concerned with criminal law. An old chestnut that will probably be inflicted upon the reader before he has proceeded far with legal studies (so why not by me?) concerns an old lady who was being given a glimpse of the Court of Chancery. She peered round and asked where was the prisoner. (According to a gloss on the tale, someone then explained to her that a Chancery judge did not try anybody except counsel.) In fact the law is divided into two great branches, the criminal and the civil,[1] and of these much the greater is the civil. Since the nature of the division must be grasped at the outset, I shall try to give a simple explanation of it.

The distinction between a crime and a civil wrong, though capable of giving rise to some difficult legal problems, is in essence quite simple. The first thing to understand is that the distinction does *not* reside in the nature of the wrongful act itself. This can be proved quite simply by pointing out that the same act may be both a crime and a civil wrong. Occasionally at a bus station there is someone who makes a living by looking after people's impedimenta while they are shopping. If I entrust my bag to such a person, and he runs off with it, he commits the crime of theft and also two civil wrongs—the tort of conversion and a breach of contract with me to keep the bag safe. The result is that two sorts of legal proceedings can be taken against him; a prosecution for the crime, and a civil action for the tort and for the breach of contract. (Of course, the plaintiff in the latter

---

[1] "Civil law" is a phrase used in several meanings. It may mean, as in the above context, the law that is not criminal law. It may also mean the law of a State as opposed to other sorts of law like international law; or it may mean Roman law. A "civilian" is a person learned in Roman law.

action will not get damages twice over merely because he has two causes of action; he will get only one set of damages.)

To take another illustration, if a railway signalman, to dumb forgetfulness a prey, fails to pull the lever at the right moment, and a fatal accident occurs on the line, his carelessness may be regarded as sufficiently gross to amount to the crime of manslaughter, and it is also the tort of negligence towards the victims of the accident and their dependants, and a breach of his contract with the Railway Executive to take due care in his work. It will be noticed that, this time, the right of action in tort and the right of action in contract are vested in different persons.

[handwritten marginal note: This is a case/scenario very similar to Pitwood which was based on omissions.]

These examples show that the distinction between a crime and civil wrong cannot be stated as depending upon *what is done,* because what is done (or not done) may be the same in each case. The true distinction resides, therefore, not in the nature of the wrongful act but in *the legal consequences that may follow it.*[2] If the wrongful act (or omission) is capable of being followed by what are called criminal proceedings, that means that it is regarded as a crime (otherwise called an offence). If it is capable of being followed by civil proceedings, that means that it is regarded as a civil wrong. If it is capable of being followed by both, it is both a crime and a civil wrong. Criminal and civil proceedings are (in the normal case) easily distinguishable: the procedure is different, the outcome is different, and the terminology is different.

In criminal proceedings the terminology is as follows. You have a *prosecutor prosecuting* a *defendant,*[3] and the result of the prosecution if successful is a *conviction,* and the defendant may be *punished* by one of a variety of punishments ranging from life imprisonment to a fine, or else may be released on probation or discharged without punishment or dealt with in various other ways.

Turning to civil proceedings, the terminology generally is that

---

[2] Cp. *per* Lord Esher M.R. in *Seaman* v. *Burley* [1896] 2 Q.B. at 346.
[3] Formerly called "prisoner" in felonies and "defendant" in misdemeanours; felonies have now been abolished as a separate class. The term "prisoner" is invidious for one who has not yet been convicted. Instead of "the defendant" the expression "the accused" is very commonly used.

a *plaintiff*[4] *sues* (*e.g.* brings an *action* against) a *defendant*. The proceedings if successful result in *judgment for the plaintiff,* and the judgment may order the defendant to pay the plaintiff money, or to transfer property to him, or to do or not to do something (injunction), or to perform a contract (specific performance). In applications for a writ of habeas corpus or for judicial review by means of an order of mandamus, prohibition or certiorari, or otherwise, the parties are called *applicant* and *respondent* respectively. In matrimonial cases in the Family Division the parties are called *petitioner* and *respondent,* and the relief sought concerns dissolution of the marriage, consequential financial arrangements, and the custody of children.[5] (There are also other kinds of civil relief, but they need not concern us here.)

It is hardly necessary to point out that the terminology of the one type of proceedings should never be transferred to the other. "Criminal action," for example, is a misnomer; so is "civil offence" (the proper expression is "civil wrong"). One does not speak of a plaintiff prosecuting or of the criminal accused being sued. The common announcement "Trespassers will be prosecuted" has been called a "wooden lie," for trespass has traditionally been a civil wrong, not (generally) a crime. (There are some statutory offences of trespass, such as trespass on a railway line; and a "squatter" or other trespasser in a house that is occupied or required for occupation generally commits an offence if he fails to leave upon request.[6])

Again, the word "guilty" is used primarily of criminals. The corresponding word in civil cases is "liable"; but this word is also used in criminal contexts.

Civil and criminal courts are partly but not entirely distinct. The *Crown Court* has almost exclusively criminal jurisdiction. Magistrates are chiefly concerned with criminal cases, but they have important civil jurisdiction over licensing and family matters. On the other hand, the county court is only civil, and so is the *High Court* apart from appeals.

Magistrates, by the way, are one and the same as justices of

---

[4] "Complainant" in magistrates' courts, *e.g.* in matrimonial matters.

[5] The petitioner *petitions* for a divorce against the respondent; and the proceedings, if successful, result in *decree* of divorce.

[6] Criminal Law Act 1977, s.7.

the peace. Over most of the country, magistrates are lay J.P.s sitting with a clerk; even the court clerk may be legally unqualified. (The "clerk to the justices" is legally qualified, but he is often occupied with administration.) In Central London and some other large towns magistrates' courts consist of a full-time stipendiary magistrate who is a lawyer.[7] Although the names "justice of the peace" and "magistrate" are synonymous, there is a slight tendency to use the former for "the Great Unpaid" and the latter for professional magistrates. Magistrates' courts are alternatively called "courts of summary jurisdiction" and "courts of petty sessions" (though the last phrase is now pretty well obsolete).

COURTS WITH CIVIL JURISDICTION

Let us look more closely at the trial of civil cases. The courts with original[8] civil jurisdiction are chiefly the High Court and county courts.

The High Court is divided into three Divisions: the *Queen's Bench Division*, the *Chancery Division*, and the *Family Division*. The first administers primarily the common law, the second primarily equity.[9] More will be said about this particular distinction in the next chapter. The Family Division was created by an Act of 1970 in place of the previous Probate, Divorce and Admiralty Division—a curious miscellany of jurisdictions (over wills, wives and wrecks, as Sir Alan Herbert put it) which were lumped together for no better reason than they were all founded (to some extent) on Roman and canon law. In 1970, wills went to the Chancery Division and wrecks to the Queen's Bench Division.

A civil trial in the High Court is before a single judge, generally sitting without a jury. The judge may sit in London or the provinces.[10] (High Court cases outside London are often

---

[7] Known in London as metropolitan magistrates.

[8] *i.e.* jurisdiction as a court of first instance: jurisdiction other than appellate jurisdiction.

[9] In 1977 a Patents Court was set up and made part of the Chancery Division.

[10] The peregrinating High Court was formerly called the Assize Court. Trials on the civil side of assizes or with a judge and jury in London were formerly said to be *"at nisi prius."* The reason for the phrase was

taken by deputy High Court judges who are in fact circuit or county court judges or plain barristers.) Some applications to the High Court are made to a Divisional Court consisting of two or more judges of the High Court.

There is almost always the possibility of an appeal from a court of trial (called a *court of first instance*). The party who appeals is the *appellant;*[11] the other is the *respondent.* For the High Court the appropriate appellate court is the *Court of Appeal (Civil Division),* consisting essentially of the Master of the Rolls and the Lords Justices of Appeal.[12] The Court of Appeal generally sits with three members, and there will be several such courts in action at the same time.

Going down the ladder again, the less important civil cases are tried in the county courts, with appeals to the Court of Appeal. As noticed before, magistrates also have some civil jurisdiction, chiefly in matrimonial matters, guardianship, adoption, and affiliation (maintenance of illegitimate children). There are lots of these courts (320 county courts, 700 magistrates' courts staffed by 24,000 lay magistrates and 52 stipendiaries); go and look at those operating in your locality. Appeals from magistrates (by means of what is called a "case stated") go to a Divisional Court—in family matters it will be composed of judges of the Family Division.[13]

The present High Court, and the Court of Appeal on its civil side, were set up by the Judicature Act 1873. The High Court superseded the old courts of Queen's Bench, Common Pleas, Exchequer, Chancery, Probate, Divorce and Admiralty, and a

---

that, when a case arose in the provinces, it was directed to be tried in London, "unless before" the trial in London the justice of assize should come into the county to try it.

[11] Emphasis on the second syllable; so also in "appellate."

[12] Occasionally Law Lords and puisne judges sit to help with the work. Lord Denning M.R. is a Law Lord, but regularly presides in the Court of Appeal.

[13] Appeals from magistrates as to the amount of a weekly maintenance payment can be heard by a single High Court judge. Another mode of appeal from magistrates is to the Crown Court; this is a full rehearing, unlike the appeal by case stated which is theoretically only on points of law. When an appeal is taken from magistrates to the Crown Court, a further appeal lies from the Crown Court to a Divisional Court on case stated.

few minor courts. The Court of Appeal superseded the old Court of Exchequer Chamber and Court of Appeal in Chancery. Together the Crown Court, High Court and Court of Appeal make up the Supreme Court of Judicature.

When an appeal is taken to the Court of Appeal (either from the High Court or from a Divisional Court), a further appeal lies (with leave) to the *House of Lords*. Why two appeals should be allowed can be explained only by reference to history. "The institution of one court of appeal may be considered a reasonable precaution; but two suggest panic," said A. P. Herbert. It is a panic that pays no regard to the resources of suitors.

One can perhaps see the beginning of a movement of opinion against our top-heavy system. Gerald Gardiner, who afterwards became Lord Chancellor, quoted the opinion of Lord Evershed in support of the following criticism.

"The cost of appeals to the House of Lords . . . has become prohibitive save to the few or to the recipient of legal aid. One appeal is enough if the appellate court is sufficiently strong, as the Court of Appeal would be if it had the present combined strength of both tribunals. The balance of advantage and disadvantage lies in favour of a strong and final Court of Appeal, able to reconsider any previous decision."[14]

The Judicature Act 1873, which was passed by a Liberal Government, would have abolished the appellate jurisdiction of the House of Lords; but the Conservatives took office before it came into force, and repealed this provision—fearing that the abolition of the Lords as a judicial body might be the thin end of the wedge leading ultimately to their abolition as a legislative body.[15] Such fears have nothing to do with the question whether a double appeal is justifiable.

It is sometimes argued that we need the House of Lords to give a unified interpretation to statutes affecting Scotland and Northern Ireland as well as England and Wales. But no appeal lies from Scottish courts to the House of Lords in criminal cases; yet no catastrophe has occurred. If an inconvenient divergence of law arises between different parts of the United Kingdom there is always Parliament to put matters right.

[14] *Law Reform Now*, ed. G. Gardiner and A. Martin (1963) 16.
[15] See Robert Stevens, *Law and Politics* (1977) 52 *et seq.*

By way of alleviation, a civil case may go on appeal direct from the High Court to the House of Lords under the "leap-frogging" procedure introduced by the Administration of Justice Act 1969. This can happen, with the consent of the parties and on certificate from the judge, if the case turns on the construction of legislation or is governed by a previous decision of the Court of Appeal or House of Lords which one of the parties wishes to overturn.

Neglecting magistrates' courts, the system of civil judicature explained above may be represented thus:

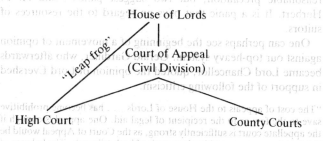

It will have been understood from what has gone before that "the House of Lords" is an ambiguous expression. It refers (1) to all the peers who choose to sit as the Upper House of the legislature (Parliament), and also (2) to a court consisting of the highest level of the judiciary. Originally the House of Lords was a single body, but a convention (understanding) grew up that only peers with exalted judicial experience should decide appeals. This was not finally established until 1844. In modern terminology it is the "Law Lords" (the Lord Chancellor, the Lords of Appeal in Ordinary, and peers who hold or have held high judicial office) who as the "Appellate Committee" of the House of Lords exercise its judicial function. The Lords of Appeal in Ordinary (like Lord Diplock and Lord Scarman) are salaried life peers appointed by way of promotion from the Lords Justices and other members of the Court of Appeal, just as the members of the Court of Appeal are appointed by promotion from the High Court. Whereas the Law Lords are truly Lords, and can take part in debates and vote in the House (though by custom the Lords of Appeal in Ordinary do so only on legal matters), the "Lords Justices" of the Court of Appeal are not Lords (peers) and cannot sit in Parliament. We refer, for example, to "Lord Justice Lawton," not "Lord Lawton."

Although, when exercising its appellate jurisdiction, the House or Lords consists exclusively of the Law Lords, it nevertheless sits in the same building as the House of Lords when meeting as a limb of the legislature; but these sittings are in a committee room instead of the House itself (except when the House is in recess).[16] Their lordships do a little play-acting by pretending to be still a legislature. They avoid saying that they are delivering judgments; instead they speak of their "opinions," or sometimes "speeches"; and they address their opinions to each other ("my Lords"), not to the parties and counsel who are their most concerned audience. Because their lordships are supposed to be speaking in Parliament, the House of Lords is not part of the Supreme Court of Judicature, even though it is the supreme tribunal.

THE CLASSIFICATION OF CIVIL WRONGS

The more important types of civil wrong may be briefly mentioned. One is the *breach of contract*. This is easy to understand, and all that the student needs to know at the outset of his studies is that a contract need not be in a formal document or indeed in any document at all. You make a contract every time you buy an apple or take a taxi.

Another civil wrong is a *tort*. This word conveys little meaning to the average layman, and its exact definition is a matter of great difficulty even for the lawyer; but the general idea of it will become clear enough if one says that torts include such wrongs as assault, battery, false imprisonment, trespass, conversion, defamation of character, negligence and nuisance. It is a civil wrong independent of contract: that is to say, it gives rise to an action for damages irrespective of any agreement not to do the act complained of. Etymologically the word comes to us from the law-French *tort,* signifying any wrong, and itself derived from the Latin *tortus,* meaning "twisted" or "wrung." And the word "wrung" is the same in origin as "wrong." (It is strange how the notion of wrong is wrapped up with that of twisting: the opposite

[16] For an interesting note, see 118 New Law Journal 1160.

of wrong is right, which is the Latin *rectus,* straight). Nowadays, however, a tort is not any wrong but only a particular kind of wrong, of which examples were given above.[17] The adjective from tort is "tortious": thus one speaks of a tortious act.

A third civil wrong is a *breach of trust.* A "trust" is not a mere obligation of honour, as the word may seem to suggest; it is an obligation enforced by the courts. Everybody has a rough idea of what a trust is; it occurs where a person, called technically a *settlor,* transfers property (such as land or shares) to another, called a *trustee,* on trust for yet another, called a *beneficiary.* (Actually the same person may combine two or even all three of these capacities; but this complication need not be considered here.) Where the trust is created by will the settlor is also called a *testator* (the name for anyone who makes a will); and an alternative name for the beneficiary is *"cestui que trust,"* an elliptical phrase meaning "he [for] whose [benefit the] trust [was created]." In this phrase *cestui* is pronounced "settee" (with the accent on the first syllable),[18] *que* is pronounced "kee," and trust as in English. Grammatically the plural should be *cestuis que trust* (pronounced like the singular); but by an understandable mistake it is sometimes written *cestuis que trustent,* as if trust were a verb.[19] The beginner will perceive by this time that several law-French words survive in our law from the time when French was the language of the upper class. In the case of a charitable trust there need be no definite beneficiary but the property is held on trust for the public as a whole or for some section of it. Thus the well-known "National Trust" preserves beautiful places for the public enjoyment, and there are many trusts for educational and religious purposes.

The only other type of civil obligation (it is not thought of as a wrong) that the beginner need hear about is the quasi-contractual obligation. Suppose that I pay you £5, mistakenly

---

[17] For a further discussion see Williams and Hepple, *Foundations of the Law of Tort* (London 1976), Chap. 1.

[18] The O.E.D. gives the pronunciation "sestwee," but this is not common among lawyers. Winfield told me that Maitland's pronunciation was the one I have given, and that is good enough authority for anyone.

[19] See Sweet in 26 L.Q.R. 196.

thinking that I owe it to you:I can generally recover it back[20] in quasi-contract. You have not agreed to pay it back, and so are not liable to me in contract; but in justice you ought to pay it back and so the law treats you as if (*quasi*) you had contracted to repay it. There are various other heads of quasi-contract besides the particular example just given, such as the obligation to repay money paid on a consideration that has failed.

COURTS WITH CRIMINAL JURISDICTION

Next, the trial of criminal cases. Crimes are divided into *indictable* (pronounced "inditeable") and *summary* offences. Indictable offences are, as the name implies, triable on indictment (pronounced "inditement"). This means that they are the more serious sort of crimes, triable by judge and jury (formerly called a petty jury) in the Crown Court.

Created by the Courts Act 1971, the Crown Court is now our main criminal court. (It has some civil jurisdiction, but only in licensing and some other minor matters.) Theoretically a single court, it is (like the High Court and Court of Appeal) in fact manifold, sitting in about 90 centres. It is the successor of the following courts (all of which used to sit with juries):

1. The criminal jurisdiction of assizes (the red-robed High Court judge on circuit);
2. Quarter sessions ("sessions" for short; here the place of the judge was taken by magistrates, or else by a professional recorder);
3. A few Crown Courts having the jurisdiction of assizes.

A criminal trial in the Crown Court is always by jury. The court is normally presided over by a *circuit judge* or *recorder,* who controls the trial and directs the jury; but it may also be constituted with a *High Court Judge.*[21] Notwithstanding their name, circuit judges do not travel a circuit; they are located in one of the circuits into which a county is divided, although they

---

[20] "Recover back," is not, in legal usage, pleonastic; *i.e.* the word "back" is not superfluous. You "recover" damages, a sum of money that you never had before. You "recover back" a certain sum of money corresponding to one that you did have at some time in the past.

[21] A judge of the Court of Appeal may sit as a High Court judge.

can take cases outside their own circuit as occasion demands. High Court judges are, on average (but only on average), more able or more experienced than circuit judges; and the theory is that they therefore try the more serious and difficult cases. But the peregrinating High Court judge is under pressure to be on his way, so while he will try a straightforward case of wounding with intent, which would be within the capacity of any judge, he will often leave a long and complicated fraud case to be tried by a circuit judge. The old name "recorder" is preserved for part-time judges who are given the same jurisdiction as circuit judges; they are allowed to continue other occupations such as practice at the Bar or as solicitors, whereas circuit judges are full time. When you visit a Crown Court you will probably see justices of the peace sitting with the circuit judge or recorder. They vote on matters of sentence, but in practice it is the professional judge or recorder who rules on the law and procedure in the course of the trial. The Crown Court sitting in the City of London (off Ludgate Hill) is still known officially as the Central Criminal Court and colloquially (never in court) as the Old Bailey (or, more frequently, the Bailey). Two of its judges (of circuit judge rank) continue to be called the Recorder and the Common Serjeant of the City of London.

Some of the centres in which the Crown Court sits are served only by circuit judges, some by High Court judges. "Practice directions" set out which indictable offences are normally allocated to a circuit judge ("lower band" offences as they have come to be called) and which require a High Court judge.[22]

Appeal from the Crown Court in criminal cases lies to the *Court of Appeal (Criminal Division).*[23] The appeal may be on law or fact or against sentence, but only the defendant can

---

[22] Technically there are four classes, not two. See Archbold, 40th ed., Chap.2, s.4.

[23] Created in 1966 and superseding the Court of Criminal Appeal, which in turn had superseded the Court for Crown Cases Reserved in 1907. The Court of Appeal (Criminal Division) sits in practice in two courts, one composed of the Lord Chief Justice, a Lord Justice of Appeal and a puisne (*i.e.* High Court) judge, and the other composed of one Lord Justice of Appeal and two puisne judges. This court and the Divisional Court occasionally sit in provincial cities such as Cardiff and Manchester.

appeal—not the Crown.[24] On a successful appeal against conviction the court will quash[25] the conviction; but it may substitute a conviction of some other offence of which the jury could have convicted.

From the Court of Appeal a further appeal lies (in important cases, with leave[26]) to the House of Lords. At this stage the appeal is open even to the prosecutor.

Crimes not triable on indictment are known as summary (formerly petty) offences; they are triable without a jury by magistrates' courts. Many crimes, though falling within the class of indictable offences, can be tried in magistrates' courts if certain conditions are satisfied; they are said to be "triable both ways."

Appeals from magistrates' courts in criminal cases are similar to those in civil cases. The defendant may appeal to the Crown Court, which rehears the whole case; there is no jury, but at least two magistrates sit with the judge or recorder. Or a case may be stated on a point of law for the decision of a Divisional Court of the Queen's Bench Division[27]; and a further appeal may be

---

[24] Apart from a purely moot appeal to settle a point of law. When a defendant is acquitted the Attorney-General may ask the Court of Appeal to rule on the law for future cases, the acquittal not being affected by the outcome of the reference: Criminal Justice Act 1972, s.36. The C.A., after giving its judgment, may also refer such cases to the House of Lords.

[25] Note the word and its spelling (neither squash nor quosh). It is cognate with modern French *casser*, as in *Cour de Cassation*. Note also that lawyers speak of *decisions* of lower courts being "reversed," while *convictions* are quashed. The verdict of a jury is "set aside."

[26] The formula is strange. The lower appeal court must certify that a point of law of general public importance is involved; and then it must appear either to that court or to the House of Lords that the point ought to be considered by the House. The C.A. frequently grants its certificate on the first point, and then refuses to grant leave on the second, in effect passing the question to the House itself. But if the matter is of general public importance (and granted that we have a second appeal court to consider it), why should not the appeal be allowed as of right? The answer has been suggested that in case of doubt the C.A. wants to leave the House to control its own list of appeals; but that is not really an answer. Cp. Prevezer in 15 Current Legal Problems 104-105.

[27] This form of appeal lies direct from a magistrates' court and also from a decision of the Crown Court on appeal from the magistrates' court.

taken from the Divisional Court (subject to restrictions) to the House of Lords. A peculiarity of the appeal by way of case stated is that it is open not only to the defendant but also to the prosecutor (whereas in trials on indictment there is no appeal from an acquittal).

The previous advice to listen to cases in court applies to every kind of court. Even when the court-room is somewhat crowded, the police and ushers will generally facilitate the entry of those who announce themselves as law students. The addresses of all courts will be found in Shaw's *Directory of Courts in England and Wales*.

The scheme of criminal courts can be represented diagrammatically as follows:

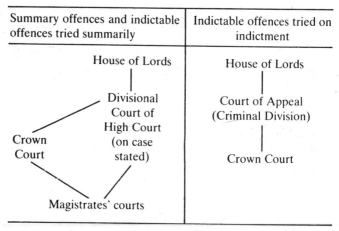

Summary offences and indictable offences tried summarily	Indictable offences tried on indictment
House of Lords Divisional Court of High Court (on case stated) Crown Court Magistrates' courts	House of Lords Court of Appeal (Criminal Division) Crown Court

The term "indictment" itself needs explanation. Originally an "indictment" was a "true bill" found by a "grand jury," *i.e.* a jury for presenting suspected offenders. The trial upon it at assizes or quarter sessions was by a "petty jury." Nowadays the grand jury is abolished, but we still retain the word "indictment" for the document commencing criminal proceedings that are to be tried by jury. The present-day indictment may be defined as a document preferred by anyone to the Crown Court, and signed by the clerk of the court. It may charge different offences in separate counts. Normally there will have been a preliminary investigation of a charge before magistrates (except that the investigation is generally reduced to a formality, unless the defendant asks for a real one), and the magistrates will have committed the defendant for trial. A form of indictment for murder is:

Court of Trial: The Crown Court held at Leeds
The Queen v. *AB*
charged as follows:
Statement of Offence.

Murder.

Particulars of Offence.

AB on the   day of   murdered JS.

Date   [Signature of officer of the court]

Prepositions have come to be used rather sloppily in criminal matters. In good usage, one is charged, tried, acquitted, convicted, or sentenced *on* (or *upon*) an indictment or count or charge. One is indicted *on* a charge of theft (or some other offence) or *on* two counts of theft. One is indicted or tried *for* theft, and the indictment/count/information/charge is *for* theft.[28] (An information is a document making a criminal charge before magistrates.) We also speak of a count or charge *of* theft. One is charged (verb) *with* theft. One pleads guilty (or not guilty) *to* a count or charge or indictment of theft, or *to* theft. One is acquitted or convicted (or found guilty) *of* theft.

OTHER COURTS

There are many courts and tribunals of special jurisdiction, chief among which are the industrial tribunals administering various legislation relating to employment. Appeals lie from the latter on some questions to the High Court and on other questions to the *Employment Appeal Tribunal,* with possible further appeals

---

[28] Some writers misguidedly say "indicted with theft," "indicted with counts of theft and robbery," "convicted of three counts," and so on. The horrible expression "summonsed for an offence" (turning the noun "summons" into a verb) has now become accepted usage, but "summoned" remains not only allowable but preferable.

to the Court of Appeal and House of Lords. Then there is the *Restrictive Practices Court,* which considers agreements that restrict prices or the conditions of supply of goods, and unfair trading practices; again an appeal lies to the Court of Appeal and House of Lords.

The House of Lords is no longer our highest court, because the *European Court* sitting in Luxembourg adjudicates upon the law of the European Community. Strictly, there are three Communities: the European Atomic Energy Commission, the European Coal and Steel Community, and the European Economic Community. The singular term is now generally used, and in practice it normally refers to the most important of the three Communities, the EEC. The decisions of the European Court are binding on British courts by reason of the European Communities Act 1972. The impact of Community law, though at present somewhat limited, grows continually; it is to be seen in company law, trade marks and other "industrial property," the law of monopolies, the control of aliens, employment law, social security, customs, and some other economic areas. An English court can ask the European Court for a ruling on any doubtful question of Community law.

Britain is a party to the European Convention on Human Rights (1953), but our Government, acting on the assumption that United Kingdom law conforms to the Convention, has made no provision for the Convention to be enforced by our courts. Any person who believes that he is aggrieved by a violation of the provisions of the Convention can complain to the European Commission of Human Rights. If the Commission finds the complaint admissible and well founded the complainant may be referred for a binding decision to the European Court of Human Rights at Strasbourg; otherwise the Council of Ministers must authoritatively decide whether there has been a breach. If the decision is in the affirmative it is to be expected that the Government will take steps to amend our law or practice accordingly. The Convention is drafted in general terms which enable the Commission and Court to make what are in reality decisions of policy under the guise of interpreting the Convention. Who would have thought, for example, that the provision protecting personal privacy means that a signatory country cannot have a law forbidding homosexual behaviour between consenting adults? Yet that is what the court has decided in relation to the law of Northern Ireland.[29]

The Judicial Committee of the Privy Council is the final court of appeal from what remains of the old colonial Empire (with remnants also of its appellate jurisdiction from the self-governing members of the Commonwealth). Its composition is much the same as that of the House of Lords when exercising appellate jurisdiction, though certain Commonwealth judges may sit in addition. It meets in a room in Downing Street. No court in Britain normally sits behind closed doors, so you can walk in boldly and listen to its proceedings.

THE TITLES OF CASES

It is helpful to know certain rules for the naming of cases. Trials on indictment are in the name of the Queen (as representing the State); thus a criminal case is generally called *Reg.* v. whomever it is—*Reg.* being short for *Regina* (pronounced "Rejyna"), and v. being short for *versus*. When there is a king on the throne, *Rex* is used instead of *Reg. Rex* and *Regina* both conveniently abbreviate to *R.,* which saves having to remember which is which. Thus *Rex* v. *Sikes* or *Reg.* v. *Sikes* may both be written *R.* v. *Sikes*. Some textbooks on criminal law even print simply *Sikes*. This last is a convenient usage for the student of criminal law.

In some types of criminal case the title of the case will not contain *Rex* or *Reg.* before the "v.," but will contain the name of a private person. This happens when the case is tried summarily before magistrates (*i.e.* justices of the peace); here the name of the actual prosecutor (*e.g.* a policeman) appears instead of the nominal prosecutor, the Queen. Again, when an appeal was taken to the House of Lords, the practice until recently was that the name of an official or private prosecutor, usually the Director of Public Prosecutions or a Government Department, was substituted for the word *Reg.* Having two names for a case was a nuisance, particularly because when the appeal was by the defendant the names of the parties became reversed. Eventually it was decided that as from 1979 criminal causes in the House of

[29] The *Dudgeon* case (1981) 131 N.L.J. 1161.

Lords should be reported under the same title as in the court below.

Civil cases will usually be cited by the names of the parties, thus: *Rylands* v. *Fletcher*. If the Queen (as representing the Government) is a party she is, in civil cases, usually called "The Queen," and similarly with the King, thus: *British Coal Corporation* v. *The King;* but *R.* may also be used.

In order to make life more difficult for us all, the name of the appellant is put first when an appeal is taken to the Divisional Court, even though he was the defendant in the court below; this means that the names may become reversed. Nattrass, an inspector of weights and measures, instituted a summary prosecution entitled *Nattrass* v. *Tesco Supermarkets Ltd.*; on appeal by the defendant company to the Divisional Court this became *Tesco Supermarkets Ltd.* v. *Nattrass,*[30] and the title stayed the same on further appeal by Tesco to the House of Lords. We need an edict saying that the titles of cases shall never change.

There are peculiar conventions in pronouncing the names of cases. (1) A criminal case, such as *R.* v. *Sikes,* can be referred to informally as "R. v. Sikes" (pronounced as written), or "Rex" (or, "Regina") "v. Sikes" (again pronounced as written). In court, however, the proper method is to call it "The King" (or, "The Queen") "against Sikes," (2) In civil cases the "v." coupling the names of the parties is pronounced "and," both in court and out of it. Thus *Smith* v. *Hughes* is always pronounced (but never written) "Smith and Hughes," and similarly *British Coal Corporation* v. *The King* (which was a civil proceeding against the Crown) is pronounced with an "and." Lawyers thus write one thing and say another.

In some cases, as where a will is being interpreted, the name of the case is *"In re"* (in the matter of) somebody or something; for instance, *In re Smith*. It is permissible to shorten this to *Re Smith.* (*Re* is pronounced "ree"). Certain applications to the courts are labelled *"Ex parte"*: *Ex p. Smith* means "on the application of Smith." In probate cases (that is, cases concerned with the proof of a will) the title *In Bonis* (*i.e.* in the Goods of) *Smith* may be met with, and in Admiralty cases the name of a ship (*e.g. The Satanita*). Other possible ways of naming cases

[30] [1972] A.C. 153.

need not be considered here, but, in order to prevent the student from being puzzled, one oddity may be mentioned. The House of Lords is often the final court of appeal for Scotland (and Northern Ireland) as well as England, and a Scots case that goes to the House of Lords may become important in English as well as Scots law. Two such important cases are *McAlister* (or *Donoghue) v. Stevenson*[31] and *Hay* (or *Bourhill) v. Young.*[32] The oddity is the alternative name in brackets, for which the explanation is as follows. In Scotland a married woman, though she takes her husband's name, does not cease for legal purposes to go also by her maiden name. When she figures in litigation, her maiden name is placed first, and her married name is given as an alternative afterwards. Nevertheless, the correct mode of citation, when brevity is desired, is by the married name.[33] The two cases above may, for brevity, be cited as *Donoghue* v. *Stevenson* and *Bourhill* v. *Young,* but not *McAlister* v. *Stevenson* or *Hay* v. *Young.*

SUBSTANTIVE AND ADJECTIVAL LAW

A distinction cutting across that between civil and criminal law is that between substantive and adjectival law. Substantive law lays down people's rights, duties, liberties and powers. Adjectival law relates to the enforcement of rights and duties: in particular, it concerns procedure and evidence. Criminal and civil procedure are different, and so are criminal and civil evidence.

The part of civil procedure that the student of substantive law most needs to know relates to pleadings. Pleadings are not, as might be supposed, pathetic speeches before judge and jury; they are dry statements on paper of the bare facts on which each party to a civil case relies. They come after the service of the writ, which commences the action, and they are exchanged between the parties before the trial in order to reveal the apple of discord to the parties themselves and to the court. In technical language their function is said to be to settle the "issues" between the parties.

---

[31] [1932] A.C. 562.
[32] [1943] A.C. 92.
[33] See Lord Macmillan in 49 Law Quarterly Review 1; 61 *ibid.* 109.

The first pleading[34] is the plaintiff's *Statement of Claim* (formerly called, in common law matters, a Declaration[35]). It may recite, for example, that the plaintiff was on the blank day of blank proceeding on foot down High Street when the defendant so negligently drove his car that he ran him down, thereby causing him personal injury and damage to his property. There will be particulars of negligence (driving too fast, on the wrong side of the road, without keeping a proper lookout, without giving warning of his approach, and so on—these particulars have become almost common form in such cases), and particulars of the injury and damage (the latter called "special damage" to distinguish it from the "general damage" that can be presumed to flow from the injury and so does not have to be specially pleaded).

Then comes the defendant's *Defence*. The defence may embody a number of defences, perhaps inconsistent with each other,[36] but they will all be found to belong to one or other of three types:

---

[34] The above statement is concerned with the Queen's Bench and Chancery Divisions. In divorce cases proceedings are commenced by a petition, and the defence is called an "answer."

[35] Any part of a declaration that in itself, if it stood alone, would have constituted a ground for action, was called a *count*. The word *count* is still used to signify the several parts of an indictment, each charging a distinct offence.

Proceedings in Chancery formerly had a terminology of their own. Underhill's description of them was as follows: "A suit in Chancery used to be commenced by a document called 'a Bill in Chancery' . . . an enormous screed . . . setting out in great detail the story of the suitor's wrongs. . . . The next step was to turn this Bill into 'interrogatories' to be answered by the defendants on oath. . . . This was called 'scraping the Defendant's conscience,' and he was obliged to answer on oath in the utmost detail, and if he failed to do so further interrogatories were administered until sufficient admissions were obtained to make out a prima facie case. . . . This practice of interrogatories was usually delegated by junior counsel (equity draftsmen) to their clerks, and at times the rough drafts were somewhat comic. [Thus:] "Did not the defendant fall down on her knees or on one and which of them and implore the plaintiff with tears in her eyes or in one and which of them to advance the said sum of £—to her husband?' " Underhill, *Change and Decay,* 77–78.

[36] Hence the tale in *Punch* of the K.C.'s son who was charged by the Head with having broken the schoolroom window: "In the first place

(1) A *traverse,* that is, a contradiction of some fact stated by the plaintiff. Using the language of Touchstone in *As You Like It,* we may call it the countercheck quarrelsome.

(2) A *confession and avoidance,* that is, an admission (confession) of the facts stated by the plaintiff, but an allegation of other facts that destroy (avoid) their legal effect, in whole or in part. "True, I did agree to buy a tame lion from you, but I was a minor at the time and the lion was not a thing reasonably necessary for my station in life." "True, I negligently ran you down, but you were guilty of contributory negligence" This may be described as the retort courteous.

(3) An *objection in point of law.* This again admits the plaintiff's facts, but objects that in law they disclose no cause of action. "True, I gave you certain advice which was wrong and on which you acted to your detriment; but I am not liable to you because in law I owed you no duty of care." It is not strictly necessary to plead an objection in point of law, for any point of law may be taken at the trial although not pleaded.

For the purpose of reading the older cases, it is desirable to know something of the old terminology and practice relating to the defence. The name "defence" for the defendant's pleading is modern. Formerly, if the defendant pleaded a traverse or a confession and avoidance, this was called a *plea;* and an objection in point of law was called a *demurrer* (law-French *demorer,* to wait or stay).[37] The demurrer was so called because the party who demurred did not proceed with his pleading but rested his case on the submission of law and awaited the judgment of the court thereon. In technical language a demurrer

---

sir, the schoolroom has no window; in the second place, the schoolroom window is not broken; in the third place, if it is broken, I did not do it; in the fourth place it was an accident." All these defences, except the last, are traverses; the last is a confession and (one hopes) avoidance.

[37] The "u" in "demurrer" is short, as also in "demurrage" (the detention of a vessel by the charterer beyond the time agreed upon, or the payment made in compensation for such detention). In the verb "demur" (from which "demurrer" is derived), and in its other derivatives "demurrable" and "demurrage," the syllable "ur" is pronounced "er."

was not a pleading. When arguing the demurrer the parties were
entitled to imagine any state of facts consistent with the
declaration. Judgment was given by the full court sitting in banc,
so that cases decided on demurrer settled the law in a peculiarly
authoritative way. Nowadays, however, the decision on an
objection in point of law, whether the objection be raised on the
pleadings or not, is made by the single trial judge, either at a
preliminary hearing which may succeed in disposing of the whole
case or after the evidence on the issues of fact has been heard.

After the defence there may sometimes be a *Reply* (formerly
called a *Replication)* from the plaintiff. This reply may take any
of the three forms of the defence, traversing the facts in defence,
confessing and avoiding them, or objecting in point of law.

The defence may also be accompanied by a *Counterclaim,*
which will result in a *Defence to Counterclaim* from the plaintiff.

It is necessary to take care in drawing pleadings, because the
judge may refuse to admit evidence on or to decide matters that
have not been properly pleaded.[38] But the court always has
power to allow an amendment of the pleadings, and, being
rightly reluctant to visit the sins of the pleaders upon their
clients, will now allow amendment wherever this occasions no
injustice to the other side, provided that the party amending
pays any costs occasioned by his mistake.[39] This power to allow
amendment diminishes the importance of the pleadings; but it

[38] See Lord Edmund-Davies in *Farrell* v. *Secretary of State for Defence*
[1980] 1 W.L.R. 179–180; I. H. Jacob in [1960] Current Legal
Problems 171.

[39] The modern attitude towards amendments was wittily explained by
Bowen L.J. in *Cropper* v. *Smith* (1884) 26 Ch.D. at 711: "There is one
panacea which heals every sore in litigation, and that is costs. I have
very seldom, if ever, been unfortunate enough to come across an
instance where a person has made a mistake in his pleadings which has
put the other side to such a disadvantage as that it cannot be cured by
the application of that healing medicine." See, however, *Soar* v.
N.C.B. [1965] 1 W.L.R. 886, from which it appears that the court may
refuse to allow a plaintiff at a late stage of the trial to raise a new case
after failure of the pleaded case. Why should not an amendmnt (with
adjournment) be allowed even then? In the county court, it is
specifically provided (by Order 9, r.8) that the delivery of a defence
does not prevent the defendant from relying on any other defence, but

must be remembered that if counsel does not ask for an amendment judgment will be given on the pleadings as they stand. Some judges, even today, when they perceive a defect in the pleadings do not call counsel's attention to it (which they could do if they were so minded), but keep silence on the point until delivering judgment, by which time it is too late for counsel to ask for an amendment. This regrettable attitude, which may still be heard defended by many lawyers, springs from the English tradition that a lawsuit is a game of legal skill in which the judge is neutral. It must also be pointed out that an appeal court regards itself as hearing an appeal on the case presented to the lower court; it will generally refuse to decide a point that was not before the court below on the facts as pleaded.

FURTHER READING

Prof. R. M. Jackson's *Machinery of Justice in England,* 7th ed., is the best general description of our courts and their working, but useful additional information is given in Radcliffe and Cross, *The English Legal System,* 6th ed., and Walker and Walker, *The English Legal System,* 5th ed.

If you have a taste for history, you will derive much pleasure and profit from J. H. Baker's *An Introduction to English Legal History,* 2nd ed. A shorter and less ambitious treatment, confined to the history of the courts, but very readable, is *English Courts of Law* by H. G. Hanbury and D. C. M. Yardley, 5th ed. Prof. S. F. C. Milsom's *Historical Foundations of the Common Law* (2nd ed.) is the best treatment of the subject, but is probably too difficult for a beginner.

all the same I have known cases lost in the county court for failure to plead the defence ultimately relied on.

A judge who allows an amendment of a statement of claim may, at his discretion, allow the defendant costs of the action up to the date of the amendment, on the ground that the plaintiff's statement of claim before that time disclosed no cause of action on which he could have succeeded.

CHAPTER 2

COMMON LAW AND EQUITY

> "You are too easily surprised," said Mr. Towkington. "Many words have no legal meaning. Others have a legal meaning very unlike their ordinary meaning. For example, the word 'daffy-down-dilly'. It is a criminal libel to call a lawyer a daffy-down-dilly. Ha! Yes, I advise you never to do such a thing. No, I certainly advise you *never* to do it."
>
> —Dorothy Sayers, *Unnatural Death*, Chap. 14.

Two technical terms of great importance that are likely to puzzle the novice are "common law" and "equity."

The law of England may be said to be composed of three great elements: common law, equity and legislation. The most important kind of legislation is the Act of Parliament (otherwise called a statute), though nowadays what is called delegated legislation, like the many government orders generally known as statutory instruments, has come to be of great importance as well. Even a layman is not likely to experience difficulty in understanding the meaning of legislation. Not so, however, with the other two terms, which need fuller discussion.

THE COMMON LAW

The phrase "the common law" seems a little bewildering at first, because it is always used to point a contrast and its precise meaning depends upon the contrast that is being pointed. An analogy may perhaps make this clearer. Take the word "layman." In the foregoing paragraph the word was used to mean a person who is not a lawyer. But when we speak of ecclesiastics and laymen, we mean by "laymen" non-ecclesiastics. When we speak of doctors and laymen, we mean by "laymen" non-doctors. Laymen, in short, are people who do not belong to the particular profession that we are speaking of. Again, take "aliens." In England if we speak of "aliens" we generally mean by that word people who are not citizens of our own country ("patrials"). But in France the French equivalent of the word would mean people who are not French citizens.

It is somewhat similar with "the common law." (1) Originally this meant the law that was not local law, that is, the law that was common to the whole of England. This may still be its meaning in a particular context, but it is not the usual meaning. More usually the phrase will signify (2) the law that is not the result of legislation, that is, the law created by the custom of the people and decisions of the judges. Within certain narrow limits, popular custom creates law, and so (within much wider limits) do the decisions of the courts, which we call precedents. When the phrase "the common law" is used in this sense it may include even local law (in the form of local custom), which in meaning (1) is not common law. Again (3) the phrase may mean the law that is not equity; in other words it may mean the law developed by the old courts of common law as distinct from the system (technically called "equity") developed by the old Court of Chancery. In this sense "the common law" may even include statutory modifications of the common law, though in the previous sense it does not.[1] Finally (4) it may mean the law that is not foreign law—in other words, the law of England, or of other countries (such as America) that have adopted English law as a starting-point. In this sense it is contrasted with (say) Roman law or French law, and in this sense it includes the whole of English law—even local customs, legislation and equity. It will thus be seen that the precise shade of meaning in which this chameleon phrase is used depends upon the particular context, and upon the contrast that is being made. When I said in the second sentence of this chapter that our law is made up of common law, equity and legislation. I meant it in a mixture of senses (2) and (3), as the context itself showed.

EQUITY

The term "equity" is an illustration of Mr. Towkington's proposition that some words have a legal meaning very unlike

---

[1] Lawyers sometimes use the term to mean only the civil-law part of the common law in sense (3), to the exclusion of the criminal law.

their ordinary one. In ordinary language "equity" means natural justice; but the beginner must get that idea out of his head when dealing with the system that lawyers call equity. Originally, indeed, this system was inspired by ideas of natural justice, and that is why it acquired its name; but nowadays equity is no more (and no less) natural justice than the common law, and it is in fact nothing else than a particular branch of the law of England. Equity, therefore, is law. The student should not allow himself to be confused by the lawyer's habit of contrasting "law" and "equity," for in this context "law" is simply an abbreviation for the common law. Equity *is* law in the sense that it is part of the law of England; it is not law only in the sense that it is not part of the common law.

The student will learn quite early in his historical studies how equity came into being. He will learn how, in the Middle Ages, the courts of common law failed to give redress in certain types of case where redress was needed, and how the disappointed litigants petitioned the King, who was the "fountain of justice," for extraordinary relief; how the King, through his Chancellor, eventually set up a special court, the Court of Chancery, to deal with these petitions; and how the rules applied by the Court of Chancery hardened into law and became a regular part of the law of the land. The most important branch of equity is the law of trusts, but equitable remedies such as specific performance and injunction are also much used. The student will learn how, in case of "conflict or variance" between the rules of common law and the rules of equity, equity came to prevail. This was by means of what was called a common injunction. Suppose that A brought an action against B in one of the common law courts, and in the view of the Court of Chancery the action was inequitable. B's proper course was to apply to the Court of Chancery for an order, called a common injunction, directed to A and ordering him not to continue his action. If A defied the injunction the Court of Chancery would put him in prison for contempt of court. Equity thus worked "behind the scenes" of the common law action; the common law principles were theoretically left intact, but by means of this intricate mechanism they were superseded by equitable rules in all cases of "conflict or variance."[2] The result justified the sarcasm of the critic who said that in England one court was set up to do injustice and another to stop it.

This system went on until 1875, when as a result of the Judicature Act 1873 the old courts of common law and the Court of Chancery were abolished, and in their place was established a single Supreme Court of Judicature, each branch of which had full power to administer both law and equity. Also, common injunctions were abolished and instead it was enacted that, in cases of "conflict or variance" between the rules of equity and the rules of common law, the rules of equity should prevail.

All this is simple to understand; what is not so easy to explain to a beginner is how we remain stuck with the distinction between law and equity. Lawyers are familiar with the proposition that the Judicature Act, although it fused the administration of law and equity, did not fuse law and equity themselves. As one writer put it: "the two streams have met and now run in the same channel, but their waters do not mix."[3] For the beginner this is a hard saying. "How," he may ask, "can one say that law and equity are still different, when they are administered by the same judges? I can understand (he may go on) that before the Judicature Act one had to know whether a particular rule was a rule of law or a rule of equity, because you had to be careful to proceed in the right court to get your rule enforced. But now courts do not matter. Why, then, should I bother to learn whether a particular rule is part of the system formerly called the common law or part of the system formerly called equity? Is

[2] The common law courts, after a famous struggle in the seventeenth century, lay passive under this process; they did not help but they did not hinder. In some cases they even took account positively of equitable doctrines. See *Master* v. *Miller* (1791) 4 T.R. at 341, 100 E.R. at 1053; *Legh* v. *Legh* (1799) 1 Bos. & Pul. 447, 126 E.R. 1002; *Bosanquet* v. *Wray* (1815) 6 Taunt. 597, 128 E.R. 1166; *International Factors Ltd.* v. *Rodriguez* [1979] Q.B. 351.

[3] Owing to the prevailing ignorance of legal history, modern courts sometimes express the heretical opinion that law and equity have become fused, so that common law remedies are available to enforce equitable rights. See *International Factors* v. *Rodriguez* [1979] Q.B. at 358A. Untraditional as this is, it is socially beneficial. However, the general proposition that law and equity are now fused is not sustainable.

anyone the worse lawyer for not knowing it?" The student cannot appreciate the full answer to this question until he has studied equity, but I think that a satisfactory preliminary answer can be given him. To start with it may be admitted that very often the student's impression is right, and it does not now matter whether a particular rule is law or equity. But sometimes it does matter. When one says that a particular rule of modern law (using that term, this time, in its wide sense) is a rule of "equity," one means that it has to be read in the light of the whole complex of rules developed by the Chancellors. These rules do not necessarily apply if the rule in question is a rule of the common law. To take an illustration of these rules developed by the Chancellors, one of them was (and is) to the effect that "he who comes to equity must come with clean hands." This rule will apply whenever the plaintiff is relying upon an equitable right, but not necessarily when he is relying on a common law right. In other words, to say that a particular right is an equitable right is shorthand for saying that all the subsidiary rules of equity apply to it, including (for instance) the rule that the plaintiff must not have soiled his hands. On the other hand, to say that a particular right is a common law right is shorthand for saying that it is to be interpreted in a common law atmosphere, leaving out of account such equitable rules as apply only to equitable rights. Thus when a modern textbook draws a distinction between law and equity, saying that at law the rule is so-and-so but in equity[4] it is such-and-such, the author is not indulging in idle verbiage nor yet in mere historical reminiscence. Although the rule is that when law and equity conflict, equity prevails, there is always the possibility that a litigant who relies on an equitable rule may for some reason find himself outside the limits of that equitable rule; and when this happens the contradictory common law rule, which may generally seem to be a dead letter, becomes very much alive.

The distinction between law and equity, as I have tried to explain it, was vividly brought home to me in a case that I listened to in my student days. It was an ejectment action brought by a landlord against his tenant, whom we will call Mr. Isaacson. The latter had what is known as an equitable lease of

---

[4] Note the prepositions—*at* law, but *in* equity.

the premises, that is to say, not a formal lease under seal, but an informal lease valid only in equity. For nearly all practical purposes these equitable leases are just as good as legal leases, and they are habitually relied on, even though they are void at law. This particular tenant, however, had broken the terms of his equitable lease, for shortly after receiving it he had assigned it to a company by the name of Saxon Ltd., and there was a covenant in the lease not to assign. Mr. Issacson somewhat disingenuously explained that he did not think this mattered, for the company was his own creation and "Saxon," he said, was none other than the latter part of his name! But Mr. Isaacson's real defence was that, although he might be liable in damages for having broken his covenant not to assign, that was not any reason for his being ejected altogether from the premises. Had the document been a legal lease this defence would have been a good one, for the lease did not contain a proviso for re-entry on breach of covenant. But unfortunately for the tenant it was an equitable lease, and by breaking an important term of it he had soiled his hands *and therefore lost his lease.*[5] Consequently the action succeeded, much, I remember, to my surprise.

The above is not the only answer to the question: What is the present difference between law and equity? But it is, I believe, the only answer that can be given in general terms without having to state exceptions; and it is the answer that is most easily apprehended by the beginner.

COMMON LAW AS MADE BY THE JUDGES

When the term "common law" is used in contrast to statutory law, it may mean either of two things, though they are closely related. It generally means the body of law produced by decided cases without the aid of legislation. Occasionally, however, the invocation of the common law refers not to previously existing law but to the power of the judges to create new law under the guise of interpreting it. Nearly all the common law in the first

---

[5] Cp. *Coatsworth* v. *Johnson* (1885) 55 L.J.Q.B. 220. But the statutory restrictions on re-entry apply: see Law of Property Act 1925, s. 146(5)(*a*). For a similar situation except that the illegality was by the landlord see *Warmington* v. *Miller* [1973] Q.B. 877.

sense is created by the common law in the second sense, that is to say by the judges in the exercise of their discretion.

How much discretion a judge has to expand the law is a complex question. Part of the answer to it will appear in Chapter 6.

CHAPTER 3

THE MECHANISM OF SCHOLARSHIP

I hold him not discreet that will *sectari rivulos*, when he may *petere fontes*.

—Coke, Preface to 4th part of Reports.

HE who wants to become a lawyer, and not merely to pass law examinations (which is not at all the same thing), must learn to use legal materials. He must get to know the way about his law library, and must acquire the habit of first-hand work among what lawyers call the sources. The great campaigner for this among teachers of law was the man affectionately known to his own generation as "F.P.," and I make no apology for repeating his words, since I cannot better them.

"We no longer make and transcribe notes and extracts, with infinite manual labour, in a huge 'commonplace book,' as former generations were compelled to do by the dearth of printed works of reference. But, since the law is a living science, no facilities of publishing and printing can ever perfectly keep pace with it. A student who intends to be a lawyer cannot realise this too soon. There is no need for him to make voluminous notes (indeed there is a great deal of vain superstition about lecture notes); but those he does take and use ought to be made by him for himself, and always verified with the actual authorities at the first opportunity. Another man's notes may be better in themselves, but they will be worse for the learner. As for attempts to dispense with first-hand reading and digesting by printed summaries and other like devices, they are absolutely to be rejected. No man ever became a lawyer by putting his trust in such things; and if men can pass examinations by them so much the worse for the examinations."[1]

Some may think that put a trifle too exuberantly,[2] but in

---

[1] Pollock, *Oxford Lectures*, 104–105.

[2] I am not quite sure what Pollock meant by "printed summaries and other like devices," which are thus absolutely to be rejected. He could not have meant textbooks, because he himself wrote several. He did

essentials the advice is sound. The great disadvantage of confining oneself to textbooks and lecture notes is that it means taking all one's law at second hand. The law of England is contained in statutes and judicial decisions; what the text writer thinks is not, in itself, law. He may have misinterpreted the authorities, and the reader who goes to them goes to the fountainhead. Besides familiarising himself with the law reports and statute book, the lawyer-to-be should get to know his way about the library as a whole, together with its apparatus of catalogues and books of reference. To quote Pollock again:

"Facility in such things may seem a small matter, but much toil may be wasted and much precious time lost for want of it. To the working lawyer these things are the very tools of his trade. He depends on them for that whole region of potential knowledge which must bear a large proportion to the actual."[3]

But this preaching; and I do not want to preach, but only to give practical advice to those who wish to hear it. Let us therefore pass at once to:

THE LAY-OUT OF THE LAW LIBRARY

Near the entrance to the library there will probably be either a catalogue of the contents of the library or a card index. In fact there may be two such catalogues or indexes, one arranged alphabetically under authors and another arranged by general subjects. They are both open to the use of readers.

Each entry contains a number of figures or letters or a combination of the two. This is known as the class mark, and it should be accurately noted, for it enables the volume to be traced in the library. You should make a point of discovering the system adopted in your library, by wandering round the shelves—assuming, of course, that it is a library in which you are allowed access to the shelves, and that it is not so large a library as to make this task impracticable. Some classifications use what may be called a decimal system, even though no decimal point

not mean case books, because after writing the above passage he went on to approve them. I suppose he was referring to what are commonly called cram books, and, so understood, any teacher would agree with him.

[3] *Ibid*. 106.

appears. For example, volumes next to each other on the shelf may be marked AF 1, AF 2, AF 22 and AF 7. If you imagine a decimal point before these numbers you will see that they are not out of order. The system enables the library staff to insert new sub-groups without altering the main order.

One has to use common sense in consulting a catalogue. Suppose you want a book by a man called Bowen-Rowlands. You should first try "Bowen," but if it is not there try "Rowlands." Libraries vary in their treatment of these hyphen-ated names. Anonymous books are usually included in the author catalogues under their titles. Thus, *Every Man's Own Lawyer*, by A Barrister, will probably be in the author catalogue under "Every," though it may be under "Barrister" or "A Barrister" or "Anonymous." Periodicals may be in the author catalogue either under their titles or grouped under the general heading of "Periodicals."

Near the catalogues or card indexes there will probably be works of reference, like dictionaries and bibliographies.

The law reports, statutes and periodicals will probably be found in special sections of the library. Usually, too, there will be special sections devoted to such subjects as Roman law, international law, jurisprudence and legal history. Most of the rest of the library will be taken up with English law textbooks. These may be arranged alphabetically under authors, starting (say) with *Abbott on Merchant Ships* and ending with (say) *Zouche on Partnership Accounts*. Or they may be classified by subject, but arranged alphabetically under authors within each subject. Where there is no subject arrangement, and it is desired to find books relating to a particular subject, it will usually be necessary to consult the subject catalogue in the library, or else one of the works mentioned later (p.174).

During the vacation it may be worth while to locate a library near your home. You may be able to obtain permission to use the library of a local university, polytechnic or technical college, or (if you are going to be a solicitor) of the local Law Society; and the larger public libraries have some law books.

We shall now look more closely at the law reports, statutes and periodicals.

LAW REPORTS

Law reports are reports of the more important cases decided by the superior courts. Not all cases are reported: only those of legal interest. The reports may be divided very roughly into the old and the new. The old run from the time of Henry VIII to 1865, and the new since that date. Before Henry VIII's time there were the Year Books, but it is highly unlikely that you will ever need to consult them.

Pre-1865 reports were produced chiefly by private reporters under their own names (the "nominate reports"). Altogether there were some hundreds of different series, though many of them ran only for a short time. Most, but not all, have been reprinted in a series known as the English Reports (abbreviated E.R.).[4] A chart supplied with the English Reports indicates the volume of the English Reports in which a particular volume of the old reports is to be found reprinted: the chart will either be found hanging in the library, or be found in a slim volume at the end of the series of English Reports. For instance, if your reference is to 1 B. & Ad. 289 (which means volume one of Barnewall and Adolphus's Reports at page 289), the chart will tell you that the corresponding volume of the English Reports reprint is volume 109. As you take down the volume from the shelf, notice the names in gilt letters at the bottom of the spine. These will tell you the order in which the old reports are reprinted in the particular volume. Volume 109 bears the legend: Barnewall & Cresswell 9–10; Barnewall & Adolphus 1–2. This indicates that 1 B. & Ad. will probably be found just beyond the middle of the book. Open the book, and you will find your page reference in heavy type at the top centre of the open pages (top outside corner in the first twenty volumes). If something goes wrong and your case eludes you, try the index at the end of the volume; failing that, Vols. 177–178 contain a complete index of all cases in the reprint.

The chart just referred to is not quite complete, because it indexes each of the old reports under one title only, whereas in fact many of the old reports were known under various titles or

---

[4] If your library does not possess the English Reports, the case you want may possibly be included in the selection called the Revised Reports.

under various abbreviations of the title. İf you are in difficulty, consult the full chart published by Professional Books. If this is not available, use the chart in Donald Raistrick, *Index of Legal Abbreviations and Citations* (1981), or the chart in *Where to Look for your Law*, supplemented in either case if necessary by the chart in 7 Cambridge Law Journal 261.

These old reports were of uneven quality, at least in the period before 1757, and need to be handled with some care. Of the worst of them many stories are told. In *Slater* v. *May* (1704)[5] a case was cited from 4 Modern, then a comparatively recent volume of reports. Upon search of the roll (that is, the official record of the case) it was found that the report in 4 Modern had omitted a material fact. Upon this Holt C.J. burst out: "See the inconveniences of these scambling reports, they will make us to appear to posterity for a parcel of blockheads." When another of the early reporters, Barnardiston, was cited before Lord Lyndhurst, the latter exclaimed: "Barnardiston, Mr. Preston! I fear that is a book of no great authority; I recollect, in my younger days, it was said of Barnardiston, that he was accustomed to slumber over his notebook, and wags in the rear took the opportunity of scribbling nonsense in it."[6] Reporters even of the nineteenth century did not always escape judicial condemnation. The one who got most kicks of all was Espinasse, who reported Nisi Prius cases between 1793 and 1807. Pollock C.B. said of him that he heard only half of what went on in court and reported *the other half*.[7] And Maule J., when a case in Espinasse was referred to, said with some emphasis that he did not care for Espinasse "or any other ass."[8] Denman C.J.'s response when a case from Espinasse was cited was:

"I am tempted to remark, for the benefit of the profession, that Espinasse's Reports, in days nearer their own time, when their want of accuracy was better known than it is now, were never quoted without doubt and hesitation; and a special reason was often given as an apology for citing that particular case. Now they are often cited as if counsel thought them of equal authority with Lord Coke's Reports."[9]

[5] 2 Ld.Raym. 1071, 92 E.R. 210.
[6] Wallace, *The Reporters*, 424.
[7] Anon., *A Lawyer's Notebook*, 43; (1938) 54 L.Q.R. 368.
[8] Biron, *Without Prejudice*, 88.
[9] *Small* v. *Nairne* (1849) 13 Q.B. at 844, 116 E.R. at 1486. Some further comments may be added from A.J. Ashton's *As I Went on my Way*,

I relate these tales only to put the researcher on his guard when dealing with some of the old reports, not to discountenance their use altogether. It sometimes happens that even poor maligned Espinasse is the only reporter to give us an important case—*Wilkinson* v. *Coverdale*,[10] which the student may perhaps come across in tort or in contract, is an example—and, as Denman C.J. indicated, he and others of like stamp are not altogether unusable, though usable only with caution. Also, this

27–28: "More decorous, though not more learned, judges than Maule always insisted that the fifth Espinasse must not be cited, and would hardly admit even the earlier volumes. Lowndes, who reported on the Northern Circuit, would barely be tolerated. It is in his rare and amusing volume that the head note is to be found,'Carlisle. Possession of trousers in Scotland evidence of larceny in England.' It was not desirable to quote the Modern Reports if you could find Lord Mansfield in any other report. Carrington and Payne depended a good deal on the number of the volume. The later it was, the less it was attended to. It would seem that Carrington, like Espinasse, went down the hill, and I have myself heard a judge refuse to hear Carrington and Kirwan cited. These reports follow Carrington and Payne in date; and the judge said he didn't believe the reporter could at that date be trusted. This was a bold commercial judge, now dead. Of Price's Reports in the Exchequer it used to be said that you could find in them anything you wanted, if you looked long enough. He was the Beavan of the common law reporters. I once looked a long time and thought I found something in Price which seemed authority worth citing in a case in which Sir Horace Davey led me. At two or three consultations running, I brought this case forward after the second leader had finished, and Sir Horace always let me read the passage to him and murmured, 'Yes that seems some authority.' I should point out to my American friends that Sir Horace did not mean what they mean by these words. But I never got him to take the book into his hands until he was arguing in court. He suddenly swerved round and said, 'Give me that case of yours,' and began turning the pages with a listless and indifferent hand—for he was very tired— and glancing at them in a lack-lustre way, said, 'Then there is a case, my Lord, in the fourth Price'—looking at the number on the back of the volume— 'which decides a number of interesting matters, including, I see', pausing at a particular page, 'the ownership of a pond in Hertford-shire, and there is somewhere', turning a few more pages, 'something that seems to bear on this matter. But, however,' ceasing to turn any more pages from sheer inanition, 'I don't think I'll cite it', handing the book back to me with a smile." (The author is mistaken as to Lowndes—the report of the case referred to is in 1 Lewin 113, 168 E.R. 980—and it was a horse, not a pair of trousers.)

[10] (1793) 1 Esp. 75, 170 E.R. 284.

sort of condemnation does not apply by any means to all the old reports, many of which are of outstanding quality.

If the student wishes to know more about these old reporters he may read Pollock's chapter in his *First Book of Jurisprudence*, 6th ed., 292 *et seq.*, or Veeder's article in (1901) 15 Harvard Law Review 1, 109, partly reprinted in 2 *Select Essays in Anglo-American Legal History*, 123, or C.G. Moran's *The Heralds of the Law* (1948). Detailed monographs are Wallace, *The Reporters*, and Fox, *Handbook of English Law Reports*.

In 1865 there commenced the semi-official "Law Reports" (with capital letters) published by the Incorporated Council of Law Reporting. At present they are published in three series, one for each Division of the High Court. They are:

the Queen's Bench Division (cited *e.g.* as [1975] 2 Q.B. 600, meaning the second volume for the year 1975 at p.600);

the Chancery Division (cited *e.g.* as [1975] 1 Ch. 800);

the Family Division (cited *e.g.* as [1975] Fam. 200).

These three series contain judgments at first instance in the three Divisions, and they also contain the judgments on appeal to the Court of Appeal. If a further appeal is taken from the Court of Appeal to the House of Lords, the decision of the Lords will be reported in a separate series called the Appeal Cases (cited *e.g.* as [1975] A.C. 100).[11] The Appeal Cases also contain cases in the Judicial Committee of the Privy Council.

Originally there were eleven series—roughly speaking, one for each of the superior courts. After the Law Reports had been running for ten years, the Judicature Act 1873 came into force, and this (since it altered the superior courts) brought about changes in the names of the series and reduced the eleven series to six. Another change occurred in 1881, when the Exchequer and Common Pleas Divisions of the High Court were incorporated in the Queen's Bench Division, with the result that the corresponding reports were likewise incorporated, reducing the series to four. A change in the mode of citation was made in 1890, when instead of quoting the volumes by number the practice was started of referring to them exclusively by the year. In 1972 the series called Probate (abbreviated P., and containing

---

[11] Sometimes the Appeal Cases contain a report of the decision in the C.A. as well as the H.L.

cases in the Probate, Divorce and Admiralty Division) was replaced by a series called Family (containing cases in the new Family Division). All these changes are shown in the table on p.39.

Take down any volume of the Law Reports and look at the beginning of a case. At the head are what are called the catchwords, indicating briefly what the case is about. They enable the reader to make sure that the case is relevant to the point he is concerned with. Then comes the headnote, which is again not part of the report but simply a summary written by the reporter. Occasionally inaccurate, it is nevertheless useful as a guide to the judgments. Occasionally the leading judgment is delivered by the senior member of the court when he is *dissenting*; if the student reads it without having consulted the headnote, he will for quite a time labour under a misapprehension as to what was decided. Obviously it is better to read the judgments of the majority first, though dissenting judgments may be valuable because they may find favour in a higher court if the point is carried further.

Generally the headnote states the short facts of the case. If they appear to be adequately summarised, it is to my mind quite permissible in ordinary cases to skip the facts as stated in detail by the judge, and to come forthwith to the part of his judgment that deals with the law. Except as above it is unwise to rely on the headnote. At the very least, one of the (majority) judgments should be read, in whole or in part. It is also very improving to read the argument for the side that lost, or a dissenting judgment if there is one, in order to appreciate that there were two sides to the question, as there always are in cases that get into the law reports.

The Incorporated Council of Law Reporting also publishes a weekly series known as the Weekly Law Reports (W.L.R.), which in 1953 replaced the earlier Weekly Notes (W.N.). The W.L.R. are bound in three volumes, the first containing cases that are not afterwards included in the Law Reports, and the second and third those cases that are expected to be superseded by the version in the Law Reports. (Sometimes, as it turns out, they are not included in the Law Reports after all.)

In addition to the Law Reports various privately owned series are still current. The most important is the All England Law

TABLE OF THE LAW REPORTS

The mode of citation is given in brackets. In the first, second and third columns, dots (. . .) are put where the number of the volume would appear in the citation. In the fourth column square brackets([ ]) are put where the year would appear in the citation.

1866–1875	1875–1880	1881–1890	1891–present
House of Lords, English and Irish Appeals (L.R. ... H.L.)			
House of Lords, Scotch and Divorce Appeals (**L.R. ... H.L.Sc.** or **L.R. ... H.L.Sc. and Div.**)	Appeal Cases (...App.Cas.)	Appeal Cases (...App.Cas.)	Appeal Cases ([ ]) A.C.)
Privy Council Appeals (**L.R. ... P.C.**)			
Chancery Appeal Cases (**L.R. ... Ch.** or **Ch. App.**)	Chancery Division (...Ch.D.)	Chancery Division (...Ch.D.)	Chancery Division ([ ]) Ch.)
Equity Cases (L.R. ... Eq.)			
Crown Cases Reserved (L.R. ... C.C., or, ... C.C.R.)	Queen's Bench Division (...Q.B.D.)		
Queen's Bench Cases* (L.R. ... Q.B.)		Queen's Bench Division (...Q.B.D.)	Queen's (or King's) Bench Division ([ ] Q.B. or K.B.)†
Common Pleas Cases (L.R. ... C.P.)	Common Pleas Division (...C.P.D.)		
Exchequer Cases‡ (L.R. ... Ex.)	Exchequer Division (...Ex.D.)		
Admiralty and Ecclesiastical Cases (L.R. ... A. & E.)	Probate Division (...P.D.)	Probate Division (...P.D.)	Probate Division ([ ]P.) Since 1972 Family Division ([ ]Fam.)
Probate and Divorce Cases (L.R. ... P. & D.)			

* Note that there is also a series called Queen's Bench Reports in the old reports (113–118 E.R.).

† After 1907 this includes cases in the Court of Criminal Appeal, later the Court of Appeal, in place of the previous Court for Crown Cases Reserved.

‡ Note that there is also a series called Exchequer Reports in the old reports (154–156 E.R.).

Reports (All E.R.). (Both the All England Reports and the Weekly Law Reports offer considerable discounts to students, newly-called barristers and newly-admitted solicitors.) The Times Law Reports (T.L.R.) ceased at the end of 1952. The Law Times Report (L.T.) became merged with the All England Law Reports at the beginning of 1948, and the Law Journal Reports (before 1947 cited as L.J.Ch., L.J.K.B., etc.) likewise became merged with the All England Law Reports in 1950. Distinguish the Law Times Reports from the Law Times Newspaper (both now defunct). Note also that many volumes of the Law Journal Reports have different page-runs for the different courts. Thus (1865) 34 L.J.C.P. 1 is not the first page of the bound volume but is in the middle of the volume. The All E.R. Reprint includes selected cases from the Law Times Reports and other earlier reports.

An advantage of having the collateral reports in the library is that if the reader wants a volume of the Law Reports and finds that it is being used by someone else, it is often more convenient to turn up the case in one of the collateral series than to wait for the Law Reports version. For citation in court the Law Reports are preferred, because the judgments they print have been revised by the judges. The Law Reports have the further advantage that counsel's argument is summarised.

The student of criminal law should seek out in his library two series of reports of particular interest to him: Cox's Criminal Cases (Cox), and the Criminal Appeal Reports (C.A.R. or Cr.App.R.). Then there are the Justice of the Peace Reports (J.P.). Before volume 96, these are usually bound at the end of the Justice of the Peace newspaper (abbreviated J.P.N.: note the independent pagination after volume 67); from volume 96 onwards they are separate. Distinguish, therefore, between (say) 96 J.P. 261, which is a reported case (the small volume), and 96 J.P.N. 261, which is a reference to the journal (the big volume). Brief reports of cases are also given in the Criminal Law Review (Crim.L.R.). Labour lawyers will need to consult the Industrial Cases Reports, the Industrial Tribunal Reports, and the Industrial Relations Law Reports. Note also the Road Traffic Reports and Lloyd's Law Reports.

HOW TO FIND A REFERENCE

In your student days you will probably be given clear references to all the cases you need to read, either in your textbook or by your lecturer. However, you may sometimes know the name of a case but not its reference. Or you may have a reference to the case but find that the report is not on the shelf, so you want a reference to the same case in another series of reports.

If the case is since 1865, start your hunt with the *Law Reports Index*. This gives the references to the case at all its stages through the courts; you will probably be looking for the reference to the last appeal, so start by looking at the references at the end of the list. The Index is particularly useful because it now gives references to the Law Reports, Weekly Law Reports, All England Reports, Criminal Appeal Reports, and other series. (Distinguish between the Table of Cases Reported and the Table of Cases Judicially Considered.) The larger index volumes cover a span of years, the latest being the *Index for 1971—1979* (red paperback). (For cases up to 1949 it was called the *Law Reports Digest*.) Cases since 1979 are listed in separate indexes for each year or parts of the current year. For more recent cases still, look at the cumulative index in the Weekly Law Reports, starting with the current number (which will tell you when the previous cumulative index was included). Cases that are too recent even for the Weekly Law Reports, being published only in some place like the Times newspaper or the Criminal Law Review, will be noted in the monthly publication called Current Law. The annual volumes of Current Law in your library may be called "Scottish Current Law"; this is the same as the English Law version except that it includes Scottish cases in addition.

Other methods can be used if for any reason this one fails. The *All England Reports Consolidated Tables and Index* gives only the All England Reports. The *Current Law Citators 1947–1977* and *1977–1979* cover all cases for the periods specified, and later cases will be found (as already said) in the annual volumes and the monthly parts of Current Law for the current year. (For the current year start with the latest monthly number, which contains a cumulative list to date.)

Current Law is helpful, but it does not always give all the

reports of the case. Failing all else, use *The Digest* (formerly called the *English and Empire Digest*), which in any event you will need for the older cases. For cases reported after January 1, 1967 the procedure is simple: consult the table of cases at the front of the annual Cumulative Supplement. This gives a reference to the volume, subject and *case number*. For cases reported before 1967 there is a slight complexity. First consult the consolidated table of cases in the blue band (*i.e.* second edition) volumes 52–54. This gives the reference to the case by volume, subject and *page number* in the blue band edition. These blue band volumes are in process of being replaced by green band (third edition) volumes. If your case is in a green band volume your page-reference will not fit, and the old blue band volume will not be on the shelf. So the only useful information the consolidated table of cases will have given you will be the volume and subject. Take down the appropriate green band volume from the shelf and look up the case again in the table of cases at the front of the volume. This will give you the *case number* within the subject. (An alternative technique is to use the reference adapter at the end of the volume; this will translate the blue band page number into the green band case number.) The official instructions on how to use The Digest are at the front of the Cumulative Supplement (1982 onwards).

If you are looking up a case in the index to a volume of the Criminal Appeal Reports, it is worth knowing that the "Table of Cases" is a snare and delusion; the true table of cases (for the Court of Appeal) is headed "Appellants and Applicants," while the table of cases decided in other courts is idiotically separated from this and concealed overleaf.

Other indexes for the older cases are the index to the English Reports (cases before 1865) and the index to the All England Law Reports Reprint (cases before 1935).

Raistrick's *Index*, already mentioned, will decipher the multitudinous shorthand names of law reports. If this work is unavailable, use one to the following: *Manual of Legal Citations*, published by the Institute of Advanced Legal Studies (1959); *Where to Look for your Law,* reprinted in Osborn's *Concise Law Dictionary* and *The Pocket Law Lexicon*; Sweet and Maxwell's *Law Finder* and *Guide to Law Reports and Statutes*; Jelf, *Where to Find Your Law*; Mozley and Whiteley's *Law Dictionary*;

volume 1 of Halsbury's *Laws of England*; volume 1(1) of the *English and Empire Digest*; the *Encyclopaedia of the Laws of England*, 3rd ed., 1: xii; Mew's *Digest*, 2nd ed., xix; Stroud's *Judicial Dictionary*, 4th ed., vol.1; the *Supreme Court Practice*, vol.1; Farrer, *Introduction to Legal Method*, 220–223; and Hicks, *Materials and Methods of Legal Research*.

The current Scottish law reports known as Sessions Cases are divided into three series all bound into one volume for the year: House of Lords, Court of Justiciary, and Court of Session. They are cited as, for example, 1978 S.C. (H.L.)100, 1978 S.C. (J.) 100 and 1978 S.C. 100; note that there are three different page-runs in each volume. See also [1958] Criminal Law Review 368.

Sometimes the reader's reference will contain two page references, thus "[1892] 1 Q.B. 273, 291" or "[1892] 1 Q.B. 273 at 291." Here the first page contains the beginning of the case and the second page the dictum to which the real reference is being made. I have known beginners spend many hours reading a case to which they were referred only for a single dictum in the middle of it. Generally speaking, if a case is quoted for a dictum there is no need to read the whole of the case.

The use of square and round brackets surrounding the dates of cases requires a word of explanation. Compare the two following references:

    Stanley v. *Powell* (1890) 60 L.J.Q.B. 52.

    Stanley v. *Powell* [1891] 1 Q.B. 86.

Why are the dates different, and why the two different sorts of brackets? To answer the second question first, the custom is to use square brackets where the date is an indispensable part of the reference to the case, round brackets where it is not. The report first cited has a volume number (60), so the date is not necessary to trace the case; the second report has no volume number, so the date is in square brackets. As to the first question, the judgment in the case was pronounced in 1890, which is therefore its true date. But some time elapses before the cases are reported in the Law Reports, and this case did not get in till 1891, which is the date in the second reference. Where cases are reported in the Law Reports it is customary to adopt the date of publication of the Law Reports version as the date of the case. The reader need not trouble to learn any of this; it is explained here simply to save bewilderment.

STATUTES

In theory there is nothing to prevent the whole of the law being set out clearly and logically in statutory form. Decided cases would then be useful only as interpreting the statutes, and important decisions could be incorporated into the statutes by amendment. In practice, human sloth, indifference and perversity have combined to keep the statute-book in a state far short of perfection. Statutes are not arranged on a rational plan, since the same subject may be divided between many statutes and the same statute may contain bits of several subjects. Statutes are amended from time to time, so that often the law has to be gathered by reading two or more statutes side by side. Relief is given when a statute and its amending Acts are gathered together into a single "consolidating" Act. This makes for convenience, but even a consolidation statute is unlikely to state the whole law on the subject with which it deals—partly because there may well be other statutes bearing on the subject, and partly because a consolidation statute does not attempt to set out the common law. The process of setting out both statute law and common law as a single, well-ordered body of law is called codification, but for reasons that it would not be flattering to examine in detail English lawyers have always been hostile (or, at best, indifferent) to this.

Statutes are cited in three ways: by the short title, which includes the calendar year (*e.g.* the Fatal Accidents Act 1846[12-13]), or by the regnal year or years and the chapter (*e.g.* 9 & 10 Vict. c. 93[14]), or by a compromise of the two (*e.g.* the Fatal Accidents Act 1846 (c.93)). Two regnal years are given (as in the foregoing example) when the session of Parliament in which the statute was passed did not fall within a single regnal year. The chapter indicates the number of the statute—formerly, the

---

[12-13] Acts passed before 1963 had a comma in the short title before the date; in 1962 a change was made and the comma was omitted. It seems sensible now to drop the comma in pre-1963 Acts as well.

[14] Pronounced as "the statute nine and ten Victoria, chapter 93," or "the ninth and tenth Victoria, chapter 93."

number in the session. It will be seen that "9 & 10 Vict. c.93" means an Act that received the royal assent in the session of Parliament beginning in the ninth year of Queen Victoria and concluding in her tenth year, being the ninety-third statute passed in that session. Since 1962, chapter numbers have referred to the calendar year.[15]

As a student you will probably have all the extracts from statutes you need in your textbook or in a book of cases, statutes and materials specially produced for your subject. If you do need to look up a statute (and you will certainly have to as a practitioner), read the advice on this in Chapter 12. In particular, there may be relevant statutes passed since your book was written. These can be traced by consulting the appropriate title in *Statutes in Force* (described in Chapter 12); and individual statutes in this publication can be ordered through any bookseller.

The main body of a statute is divided into sections, and sections may by subdivided into subsections. When there are subsections they comprise the whole of the section—there is no opening part of the section before the subsections. A subdivision following an opening part is called a paragraph. Subsections have a number in brackets while paragraphs have an italicised letter in brackets. Here is an example drawn from the Theft Act 1968 section 21, which establishes the crime of blackmail. Section 21 opens immediately with subsection (1).

> (1) A person is guilty of blackmail if, with a view to gain for himself or another or with intent to cause loss to another, he makes any unwarranted demand with menaces; and for this purpose a demand with menaces is unwarranted unless the person making it does so in the belief—
>
> *(a)* that he has reasonable grounds for making the demand; and
> *(b)* that the use of the menaces is a proper means of reinforcing the demand.

You would cite this as subsection (1), and the paragraphs as paragraph *(a)* and paragraph *(b)* respectively. In informal speech

---

[15] They do things better in some other parts of the Commonwealth like the provinces of Canada, which issue current statutes without a number. At the end of the year the statutes are arranged alphabetically and only then given a number. United Kingdom Statute Law Committee, please copy.

lawyers sometimes refer to "section 1 subsection (1)" as "section 1 sub (1)," and so on.

As a student you are not likely to have much to do with Statutory Instruments ("S.I."—formerly known as Statutory Rules and Orders—"S.R. & O."), though exceptionally you may have to consult them.[16] When referring to Statutory Instruments, instead of calling the particular provisions of the Instrument "section" and "subsection" as with statutes, one calls them "articles" or "rules" and "paragraphs" respectively.

Some statutory instruments are made in order to give effect to European Community law. A substantial part of Community law takes effect directly on individuals and affects private rights and duties; this is true for some provisions of the Treaty of Rome and for nearly all *regulations* made under the treaty. These regulations are expressly incorporated into our law by statutory instruments under the European Communities Act 1972; but if for any reason a statutory instrument fails to express part of a regulation that is directly applicable to citizens of the Community, the regulation itself retains full effect. The organs of the Community also produce *decisions* and *directives*, which do not generally affect our law directly, but again may be incorporated into statutory instruments.[17] The most that the ordinary lawyer can hope for is to know when Community law *may* affect a particular case; after that, unless a clear answer is given in his books of reference, he will have to consult a specialist in Community law.

PERIODICALS

Legal periodicals contain articles of great importance for the lawyer and student.

Special mention must be made of the Law Quarterly Review

---

[16] See Chapter 12.

[17] A sketch of law-making in the Community will be found in Michael Zander, *The Law-Making Process* (1980) 259–264. For a fuller study see Wyatt and Dashwood, *The Substantive Law of the EEC* (1980). A useful short discussion of the doctrine of direct effect is by Hacker in 129 New Law Journal 43.

(L.Q.R.), which is published quarterly, the Modern Law Review (M.L.R.), published every two months, and the Cambridge Law Journal (C.L.J.), published twice yearly; students may obtain them at greatly reduced rates. Current Legal Problems appears annually. New entrants on the scene are Legal Studies (successor to the Journal of the Society of Public Teachers of Law), the Oxford Journal of Legal Studies, and the Journal of English Legal History.

The legal weeklies, the New Law Journal (N.L.J.), Solicitors' Journal (S.J.) and Justice of the Peace (J.P.N.) are published chiefly for practitioners; the best coverage is in the New Law Journal, which is available to students at half price (£16.80 including postage). The monthly Law Notes is intended for students and costs £6.80 per annum; it contains summaries of recent cases which may be found useful, but readers who follow the cases in one of the series of law reports will derive much more profit from the New Law Journal. Specialist publications include Public Law, the Criminal Law Review, the Conveyancer, the Journal of Planning and Environment Law, Family Law, the Industrial Law Journal, and the International and Comparative Law Quarterly. Space does not allow mention of the numerous periodicals published overseas, or of various others published in the United Kingdom.

The Times newspaper is available to students at half price. Particulars can be obtained from a newsagent.

Further information on the use of a law library will be given in Chapter 12.

I should not need to remind my readers not to deface library books, however urgently the text may seem to need correction, emphasis or comment. It is distracting to have to endure the handiwork of other readers.

CHAPTER 4

METHODS OF STUDY

Learning by study must be won;
'Twas ne'er entailed from son to son.

—Gay, *Fables*, II, ii.

TEXTBOOKS

How is my time better spent: sitting in the library reading cases in the reports, or stewing over a textbook in my own room? This is a question often put by beginners, and it is a hard one to answer. One can, of course, answer it discreetly by saying: do both. But then the question is: in what proportion? What is the relative importance of the two modes of study?

Before answering this question let me remind the reader that when studying law he has not one aim but two. His primary and most important aim is to make himself a lawyer. His secondary (but also very important) aim is to pass his law examinations with credit.

Now to a large extent these two aims can be pursued by the same means. For both purposes one must study cases, either in the original law reports or in case books. It is through applying oneself to cases that one gets to understand how legal problems present themselves and how legal argument is conducted. That understanding is important whether one's object is to solve examination problems or to give sound opinions on points of legal practice.

But there is one difference between preparation for practice and preparation for examinations. For the practising lawyer, having a large field of what Pollock called potential knowledge is more important than having a small amount of actual knowledge. What the practitioner needs is a grasp of general legal principles, a sound knowledge of practice and procedure, an ability to argue, and a general knowledge of where to find the law he wants. But it is not essential for him—though, of course, it is a great help—to carry much law in the mind.[1] To shine at examinations, on the other hand, one must not only know how to argue, and be able to display a first-hand knowledge of the sources; one must also be able to parrot a considerable number of rules and authorities. From the examination point of view there is a danger in discursive reading that is not accompanied by a considerable amount of learning by rote.

Teachers of law regret this, but they have not agreed upon effective counter-measures. It is true that the introduction of problems into examination papers has done something to redress the balance between intelligence and memory; but too much memorising is still required. Often it seems to smother constructive thought. Some examination scripts are positively shocking for the amount of word-perfect memorising that they display, coupled with lack of individuality. Copies of statutes are now allowed to be used in some law examinations. The result is not to lower the standard of the examination but to raise it, for it means that the examination can be made more starkly a test of intelligence and lawyerly ability. There is no reason why case books should not be permitted, or at least lists of names of cases. In the United States, some teachers allow their pupils to take in to the examination all material that they have prepared themselves.

But I must not vex my present readers with problems of educational reform. My reason for writing the above was merely to underline the importance, as matters now stand, of memory work. It is distressing when a student who has worked

---

[1] There is an old tale of a solicitor who won great renown for his deep knowledge of the law. His secret was this. He had had three copies of *Every Man's Own Lawyer* bound to resemble law reports and lettered respectively "3 Meeson and Welsby," "1 Term Reports" and "7 Manning and Granger ." When a client propounded a legal question, the solicitor would ring for his clerk and say: "Bring me 3 Meeson and Welsby," or "1 Term Reports," or "7 Manning and Granger." When the volume came he would gravely look up the point and then say triumphantly: "Ah! here it is. I thought so. The very authority we wanted." The solicitor was not such a fraud as a layman hearing this story might think. At least he knew his way about that particular book better than his clients did.

industriously and read widely fails to achieve his due place in the examination merely because he has not committed a due proportion of his reading to memory.

There is another observation to be made about the learning of law through the medium of textbooks. It is an observation that everyone inured to learning has already made for himself, but it is, perhaps, worth putting on paper for the sake of those whose acquaintance with this discipline has hitherto been slight. It is this. The more often a book is read, the easier and quicker it is to read (which is obvious), and the more it repays the reading (which is, perhaps, not quite so obvious). When a book on an unfamiliar subject is read for the first time it is rather heavy going, and one seems not to remember very much of it. The second reading is both easier and more interesting, and more (but still not much) is remembered. Many people take their examination at this point. Had they had the perseverance to read through the book a third, fourth and fifth time, they would have found that each successive reading came more easily and that the residue left in the mind each time went up in geometrical progression.

While on the subject of memory work it is worth pointing out that learning by heart is best performed in short periods distributed over as long a time as possible. For instance, it is better to devote one hour a day to revision than six hours at a stretch once a week. By the same token, you can learn the same amount in less learning time by distributing your learning evenly over term and vacation than by crowding your learning into the term and leaving the vacations an academic blank. The greater the gaps you leave between your periods of learning, the less learning you have to do.[2]

Psychological studies have shown that what is involved is the "ageing" of learning. Learning can be increased in strength by sleep or a rest period. It seems, therefore, that more learning can be accomplished in, say, three hours by taking a ten-minute rest period in the middle than by working continuously. Also, "overlearning" delays forgetting.[3] If, therefore, you read a

---

[2] See the experiment described by Ian M.L. Hunter, *Memory* (Penguin Books, 1957), 58.

[3] Peter McKellar, *Experience and Behaviour* (Pelican Books, 19⁄ 137–138.

chapter of a book at night, try to read it again first thing in the morning, even though you feel you know it.

"It has been found," says a psychologist, "that when acts of reading and acts of recall alternate, *i.e.* when every reading is followed by an attempt to recall the items, the efficiency of learning and retention is enormously enhanced."[4] This means that learning is best done by reading a paragraph or page or similar convenient amount, and immediately reciting the gist of it: it has been found better to recite aloud than to perform the recall in the head. If you find that you cannot remember the passage properly, read it again and then try another recall. The longer the passage that you set yourself for recall the better; in other words, read as much at a time as you will be able to reproduce at the next recall. Tests have shown that when time is thus distributed between reading and recall, fifty per cent more is remembered than when the same time is spent merely in reading the passage over and over.[5]

Heavy footnotes to a book are sometimes distracting, and it is then a good plan to read the book through a first time without looking at the footnotes.

It is a mistake to spend valuable time in digesting a textbook on paper, unless the digest consists of little more than subject-headings and names of cases. Mere transcription from a book that one owns oneself is certainly folly. "Many readers I have found unalterably persuaded," wrote Dr. Johnson, "that nothing is certainly remembered but what is transcribed: and they have therefore passed weeks and months in transferring large quotations to a commonplace book. Yet, why any part of a book, which can be consulted at pleasure, should be copied I was never able to discover. The hand has no closer correspondence with the Memory than the eye. The act of writing itself distracts

---

[4] C. A. Mace, *The Psychology of Study*, 2nd ed. 38. Those who find it difficult to settle down to University studies may find further help in T.H. Pear, *The Art of Study* (1930), Chaps. 6–8.

[5] Ian M.L. Hunter, *op. cit.* 54. Sir Cyril Burt, who also gave the above advice, added: "Exploit your strongest form of imagery; if you are a visualiser, invent mental pictures; if you hear things easily in your mind's ear, use rhythms, rhymes, and alliterations" (*The Listener,* December 7, 1950).

the thoughts, and what is twice read is commonly better remembered than what is transcribed."[6]

Some teachers of law do not recommend the use of case books. In their view, the only way to become a proficient lawyer is to sit down in the library and read cases, not contenting oneself with the headnote or any other simplified version of the case, but reading through the whole of the statement of facts and the whole of the judgments. Faced with such a counsel of perfection the student may well echo from the heart the words of Doderidge J., written when legal literature was but a fraction of its present bulk: *"Vita brevis est, ars longa,* our life is short and full of calamities, and learning is a long time in getting."[7] A teacher must consider, before he gives advice like the above, the amount of time actually available to a law student for his studies. Taking first those at the universities, their period of residence is only about six months in the year, and few work for more than eight months in the year altogether. In that time they have to cover four or five subjects. This means an average of between six and eight weeks for each subject. Into this alarmingly short space they must fit attendance at lectures, the reading of the textbook, wider reading in the library, and revision, as well as the manifold activities that very properly occupy the undergraduate outside his work. Those attending technical colleges or studying for professional examinations, particularly those engaged in office work during the day, will probably have less rather than more time than undergraduates.

It becomes obvious, then, that time must be husbanded. Granting that the student must read cases, it is to my mind a permissible economy of time to buy a good case book for each department of law that is being studied. Using a case book has two advantages for the learner. First, the case book saves him some of the trouble (beneficial, but time-consuming) of making his own notebook of cases. Secondly, it does something to eliminate immaterial facts, thus helping in the search (again

---

[6] *The Idler,* No. 74.
[7] *The English Lawyer* (1631), 38.

beneficial, but again time-consuming) for the facts that are legally material.

It should be added that the use of case books by no means dispenses with the need for reading the original reports. For one thing, many of the more important cases in the case book can profitably be read in full in the law reports, using the case book version only for revision. Also, there are bound to be many cases that the keen student will come across and want to read that are not in his case book: among them, cases decided since the case book went to print.

To the student of modest means the high price of law books is intimidating, but it is false economy to do without basic works. Many are now available at reasonable prices in paperback. Money can sometimes be saved by buying secondhand books, but the beginner who does this should be careful never to buy anything but a latest edition, except on his teacher's advice.

The following is a London firm specialising in secondhand and new law books. A postcard will bring a quotation.

Wildy & Sons Ltd., Lincoln's Inn Archway, Carey Street, London, WC2A 2JD.[8]

LECTURES AND CLASSES

In the Middle Ages lectures were necessary because of the shortage of books. Now that printing has been with us for some hundreds of years, is there any need to continue the lecture system?

This is a vexed question, and perhaps the only comprehensive answer is that it depends upon the particular lecturer and the particular lectures. But, speaking generally, lectures may be said to possess several merits as a means of instruction. They can quicken interest. To listen to a competent lecturer makes a welcome change from the reading of books. The lecturer, too, can help his audience by giving the "basis and essentials" of the subject, elucidating the broad principles and indicating what is matter of detail. He can dwell on the parts of the subject that in

---

[8] Professional Books Ltd., Milton Trading Estate, Abingdon, Oxon. OX14 4SY also sells law books, old and new, particularly runs of law reports and periodicals. Frognal Rare Books, 18 Cecil Court, Charing Cross Road, London WC2N 4HE specialises in collector's items.

his experience cause special difficulties. Another point in his favour is that by varying his emphasis he can make himself more readily understood than can the toneless words of a book. Finally, the lecturer can bring textbooks up to date, and in a smallish class he can solve individual difficulties.

Some lecturers regard it as their sole function to stimulate and inspire; they do not particularly want notes to be taken. Certainly there is no greater waste of time than to sit through the average lecture making notes mechanically without thinking what they are about. Either concentrate on the lecture and rely upon your books for acquisition of facts, or form the habit of taking notes and at the same time of following the line of argument. It may set an edge upon your attention if you imagine that you are due to be tested in the subject immediately after the lecture. Another inestimable habit (though few cultivate it) is of spending a part of each evening reading through all the notes taken in the day.

Some lecturers are blamed for saying too many valuable things in too short a time, making it difficult for the pens of their audiences to keep pace with them. To meet this, use abbreviations. The following are particularly useful:

H	husband	W	wife
L	landlord	T	tenant
M	master	S	servant
P	plaintiff	D	defendant
P	principal	A	agent
V	vendor	P	purchaser

In land law it is customary to refer to imaginary pieces of land as Blackacre, Whiteacre, etc. The conventional abbreviations for these are Bacre, Wacre, etc.

Some traditional abbreviations make use of the stroke,/. Apart from a/c, account, they all represent two words, the stroke being placed between the initial letters of each:

b/e	bill of exchange
b/l	bill of landing
b/n	bank note
b/s	bill of sale
h/p	hire purchase
p/n	promissory note

This method can, of course, be extended to other common legal phrases:

a/b	act of bankruptcy
a/t	abstract of title
A/P	Act of Parliament
b/f	bona fide
e/r	equity of redemption
l/a	letters of administration
n/i	negotiable instrument
n/k	next of kin
p/a	power of appointment
p/p	personal property, part performance
p/r	personal representative
r/p	real property
r/c	restrictive covenant
s/g	sale of goods
s/p	specific performance

Alternatively the initial letters may be separated by periods:

b.f.(p)	bona fide (purchaser)
c.q.t.	*cestui que trust* (c.q.tt., *cestuis que trust*)
p.f.	prima facie

Or they may even be joined up:

DHSS	Department of Health and Social Security

Another traditional method of abbreviation is to write the first pronounceable part of the word and then write the ending. Common examples of this method are *assn* for *association*, *dept* for *department* and *insce* for *insurance*.

If you fail to catch or understand a particular sentence, no lecturer minds being asked to repeat or amplify it. Some lecturers invite questions and argument; in that case see that you play your part.

It need hardly be added, after what has already been said about transcription, that the making of a fair copy of one's own lecture notes is a dismal waste of time.

Considerably more important than the average lecture is the discussion class, generally called a class, supervision or tutorial. And of discussion classes, the most beneficial are those in which the discussion is centred on legal problems. With regard to these classes my injunctions are limited to two; first, attend them, and secondly, prepare for them by attempting to work out the problems for yourself before the class. Half the value of the class is missed if you sit supinely back and let the instructor or the other members of the class do the problems for you. The larger the class, the less likely it is that you will be pressed to speak, and the more important it is that you should speak—in order to cultivate self-possession and to get used to the sound of your own voice in public.

Talking about your work, whether in class or with a friend, has the further very important advantage of helping the memory. To quote one of our psychologists again: "Some form of action or of expression would seem to be essential to unimpaired retention. It seems that good conversationalists and great talkers generally have good memories. It is over-simple to suppose that this is due to the fact that, having good memories, they are well supplied with topics of conversation. The reverse connection would seem to be involved. What is talked about is more firmly impressed upon the mind. Such men when they read a book immediately discuss it with a friend, thus unconsciously employing the potent principle of active repetition."[9]

Apart from this necessary conversation, form the habit of working a full morning, because this is the part of the day when you are freshest. Do not do minor chores in the morning. As for the rest of the day, you will wish to make your own choice between the afternoon and evening for work, but at either time you will find that alcohol is totally inconsistent with study.

In conclusion, a few words on a comparatively humble matter, that of materials. The use of bound lecture notebooks is not to be recommended, because they are cumbrous and inelastic. If you use such notebooks and have three or four lectures to attend in a morning, this means a considerable weight and bulk to be carried about. Also, if you want to expand the lecturer's remarks with notes of your own you will find it difficult to do so within the confines of the notebook. On both counts the loose-leaf system is greatly preferable. The student who adopts this system needs to take with him to lectures only a single loose-leaf notebook, the day's work being transferred to larger specialised files in the

[9] C.A.Mace, *op. cit.,* 40–41.

evening. Notes taken down in this form can be rearranged and expanded at pleasure.

THE STUDY OF HISTORY

I suppose that most English students have some recollection of the order and the dates of the kings and queens of England. They will find such knowledge necessary in the study not only of constitutional but of purely legal history, for regnal years are the foundation of legal chronology. Overseas students, and others whose historical knowledge is shaky, may possibly be glad of the following mnemonic rhyme, which was once learnt by little Victorian boys and girls; I set it out with the corresponding regnal years at the side:

First William the Norman	1066–1087.
Then William his son;	1087–1100.
Henry, Stephen, and Henry,	1100–1135, 1135–1154, 1154–1189.
Then Richard and John;	1189–1199, 1199–1216.
Next Henry the third,	1216–1272.
Edwards, one, two and three,	1272–1307, 1307–1327, 1327–1377.
And again after Richard	1377–1399.
Three Henrys we see.	1399–1413, 1413–1422, 1422–1461.
Two Edwards, third Richard,	1461–1483, 1483, 1483–1485.
If rightly I guess;	
Two Henrys, sixth Edward,	1485–1509, 1509–1547, 1547–1553,
Queen Mary, Queen Bess,	1553–1558, 1558–1603.
Then Jamie the Scotchman,	1603–1625.
Then Charles whom they slew,	1625–1649.
Yet received after Cromwell	[1649–1660].
Another Charles too.	1649[10] (1660)–1685.
Next James the second	
Ascended the throne;	1685–1688.
Then Good William and Mary	
Together came on.	1689–1702.
Till, Anne, Georges four,	1702–1714, 1714–1727, 1727–1760,
	1760–1820, 1820–1830.
And fourth William all past,	1830–1837.
God sent Queen Victoria:	1837–1901.
May she long be the last!	

---

[10] Although Charles did not become king *de facto* until 1660, his regnal years were computed from the death of his father in 1649.

A racier version, and one easier to remember, is:

> Willy, Willy, Harry, Ste,
> Harry, Dick, John, Harry 3;
> One, two, three Neds, Richard 2,
> Henry 4, 5, 6. Then who?
> Edward 4, 5, Dick the Bad,
> Harrys twain and Ned the Lad;
> Mary, Bessie, James the Vain,
> Charlie, Charlie, James again;
> Will and Mary, Anna Gloria,
> Georges four, Will, Victoria.

Perhaps it is time to add to the edifice:

> Edward, George, then Edward 8,
> George; now Bess is Head of State.[11]

If the regnal years are not already known, and the task of learning them all seems too great, the student should at least notice the sovereigns whose reigns commenced at or shortly after the turn of each century. Knowledge of this, combined with a knowledge of the order of the sovereigns, will place every sovereign in his proper century. The sovereigns just referred to are:

Henry I	1100
Henry III	1216
Edward II	1307
Henry V	1413
Henry VIII	1509
James I	1603
Anne	1702
George IV	1820

Not only regnal years but dates in general are often a bugbear to students of history. The intelligent way to remember dates is to memorise a few key dates, and then to remember others by working backwards and forwards from these. For instance, Lord Mansfield became Chief Justice of the King's Bench in 1756, an easy date to remember and an important one. Suppose that it is desired to remember also that Blackstone delivered his first

---

[11] These lines are not my composition. If the author will communicate with me I shall be happy to give him due credit in the next edition.

course of lectures on English law in 1753. By relating this in the mind to 1756, and noticing the difference in years (3), the one will become linked to the other, and both can be recalled together. In time the same date can be related to several other dates, so that all important dates become interlocked in the mind. This method of memorising helps to build up the sense of historical perspective, which is the only rational justification for remembering dates.

Two useful dictionaires that may be found in the library are *Dictionary of British History*, edited by S. H. Steinberg, and *The Dictionary of English History* by Low and Pulling.

CHAPTER 5

TECHNICAL TERMS

'Zounds! I was never so bethump'd with words.

—Shakespeare, *King John*, II, i.

DICTIONARIES

AT first the beginner will find himself rather lost among the many technical terms used in a report, and will find some difficulty with Latin and law-French phrases and maxims.[1] Many are the tales that are recounted of these difficulties. There was the youth who innocently asked whether the phrase *en ventre sa mère* meant the same thing as *in loco parentis*. There was the examination candidate who expressed the opinion that the whole of Lord Atkin's speech in *Donoghue* v. *Stevenson* was *per incuriam*. To two other candidates belongs the credit of suggesting that *fructus naturales* means illegitimate children, and that *animus revertendi*

---

[1] The law-French phrases survive from the time when French, or rather Anglo-Norman, was the language of the courts. See Pollock, *First Book of Jurisprudence* (6th ed., 1929), 297–302; Holdsworth, *History of English Law*, ii, 477–484; Theo. Mathew in 54 L.Q.R. 358.

Latin was formerly the language for official documents, like writs; and sometimes survives in the names of writs. Also, maxims are usually in Latin because they are derived from Roman law or because they were invented by medieval jurists.

In 1730 Parliament passed an Act abolishing law-Latin in legal proceedings. But it was found that technical terms like *nisi prius, quare impedit, fieri facias* and *habeas corpus* were (as Blackstone put it) "not capable of an English dress with any degree of seriousness," and so two years later another Act was passed to allow such words to be continued "in the same language as hath been commonly used."

means the transmigration of souls. Weak latinity may also result in ungrammatical constructions. Thus the word *"obiter"* in *"obiter dictum"* (a judge's "saying by the way" or "passing remark") is not a noun: one should not write, as another examinee did, that a lawyer in reading cases needs to "hack his way through the *obiter* to reach the actual decisions."

A law dictionary can assist in such troubles. Three suitable for students, in order of price, are L.B. Curzon's *A Dictionary of Law* (£3.50), Osborn's *Concise Law Dictionary* (£3.65), and Mozley and Whiteley's *Law Dictionary* (9th ed. £5). A magnificent dictionary-encyclopaedia is David M. Walker's *The Oxford Companion to Law* (1980). As its name implies, it is not limited to English law but gives a general view of other common-law countries and foreign systems, as well as of legal philosophy; legal history is catered for, and there are brief biographies of judges and jurists. A splendid book to have on your shelf, if your purse will reach to it (£17.50); anyway you will probably find it in the reference section of your Law School or public library. Note also Earl Jowitt's *Dictionary of English Law,* which is founded upon earlier works by Wharton and Byrne.

Alternatively, a good English dictionary can afford considerable assistance on the meaning of individual English words, though not, of course, on Latin maxims. The cheapest short dictionary is the paperback Penguin (£2.25); the best are the *Concise Oxford Dictionary*, 6th ed. (£5.75) and *Collins English Dictionary* (£7.95)—either is an investment for a lifetime.

PRONUNCIATION

A few words may be said about pronunciation. Latin words and phrases are generally pronounced by lawyers in the same old barbaric way as they were in the Middle Ages,[2] that is to say, as

---

[2] There is a medieval tale, told me by an assistant in the Record Office, of some nuns who needed extra help about the convent and who accordingly sent down to the village by word of mouth for *servitia*. The request was understood by the villagers as a request for *cervicia*, an ale-feast, and they acted accordingly. The anecdote shows that the "c" in *cervicia*, and probably also the "t" in *servitia*, were pronounced like "s."

if they were English. To those who have been taught the new style of pronunciation at school this occasions some difficulty. *C* and *g* are soft where they would be in English,[3] and the pronunciation of such syllables as *atio* in *ratio decidendi* is also anglicised ("rayshio deesidendy"). Long vowels are pronounced as in English (the sounds being those in the names of the vowels).[4] Moreover, whether the vowel is to be pronounced long or short depends more upon English rules than upon Roman ones.(1) In words of two syllables, the first vowel is pronounced long even though it was short in Latin. Examples are bonus, onus, opus, genus ("jeenus"), *capias* ("caypias"), *mens rea* ("mens reeah"), *modus vivendi* ("mohdus vivendy"), nisi prius ("nysy[5] pryus"), *ratio decidendi* ("rayshyoh deesidendy"), *sine die* ("synee dyee"), and *vice versa* ("vysee"). This lends point to Mr. Punch's translation of *pendente lite*[6] as "a chandelier." (2) In words of three or more syllables derived from the Latin, vowels are generally pronounced short before the penultimate syllable, whether or not they were short in classical Latin. This is seen in the ordinary English words codicil, general and genera, ominous and operate. (Strictly, we should pronounce "economic" and "devolution" in the same way with a short first vowel, but they have become lengthened by usage.) It will be seen that the preferable pronunciation of *obiter*, according to the rule, is with a short *o*.

[3] Hence R.H. Barham's lines in allusion to Sir C. Wren's epitaph in St. Paul's Cathedral:
    And, talking of epitaphs, much I admire his,
    "Circumspice, si monumentum requiris,"
    Which an erudite verger translated to me,
    "If you ask for his monument, Sir—come—spy—see!"

[4] But there are no immutable rules, any more than there are in the pronunciation of English. Thus *si* is pronounced "see" by old and new school alike, though to be consistent the old school should pronounce it "sy," as indeed it does in the world *nisi*.

[5] There is an anecdote of how Lord Hewart C.J. "put down" counsel who applied for a rule *nisi* (pronouncing it "nysy," which was correct). Lord Hewart listened in silence and then said: "The judgment of the court will be short, like the first *i* in *nisi*. In this he displayed both his classical education and his ignorance of the rules of English pronunciation. The lawyer's traditional pronunciation of "patent" with a short *a* breaks the rule.

[6] "While the suit is pending."

Law-French words are pronounced much as they were in the Middle Ages; it is a solecism to utter them as if they were modern French. The pronunciation is, indeed, much nearer to modern English than it is to French. Thus the town crier quite correctly said "Oy-ez," not "Oy-ay.' The following are pronunciations of legal terms deriving from medieval French.

attorn		(-er)
attorney		
autrefois acquit		(oterfoyz, with "acquit" and "convict"
autrefois convict		pronounced as usual in English)

detinue (det-)
distress damage feasant (feezant)
emblements (embliments)
formedon ("e" pronounced indeterminately, as in "added")
feme sole[7] (femm)
feme covert (cuvert)
feoffment (feff-)
laches (laytshiz)
lien (lee-en or leen)
mesne (meen)

misfeasance		(-feez-)
nonfeasance		

pur autre vie (pur öter vee)
que (in the phrase "in the *que* estate" and in *cestui que trust*; pronounced kee)
seisin (-eez-)
semble—anglicised as written
Statutes of Jeofails (jefailz)[8]
venue (accent on the first syllable)
villein (villen)

In some instances lawyers still jealously retain the archaic pronunciations of English words. The noun "record" is pronounced like the verb, with the stress on the second syllable.[9] The term for an insured person, "assured," has the last syllable pronounced like "red" and stressed. In "cognisance," "recogni-

---

[7] Another tale concerns counsel who departed from usage by pronouncing this phrase "femmee sole." The judge pricked up his ears and said, "What is that? I have heard of a camisole, but not of a femmee sole."

[8] So the O.E.D. Sutton, *Personal Actions* 119, gives "jeefailz."

[9]   Condemn the fault, and not the actor of it?
    Why, every fault's condemn'd ere it be done.
    Mine were the very cipher of a function,
    To fine the faults whose fine stands in record,
    And let go by the actor.
    —Shakespeare, *Measure for Measure*, II, ii.
    Then turning to the Judge, he cry's, My Lord,
    (And thus runs o'er their Crimes upon record).
    —Edward Ward, *A Journey to H——, or a visit paid to the D——*
    (or, *The Infernal Vision*), Part I, Canto II (A.D. 1700–1705).

sance" and "cognisable" we refuse to "take cognisance of" the intrusive "g" in speaking, though we do in writing. (The "g" comes through latinising the law-French word *conusance*). In these words the lawyer's pronunciation is different from the layman's. Lastly, the "committee" of a person of unsound mind was a single person to whom the care of such person was entrusted by the court, the stress being on the last syllable. Committees are no long appointed.

LEGAL ABBREVIATIONS

Legal abbreviations are another frequent source of vexation to a beginner. The possession of a law dictionary is again a great help, but something may be said here of the more common abbreviations and short-cut terms seen in print.

First, as to the titles of judges.[10] "Smith J." means "Mr. Justice Smith" (or Mrs. Justice Smith, as the case may be), and when speaking of him in public he will be given that full title. Never say "Justice Smith" or (except for a circuit or county court judge) "Judge Smith"; these are Americanisms, to be shunned and avoided on this side of the Atlantic. The plural abbreviation is JJ.: "Smith and Byles JJ.," which is read out as "Mr. Justice Smith and Mr. Justice Byles." Similarly, the following letters placed after the names of the judges have the following meanings:

B.	=	Baron [of the Exchequer]. A member of the former Court of Exchequer—not to be confused with Barons who are peers. Plural BB. Title now obsolete.
C.B.	=	Chief Baron: the head of the former Court of Exchequer. Title now obsolete.
C.J. (or L.C.J.)	=	(Lord Chief Justice. Head of the Q.B.D. and of the C.A. (Criminal Division).
J.A.	=	Justice of Appeal. Title found between 1875 and 1877, and now obsolete.[11]
L.C.	=	Lord Chancellor. Head of the judicial system.
L.J.	=	Lord Justice. Member of the C.A. Plural L.JJ.: Lords Justices.
M.R.	=	Master of the Rolls. Member (and virtually head) of the C.A. (Civil Division).
P.	=	President. Head of the Family Division (formerly Probate, Divorce and Admiralty Division).
V.C.	=	Vice-Chancellor. In effect head of the Chancery Division.

[10] Sometimes called puisne (pronounced "pewny"—ew as in few) judges, meaning any judge of the High Court (or the older courts that it replaced) other than the chiefs.

[11] See 61 L.Q.R. 231.

Do not omit or abbreviate "Lord" before the name of a judge who is a Law Lord or other peer. Thus you will write "Lord Hailsham L.C." not "Hailsham L.C." and similarly "Lord Lane C.J.", (or "Lord Lane L.C.J."). These are read out as "Lord Hailsham, Lord Chancellor" and "Lord Lane, Chief Justice" (or "Lord Chief Justice"). In the case of Chief Justices who were not peers, like Rufus Isaacs, the written designation is "Isaacs C.J." (or "L.C.J."), which is read out as "[Lord] Chief Justice Isaacs." "Ormrod L.J." is read out as "Lord Justice Ormrod." "Ormrod and Watkins L.JJ." are "Lords Justices Ormrod and Watkins." Lord Denning M.R. is "Lord Denning, Master of the Rolls." Where this last office is not held by a peer the former usage was that one had to remember the holder's Christian name when speaking of him, so "Pollock M.R." was "Sir Ernest Pollock, Master of the Rolls," and "Brett M.R." was "Sir Baliol Brett, Master of the Rolls."[12] But at the present day it would be acceptable to say "Pollock, Master of the Rolls," and so on. A living judge like Megarry V.-C. should certainly be referred to as "Sir Robert Megarry, Vice-Chancellor."

Certain abbreviations and shorthand expressions supply a convenient mechanism for referring to authorities. A librarian once showed me a request form filled in by a reader asking for a supposed book called *"Ibid."* Evidently the reader had seen this referred to many times in footnotes, and thought that it must be an extremely important book, written perhaps by an eminent Persian. Of course, *"ibid."* is short for *ibidem,* meaning "in the same place"; it is simply a way of repeating a reference previously given. Similarly, *op. cit.* means the book previously cited, and *loc. cit.* means the page previously cited in the book previously cited. *Passim* means "everywhere in the book." S.C. means "same case" (*i.e. ibid.* as applied to a reported case), and S.P. "same principle." Other compendious expressions are *per, semble, aliter* (or *secus*) and *contra. Per* generally means "statement by": thus *"per* Lord Wilberforce" following a quotation means that the remark quoted is that of Lord Wilberforce. *Per curiam* and *per incuriam* are not opposites. *Per curiam* means that the statement is by the whole court. *Per incuriam* means that a judge's remark was made by mistake.

[12] 79 L.Q.R. 190.

Semble is law-French for "it seems" or "it seems that" (when the authority for a proposition is weak or not completely satisfactory; usually it indicates an *obiter dictum*). *Aliter* and *secus* means "otherwise" and *contra* refers to an authority contradicting what one has first said. Thus one can write "*Semble* the phrase 'carcase or portion of a carcase' in this statute does not include a sausage—see *per* Tripe L.J., *obiter*, in *Sage* v. *Onions* (C.A.); *contra, Ham* v. *Eggs* (Div.Ct.); *aliter* if the sausage meat is not yet minced." This may not be an elegant style but it does represent an economy of effort, which to some minds has a beauty of its own.

CHAPTER 6

CASE LAW TECHNIQUE

Mastering the lawless science of our law,
That codeless myriad of precedent,
That wilderness of single instances,
Through which a few, by wit or fortune led,
May beat a pathway out to wealth and fame.

—Tennyson, *Aylmer's Field.*

RATIO DECIDENDI AND OBITER DICTUM

ENGLISH courts make a habit of following their previous decisions within more or less well-defined limits. This is called the doctrine of precedent. The part of a case that is said to possess authority is the *ratio decidendi,* that is to say, the rule of law upon which the decision is founded. Finding the *ratio decidendi* of a case is an important part of the training of a lawyer. It is not a mechanical process but is an art that one gradually acquires through practice and study. One can, however, give a general description of the technique involved.

What the doctrine of precedent declares is that cases must be decided the same way when their material facts are the same. Obviously it does not require that *all* the facts should be the same. We know that in the flux of life all the facts of a case will never recur; but the legally material facts may recur and it is with these that the doctrine is concerned.

The *ratio decidendi* of a case can be defined as the material facts of the case plus the decision theron.[1] The same learned writer who advanced this definition went on to suggest a helpful formula. Suppose that in a certain case facts A, B and C exist;

---

[1] Goodhart, "Determining the *Ratio Decidendi* of a Case." *Essays in Jurisprudence and the Common Law* (1931) 1.

and suppose that the court finds that facts B and C are material and fact A immaterial, and then reaches conclusion X (*e.g.* judgment for the plaintiff, or judgment for the defendant). Then the doctrine of precedent enables us to say that in any future case in which facts B and C exist, or in which facts A and B and C exist, the conclusion must be X. If in a future case facts A, B, C and D exist, and fact D is held to be material, the first case will not be a direct authority, though it may be of value as an analogy.

What facts are legally material? That depends on the particular case, but take as an illustration a "running down" action, that is to say, an action for injuries sustained through the defendant's negligent driving of a vehicle. The fact that the plaintiff had red hair and freckles, that his name was Smith, and that the accident happened on a Friday are immaterial, for the rule of law upon which the decision proceeds will apply equally to persons who do not possess these characteristics and to accidents that happen on other days. On the other hand, the fact that the defendant drove negligently, and the fact that in consequence he injured the plaintiff, are material, and a decision in the plaintiff's favour on such facts will be an authority for the proposition that a person is liable for causing damage through the negligent driving of a vehicle.

The foregoing is a general explanation of the phrase "the *ratio decidendi* of a case." To get a clearer idea of the way in which a *ratio decidendi* is extracted, let us take a decided case and study it in detail. I set out below the case of *Wilkinson* v. *Downton*,[2] where the plaintiff was awarded damages by a jury for nervous shock, and the trial judge then heard argument on the question whether the verdict could be upheld in law. The first part of the judgment, which is all that needs be considered here, runs as follows.

WRIGHT J. In this case the defendant, in the execution of what he seems to have regarded as a practical joke, represented to the plaintiff that he was charged by her husband with a message to her to the effect that her husband was smashed up in an accident, and was lying at The Elms at Leytonstone with both legs broken, and that she was to go at once in a cab with two pillows to fetch him home. All this was false. The effect of the statement on the plaintiff was a violent shock to her nervous

[2] [1897] 2 Q.B. 57.

system, producing vomiting and other serious and permanent physical consequences at one time threatening her reason, and entailing weeks of suffering and incapacity to her as well as expense to her husband for medical attendance. These consequences were not in any way the result of previous ill-health or weakness of constitution; nor was there any evidence of predisposition to nervous shock or any other idiosyncrasy.

In addition to these matters of substance there is a small claim for 1s. 10½d. for the cost of railway fares of persons sent by the plaintiff to Leytonstone in obedience to the pretended message. As to this 1s. 10½d. expended in railway fares on the faith of the defendant's statement, I think the case is clearly within the decision in *Pasley* v. *Freeman* (1798) 3 T.R. 51. The statement was a misrepresentation intended to be acted on to the damage of the plaintiff.

The real question is as to the £100, the greatest part of which is given as compensation for the female plaintiff's illness and suffering. It was argued for her that she is entitled to recover this as being damages caused by fraud, and therefore within the doctrine established by *Pasley* v. *Freeman* and *Langridge* v. *Levy* (1837) 2 M. & W. 519. I am not sure that this would not be an extension of that doctrine, the real ground of which appears to be that a person who makes a false statement intended to be acted on must make good the damage naturally resulting from its being acted on. Here there is no *injuria* of that kind. I think, however, that the verdict may be supported upon another ground. The defendant has, as I assume for the moment, wilfully done an act calculated to cause physical harm to the plaintiff—that is to say, to infringe her legal right to personal safety, and has in fact thereby caused physical harm to her. That proposition without more appears to me to state a good cause of action, there being no justification alleged for the act. This wilful *injuria* is in law malicious, although no malicious purpose to cause the harm which was caused nor any motive of spite is imputed to the defendant.

It remains to consider whether the assumptions involved in the proposition are made out. One question is whether the defendant's act was so plainly calculated to produce some effect of the kind which was produced that an intention to produce it ought to be imputed to the defendant, regard being had to the fact that the effect was produced on a person proved to be in an ordinary state of health and mind. I think that it was. It is difficult to imagine that such a statement, made suddenly and with apparent seriousness, could fail to produce grave effects under the circumstances upon any but an exceptionally indifferent person, and therefore an intention to produce such an effect must be imputed, and it is no answer in law to say that more harm was done than was anticipated, for that is commonly the case with all wrongs.

The reader will notice that the judge does not cite any authority for his decision that the £100 is recoverable. The only authorities he cites are authorities on which he says he prefers not to rely. The reason is that at the date when the case was decided there was no English authority on the general question whether it was a tort intentionally to inflict bodily harm on another. There was, indeed, the very ancient tort of battery, which is committed when D hits or stabs or shoots P. But Downton committed no battery upon Mrs Wilkinson; nor did he assault her by threatening a battery. Consequently, the case was one "of first impression," and the judge decided it merely on common-sense principles. It would be a grave reproach to a civilised system of law if it did not give a remedy on such facts.

Let us now see how the *ratio decidendi* is to be extracted. This is done by finding the material facts. The judge has already done much of the work for us, because he has omitted from his judgment many of the facts given in evidence that were obviously irrelevant to the legal issue—*e.g.* the address at which the plaintiff lived. But the judgment mentions the address at which the husband was supposed to be lying, which also is clearly irrelevant. As a first step in boiling it down we may say that the essential facts, and the pith of the judgment, were as follows:

> The defendant by way of what was meant to be a joke told the plaintiff that the latter's husband had been smashed up in an accident. The plaintiff, who had previously been of normal health, suffered a shock and serious illness. Wright J. held that the defendant was liable, not perhaps for the tort of deceit but because the defendant had wilfully done an act calculated to cause physical harm to the plaintiff, and had in fact caused such harm.

The above would represent the sort of note that an intelligent student would make of the case. How are we to frame the *ratio decidendi*? There are two main possibilities.

The first would be to take such of the detailed facts as may be deemed to be material, plus the decision on the facts. This would result in the following rule: that where the defendant has wilfully told the plaintiff a lie of a character that is likely (a clearer word than "calculated") to frighten and so cause physical harm to the plaintiff, and it has in fact caused such harm, the defendant is liable, in the absence of some ground of justification.

This *ratio* omits to specify the particular lie told by the defendant, because this was immaterial. What mattered was not the particular lie as to the plaintiff's husband's alleged injury, but the more general fact of lying. The particular lie told by the defendant was material only in the sense that it was the sort of lie that was likely to frighten and cause physical harm to the plaintiff.

But, it may be objected, such a *ratio* would be too narrow, because the learned judge evidently intended to lay down a wider rule. He did not confine his judgment to lies, but spoke only of wilfully doing an *act* which is calculated to and does cause physical harm; and this gives us the true *ratio*. It was immaterial that the particular form of mischief perpetrated by the defendant took the form of a verbal lie; it might have been some other act likely to cause harm, and the legal outcome would have been the same. This, indeed, is common sense. A person with Downton's juvenile sense of humour who dresses up as a ghost, or who puts a squib under somebody else's chair, would doubtless find himself in the same legal category as Downton.

Again, the judge did not speak of fright when he formulated the principle of his decision. He spoke of causing physical harm, which is much wider. On this principle, an outrageous *threat* causing suffering is a tort. In a subsequent case[3] which approved *Wilkinson* v. *Downton,* the defendant threatened to arrest and prosecute the plaintiff, a foreign servant-girl, if she did not give certain information; the defendant knew that any charge he brought against the girl would be quite unfounded, and the girl became ill with distress. It was held that she had a good cause of action. Another application of the principle occurs where the harm operates directly on the plaintiff's body, not indirectly through the mind—as where the defendant blackens a towel with which the plaintiff is about to wipe his face, or secretly adds poison to the plaintiff's drink. Although these situations have not been the subject of reported decisions; there is no doubt that they would fall under the principle of *Wilkinson* v. *Downton.*

The reader may now be feeling rather puzzled to the meaning of *ratio decidendi.* We started off with a possible narrow *ratio decidendi* of the case, incorporating the fact of lying and the fact of fright. Then we passed to a wider *ratio,* which evidently accords with common sense as well as with the language of the judgment, in which the facts of lying and fright have disappeared. How can this be reconciled with our definition of *ratio decidendi* as the material facts plus the decision thereon? Were

[3] *Janvier* v. *Sweeney* [1919] 2 K.B. 316.

not the lie and the fright material facts in *Wilkinson* v. *Downton*? If there had been no lie and no fright, and no equivalent facts in their place, the plaintiff would not have won. What exactly do we mean by a "material fact"?

The answer is that we have not been using this expression in a consistent way, and it is necessary to restate the position in more exact language. What is really involved in finding the *ratio decidendi* of a case is a process of abstraction. Abstraction is the mental operation of picking out certain qualities and relations from the facts of experience. Imagine a baby in whose household there is a terrier called Caesar. The baby will be taught to call this dog "bow-wow," because, "bow-wow" is easier to say than "Caesar." If he sees another dog he will guess or be told that this other dog is to be called "bow-wow" as well. This is an example of one of the baby's earliest feats of abstraction. Abstraction comes through the perception of similarities between individual facts, and all language and all thinking depend upon it.

The next point to be noticed is that this process of abstraction may be carried to progressively higher flights. The individual dog Caesar is, at a low level of abstraction, a terrier; at a higher level he is a dog; higher still, a mammal and then an animal and a living thing. In the same way a man might say that he was born at the Piccaninny Nursing Home; in London; in England; in Europe. All these are "facts," but they are facts belonging to different levels of abstraction.

We are now in a better position to state the *ratio decidendi* of a case. The ascertainment of the *ratio decidendi* of a case depends upon a process of abstraction from the totality of facts that occurred in it. The higher the abstraction, the wider the *ratio decidendi*. Thus a rule that "it is a tort to tell a lie that is likely to and does cause fright and consequent physical harm" is a narrow rule, belonging to a low level of abstraction from the facts of the particular case in which it was laid down; leave out the reference to fright, and it becomes wider; replace "tell a lie" by "do any act with intent to affect the plaintiff in body or mind" and it becomes wider still. It is the last rule that is the *ratio decidendi* of *Wilkinson* v. *Downton*. We carry on the process of abstraction until all the particular facts have been eliminated except the fact of the doing of an act that is intended to affect the plaintiff adversely and is likely to cause physical harm, and the fact of the occurrence of such harm.

How do we know when to stop with our abstraction? The answer is: primarily by reading what the judge says in his judgment, but partly also by our knowledge of the law in general, and by our common sense and our feeling for what the law ought to be. It so happens that in the case we have been considering the learned judge formulates the rule fairly clearly, but sometimes the rule stated in the judgment incorporates facts which as a matter of common sense are not essential, and sometimes it goes to the opposite extreme of being too sweeping—as can be demonstrated either by the use of common sense or by referring to other decided cases. The finding of the *ratio decidendi* is not an automatic process; it calls for lawyerly skill and knowledge.

DISTINGUISHING

Certain general truths implicit in the foregoing discussion may now be stated more explicitly.

In the first place, a case may have not one but several *rationes decidendi,* of ascending degrees of generality. We have seen two or three possible *rationes* in *Wilkinson* v. *Downton.* The third was accepted not only because it was stated by the judge but also because it accorded with common sense and with other authorities. Sometimes a judge will lay down a rule that is narrower than is required by common sense, and a later court may then say that the rule ought to be read more widely, by abandoning some limitation unnecessarily expressed in it. Indeed, one such unnecessary limitation can be found in the judgment in *Wilkinson* v. *Downton.* The rule stated by Wright J. refers to a person who has "wilfully" done an act calculated to cause physical harm, and the primary meaning of a "wilful" act is one that is done with the intention of bringing about a particular consequence.[4] Downton did not, perhaps, intend to cause Mrs

---

[4] "Wilful act," or "doing an act wilfully," is a telescoped expression. In a sense, every act is wilful, or it is not an act but merely a spasm. In legal discussions, the notion of wilfulness or intention usually refers to the *consequences* of conduct; it is the consequence that is intended, or wilfully brought about, not the movement of the defendant's body that constitutes the act. Where mere movement is referred to, "intention" connotes knowledge of the circumstances.

Wilkinson a serious illness, but he did intend to frighten her, and that was sufficient. But, as a matter of common sense, the rule should be extend also to one who is merely *reckless* as to the harm in question (and the word "wilful" is, indeed, capable of extending to recklessness). If Downton had made the lying statement to Mrs Wilkinson in order to persuade her to accompany him for some secret end of his own, realising that the statement would be likely to frighten her but not desiring (and therefore not intending) the fright itself, his liability should be just the same as for a tort of intention. This was the essential position in the case of the foreign servant-girl referred to before: what the defendant intended in that case was to put pressure upon the girl to make her talk; he must have foreseen the possibility of causing her great distress, but his mind was directed towards making her do what he wanted, not towards distress. In analysis, the case is one of recklessness as to the plaintiff's fright, not one of intention as to the fright; but the legal liability should be, and is, the same.[5]

One may argue that there is another unnecessary limitation contained in the judgment in *Wilkinson* v. *Downton*. The judge referred to the fact that the plaintiff had been in normal health, yet it is not possible but probable that the decision would have been just the same even if her health had previously been poor—for the fact that the plaintiff is in poor health can be no excuse to a defendant who tells her a cruel lie that would be

[5] A word may here be added upon the meaning of the word "calculated," which Wright J. used in his judgment. Judges are fond of this word, but it is an unfortunate expression because it suggests a meaning which it is not intended to convey. Originally, "calculated to" bore its literal meaning of "intended to," but in time it came to mean merely "likely to," and it is in this sense that Wright J. uses it. What the learned judge means is that the defendant intended to give the plaintiff a fright (this was the "wilful act"), and what he did was likely ("calculated") to cause the injury it did, even though the defendant did not intend to cause the full degree of the injury that occurred. The judge's decision would not apply (1) if the defendant merely acted carelessly in passing on information which was not true (for then there would be no "wilful act"), or (2) if, although the defendant intentionally told a lie and intended to cause the plaintiff some slight perturbation, a reasonable man would not have foreseen that the plaintiff would be seriously upset (for then the lie would not be "calculated" to cause physical harm).

likely to cause her physical harm. The fact that the particular plaintiff had been in good health removed a complication that the judge might otherwise have had to consider, and for that reason he referred to it; but all the same a later court may, on mature consideration and when the question arises, decide that the limitation is unnecessary.

Conversely, it sometimes happens that a judge will lay down a rule that is unnecessarily wide for the decision of the case before him; a later court may say that it is too wide, and needs to be cut down.

This point leads on to the second. The phrase "the *ratio decidendi* of a case" is slightly ambiguous. It may mean either (1) the rule that the judge who decided the case intended to lay down and apply to the facts, or (2) the rule that a later court concedes him to have had the power to lay down. The last sentence is rather clumsy, but what I mean is this. Courts do not accord to their predecessors an unlimited power of laying down wide rules. They are sometimes apt to say, in effect: "Oh yes, we know that in that case the learned judge purported to lay down such and such a rule; but that rule was unnecessarily wide for the decision of the case before him, because, you see, the rule makes no reference to fact A, which existed in the case, and which we regard as a material fact, and as a fact that ought to have been introduced into the *ratio decidendi.*"[6] One circumstance that may induce a court to adopt this niggling attitude towards an earlier decision is the necessity of reconciling that decision with others. Or again, the court in the earlier case may have enunciated an unduly wide rule without considering all its possible consequences, some of which are unjust or inconvenient or otherwise objectionable. Yet another possibility is that the earlier decision is altogether unpalatable to the court in the later case, so that the latter court wishes to interpret it as narrowly as possible.

This process of cutting down the expressed *ratio decidendi* of a case is one kind of "distinguishing." It may be called "restric-

---

[6] A common form of statement is to say that the earlier judges "were speaking of, and their language must be understood by reference to, the particular facts which were brought before them in that case": 62 L.J.Ch. 126.

tive" distinguishing, to differentiate it from the other kind, genuine or non-restrictive distinguishing. Non-restrictive distinguishing occurs where a court accepts the expressed *ratio decidendi* of the earlier case, and does not seek to curtail it, but finds that the case before it does not fall within this *ratio decidendi* because of some material difference of fact. Restrictive distinguishing cuts down the expressed *ratio decidendi* of the earlier case by treating as material to the earlier decision some fact, present in the earlier case, which the earlier court regarded as immaterial,[7] or by introducing a qualification (exception) into the rule stated by the earlier court.

Wilkinson v. *Downton* has not been cut down, because the wide principle has commended itself to later judges.[8] If, however, a case ever arises in which Wright J.'s wide rule is thought to carry the law too far, the decision can be restrictively distinguished.

I have stressed this matter of distinguishing because it plays a most important part in legal argument. Suppose that you are conducting a case in court, and that the other side cites a case against you. You then have only two alternatives (that is, if you are not prepared to throw your hand in altogether). One is to submit that the case cited is wrongly decided, and so should not be followed. This is possible only if the case is not binding on the court. The other is to "distinguish" it, by suggesting that it contains or lacks some vital fact that is absent or present in your client's case. Sometimes you may have the sympathy of the judge

---

[7] Dr. Goodhart in the article cited above, p.68, n.1, says that (1) it is for the judge who decides the case, and for him alone, to determine what facts are material, and the judge may express his decision that facts are immaterial merely by leaving them out of the rule of law that he propounds. But on the other hand (2) the *ratio decidendi* of a case is not necessarily the rule of law stated by the judge, because that may be too wide. It seems to me that these two statements are contradictory, and the truth I take to be that the second is right and the first wrong. The rule stated by the judge may be "too wide" in the view of the later court, and that means that the judge has not an unlimited discretion to jettison fact as being immaterial. For Dr. Goodhart's reply to a controversy on this question, see 22 M.L.R. 117.

[8] The only English case in which *Wilkinson* v. *Downton* was directly relevant was *Janvier* v. *Sweeney*, p.71, n.3. But the validity of the principle is amply supported by American decisions.

in your effort to distinguish it, even though the distinction you suggest involves tampering with the expressed *ratio decidendi* of the precedent case and even though you have no authority for the suggested distinction. Your judge may be gravely dissatisfied with the case and yet, owing to our excessively strict doctrine of precedent, it may be impossible for him to overrule it. In such circumstances it is simply human nature that he will distinguish it if he can. He may, in extreme and unusual circumstances, be apt to seize on almost any factual difference between this previous case and the case before him in order to arrive at a different decision.[9] Some precedents are continually left on the shelf in this way; as a wag observed, they become very "distinguished." The limit of the process is reached when a judge says that the precedent is an authority only "on its actual facts." For most practical purposes this is equivalent to announcing that it will never be followed. It is not suggested that this extreme form of distinguishing is a common occurrence, for generally judges defer to the decisions of their predecessors both in the letter and in the spirit, even though they dislike them. But restrictive distinguishing does happen, and the possibility of its happening makes it of great importance to the lawyer.

OBITER DICTA

In contrast with the *ratio decidendi* is the *obiter dictum*. The latter is a mere saying by the way, a chance remark, which is not binding upon future courts, though it may be respected according to the reputation of the judge, the eminence of the court, and the circumstances in which it came to be pronounced. An example would be a rule of law stated merely by way of analogy or illustration, or a suggested rule upon which the decision is not finally rested. The reason for not regarding an *obiter dictum* as binding is that it was probably made without a

---

[9] Perhaps Pollock C.B. had restrictive distinguishing in mind when, in a letter to his grandson, "F.P.," in 1868, he made the following remark: "Even Parke, Lord Wensleydale (the greatest legal pedant that I believe ever existed) did not always follow even the House of Lords; he did not overrule—oh no! but he did not *act upon* cases which were *nonsense* (as many are)." Hanworth's *Lord Chief Baron Pollock* (1929), 198.

full consideration of the cases on the point, and that, if very broad in its terms, it was probably made without a full consideration of all the consequences that may follow from it; or the judge may not have expressed a concluded opinion.

An example of an *obiter dictum* occurs in *Wilkinson* v. *Downton* when the learned judge is considering the argument that the plaintiff is entitled to recover damages for the tort of deceit. At first sight this may seem a good argument, because the defendant could certainly be said in a popular sense to have deceived the plaintiff. But it is generally taken to be essential for the tort of deceit that the defendant should have intended the plaintiff to have acted on the statement, and that the plaintiff should have so acted to his detriment, for which detriment he now claims damages. Mrs Wilkinson recovered 1s. 10½d. as damages for deceit, because this was a sum of money that she had spent in reliance on the defendant's deceitful statement. But the fact that she became ill was not an act of reliance upon the statement. It was a spontaneous reaction to the statement. Consequently, the learned judge preferred not to rest his judgment upon this ground. He did not positively pronounce against it, but his words seem to indicate that he thought that as the law now stands the claim could not properly be based on the tort of deceit. One may say, therefore, that there its a very tentative dictum against the plaintiff on this particular issue. But the point was not finally decided, and in any case was not made the ground of the decision, and so the observations made upon it were *obiter*.

There is another kind of *obiter dictum*, which perhaps is not, properly speaking, an *obiter dictum* at all, namely a *ratio decidendi* that in the view of a subsequent court is unnecessarily wide. It is not an *obiter dictum* in the primary meaning of that phrase, because it is constructed out of the facts of the case and the decision is rested upon it. But, as we have seen, later courts reserve the right to narrow it down, and in doing so they frequently attempt to justify themselves by declaring that the unnecessarily wide statement was *obiter*. The real justification for the practice of regarding what is really *ratio decidendi* as *obiter dictum*, that is to say for restrictive distinguishing, is the undesirability of hampering the growth of English law through the too extensive application of the doctrine of precedent. A court may restrictively distinguish its own decisions, or those of a court on the same level, but it will not generally dare to do this with the decisions of courts superior to it in the hierarchy, particularly the House of Lords.

It is frequently said that a ruling based upon hypothetical facts is *obiter*. This is often true. Thus if the judge says: "I decide for the defendant; but if the facts had been properly pleaded I should have found for the plaintiff," the latter part of the statement is *obiter*. But there is at least one exception. In the past, when the defendant pleaded an "objection in point of law" (the former "demurrer"), legal argument might take place on this before the trial, and for the purpose of the argument and the decision it was assumed that all the facts stated in the plaintiff's pleadings were true. A decision pronounced on such assumed facts is not an *obiter dictum*. However, the practice of arguing the law before adducing evidence is now virtually obsolete.

If a decision would otherwise be a binding authority, it does not lose that status merely because the point was not argued by counsel (this will be important only as a way of attacking a decision that is of merely persuasive authority). But what is called a decision *sub silentio* is not binding: that is to say, one in which the existence of the particular point was not perceived by the court, so that it was not discussed in the judgment.[9a] This is so, at least, where the precedent case is that of the same court. The House of Lords would probably regard its own decision *sub silentio* as binding on the Court of Appeal.

HOW MUCH OF A CASE TO REMEMBER

A question that frequently vexes the beginner is: how many of the facts of a case should he remember, for the purpose of learning the law and for the purpose of making a good showing in the examination? Ought he to try to remember (1) all the facts stated in the report, or (2) a selection of those facts, or (3) only those facts that are incorporated in the statement of the *ratio decidendi*? Take again as an illustration the case of *Wilkinson* v. *Downton*. The three possibilities just referred to are exemplified by (1) the passage from the judgment on pp. 68–69, above, (2) the first attempt at condensation on p. 70 and (3) the statement of the *ratio decidendi* on p. 72.

[9a] *Barrs* v. *Bethell* [1981] 3 W.L.R. 874.

The answer to the question is that both (2) and (3) should be remembered. (1) is obviously ruled out; it would be a waste of effort to remember every minor circumstance that may be stated in the report, such as the fact that Mr Wilkinson was alleged to be lying at The Elms at Leytonstone. On the other hand, (3) is as obviously included, for it is the pith and marrow of the law. About the necessity for remembering (2) the reader may be inclined to be argumentative. He may contend that he is learning to be a lawyer, not a chronicler of tragedies, and that if he learns the rules of law there is no need for him to burden his memory with the facts of cases that as a matter of history gave rise to those rules.

There are two answers to this objection, the first of interest to examination candidates only, and the second of wider interest.

The first answer is that examiners are suspicious creatures, and in particular they are suspicious of "footnote" knowledge. Suppose that in the examination your only reference to *Wilkinson* v. *Downton* is as follows: "A person is liable in tort if he causes physical injury by an act intended to affect the plaintiff adversely and likely to cause injury: *Wilkinson* v. *Downton.*" The rule is correct and the name of the case is correct; and you may in fact have satisfied yourself that the rule is deducible from the case; but the examiner will not know it. For all he knows, you saw the rule in your textbook and the name of the case in a footnote. To dispel his suspicion, you must give some statement of the concrete facts.

The second answer is more important, but we need spend no further time over it because enough has really been said on it already. It is a mistake to suppose that every case has one and only one fixed and incontrovertible *ratio decidendi*. What exactly is the *ratio decidendi* of a case is often a matter for much argument. Also, the pick-lock art of distinguishing depends upon a critical examination of all the facts of the case that might by any possibility be regarded as material. If, therefore, there is any sort of doubt about the correctness of a decision, or about its limits, as many of the facts as can conceivably be looked upon as material should be remembered.

There are some cases, however, where nothing more than the simple *ratio decidendi* need be remembered, because apart from the facts stated in the *ratio decidendi* the case contains no facts except the trivialities of date, amount, etc. An illustration is *Byrne* v. *Van Tienhoven*.[10] The facts of this case were as follows:

October 1.—The defendants in Cardiff by letter offered to sell to the plaintiffs 1,000 boxes of Hensol Tinplates.
October 11.—The plaintiffs received this letter. The plaintiffs wired to defendants. "Accept thousand Hensols." But
October 8.—The defendants posted a letter revoking their offer, ending "and we must consider our offer to be cancelled from this date."
October 20.—The plaintiffs received second letter.

It was held that there was a good contract and that the defendants' revocation of their offer was ineffective.

The reason why the above facts are set out in a case book is to show the student how the legal question as to revocation of offers is likely to arise in practice. By digesting the facts in his own mind, and seeing how the problem arises out of them, the student is preparing himself to answer examination problems and to deal with cases in his legal practice. But this does not mean that he is expected to memorise any of the particular facts of *Byrne* v. *Van Tienhoven*. All the facts of this case are immaterial except the fact that the offerors attempted to revoke their offer by a letter that did not arrive until after the offerees had accepted; and the *ratio decidendi* is that such a revocation is ineffective. If this is grasped, all the rest of the facts can be forgotten.

DIVERGENT OPINIONS

The establishment of the *ratio decidendi* is more complicated when different members of a composite court express different opinions. The problem is particularly acute for the House of Lords, where all the members commonly express separate opinions, which may show great diversity. As a result, their lordships not infrequently make the law more uncertain than it was before the appeal.

Where the opinions of different judges differ so greatly that there is no majority for any single view, all that can be done, to ascertain the *ratio decidendi,* is to add up the facts regarded as material by any group of judges whose votes constitute a majority, and to base the *ratio* on those facts. The result is to

[10] (1880) 5 C.P.D. 344.

confine the *ratio* to its narrowest form. For example, if Lords L
and M hold that the material facts are A and B, while Lords N
and O hold that they are A, B and C, and Lord P dissents, the
ratio decidendi must require the presence of A, B and C. It
seems, however, that the confusion of opinion may be such that
there cannot be said to be a *ratio decidendi*. This is so where, of
the three majority lords, Lord L holds that the material facts are
A and B, Lord M holds that they are A and C, and Lord N holds
that they are A and D, while Lords O and P dissent. It would be
wholly artificial to say that the *ratio* requires the presence of A,
B, C and D, since this is not the view of any one of the lords.[11]

Further complications can arise. The minority lords, O and P,
may agree with Lord L in thinking that if the facts were A and B
the conclusion would be X, but they may hold that there is
insufficient evidence that fact B existed, and for this reason
conclude that the answer in this case is not X. So on the abstract
point of law there is a majority of the House (L, O and P) in
favour of L's view. Yet, strictly speaking, the expressions of
opinion by O and P are *obiter*. All that can be said is that the
joint opinion of L, O and P will carry great weight with lower
courts, even though it is not binding.

THE NAMES OF CASES

Another question frequently asked by law students is as to
remembering names of cases. The questioner realises, of course,
that he is expected to read cases and to quote them, where
relevant, in his answers; but must he behave as though he were
learning the telephone directory?

The first and most important reply to the question is this:
Never refrain from referring to a case in the examination merely
because you have forgotten its name. The name is the least
important part of the case. Most important is the rule of law
contained in the case; next important are the facts; even the
name of the court that decided the case is of more legal value
than the proper names of the parties. If the name of the case is
imperfectly remembered the approximate name can be given,

[11] See Sir Rupert Cross in 93 L.Q.R. 378. He took the view that the
opinion of a majority of the majority can be controlling, even though
it is a minority of the whole House (see at p.381); *sed quaere*.

with a question mark in brackets; thus, *Derry* v. *Peek* [12] might be rendered as "*Perry* v. *Deek* (?)." Or the cases can be referred to by the name of the plaintiff if that only is remembered: *e.g.* "*Derry's* case." Or the name of only the defendant may be given—though in this case it is desirable to make it plain that the name is that of the defendant: *e.g.* "in an action against one *Peek*," or "in . . . v. *Peek*." Or the case can be identified by reference to some salient fact: *e.g.* "in the case concerning the tramway company's power to use steam." Even if both name and facts are forgotten, the student can at least indicate that there is authority for his proposition by saying: "In one case it was held that . . . "

But although the name is the least important part of the case, it is not altogether without importance. For the immediate purpose of the examinaton a script in which cases are referred to by name has naturally a more "finished" appearance than one that merely refers to "cases" in the air. Moreover, in your professional life (if, indeed, you intend to make the law your profession), you will find that a memory of the names of leading cases will be of help. If you are turning up a point of law in a practitioner's book, and happen to remember a case bearing upon it, you will usually find that by tracing the case through the case index you will come upon that portion of law in the book more quickly than by any other method.

In order, then, to lay the foundation of a sound legal knowledge, it behoves the student to make some effort to remember the names of the outstanding cases. Many of these, the most important, will be acquired simply through pondering over and discussing the cases themselves. For the rest, the amount of energy that he puts into the memorising of their names must be left to the individual. Certainly no more than a very small part of his time should be devoted to this task, and too much should not be attempted. Some students find it useful to compile a wall chart of cases (with an identificatory tag in brackets following the name), which they ruminate upon over their breakfast marmalade. Or a short recital of the cases can be recorded on tape. Another suggestion is to tabulate the cases on

[12] (1889) 14 App.Cas. 337.

postcards, carrying a selection of them in the pocket and revising them from time to time at odd moments.

The precise date of a case need never be committed to memory, but if it is a very old case the century to which it belongs may be mentioned, for extreme old age sometimes weakens its authority. And it may be important to say that a case was decided before the passing of a particular statute.

THE HIERARCHY OF AUTHORITY

For my part I consider, as I have said already, that more important than the name of the case is the rank of the court in which it was decided. To mention the court that decided a case is a mark of awareness of the doctrine of precedent, with its hierarchy of authority. The rule is that every court binds lower courts[13] and that some courts bind even themselves. When the appellate court reverses or overrules a case in the court below, the case so reversed or overruled loses all authority. *Reversal* is when the same case is decided the other way on appeal; *overruling* is when a case in a lower court is considered in a different case taken on appeal, and held to be wrongly decided.

In 1966 the House of Lords declared (departing from its previous practice) that it would not be bound by its own decisions.[14] The day after the declaration, Osbert Lancaster's cartoon in the *Daily Express* portrayed one Law Lord saying to another: "I say, Uptort, I can't get used to the fact that we can

---

[12] *Broome* v. *Cassell & Co. Ltd.* [1972] A.C. 1027. But it seems that, exceptionally, the decision of the Crown Court in the exercise of its appellate jurisdiction will not be a binding precedent for magistrates' courts in other cases: see 140 J.P.N. 242.

   Whether a court is "lower" depends not only on whether an appeal lies from it to the other court but, additionally, on whether the latter court is inherently higher in rank. Thus a Divisional Court of the High Court exercising its appellate jurisdiction from magistrates regards itself as bound by decisions of the Court of Appeal even though the further appeal in these cases goes not to the Court of Appeal but direct to the House of Lords. See Sir Rupert Cross, *Precedent in English Law,* 3rd ed., 121. It is not clear whether a ruling on a point of law made by a judge sitting in the Crown Court with a jury is binding on magistrates' courts.

[14] *Practice Statement* [1966] 1 W.L.R. 1234.

ever have been wrong." Their lordships are still extremely disinclined to exercise their new-found freedom.[15]

The Court of Appeal generally binds itself, both on the civil and on the criminal sides. There has been a steady stream of criticism by writers of this "autolimitation" of the court, at any rate in civil cases, for when a decision of the Court of Appeal is plainly wrong, it seems absurd that the parties should be put to the expense of a further appeal to the House of Lords in order to get it set aside.[16] When an appellant perceives that he cannot succeed in the Court of Appeal because a precedent stands in the way, he will save himself money if he can obtain leave to use the "leapfrogging" procedure before referred to, and go direct to the House of Lords.

In certain exceptional cases it is recognised that the Court of Appeal can refuse to follow one of its own previous decisions.[17] Although the precise scope of the exceptions is not fully agreed, it is generally thought that they are mainly as follows. (1) Where, by inadvertence or otherwise, the court arrives at inconsistent decisions, a later court must necessarily choose between them. It is not bound to follow either the earlier or the later. (2) The court is bound to refuse to follow its earlier decision that has been overruled by the House of Lords or that cannot stand with a later decision of the House (*i.e.,* has been impliedly over-ruled). (3) It need not follow its own decision given *per incuriam* (by oversight), as where a relevant statute was not considered, or was misconstrued because the court overlooked part of its provisions or arrived at a conclusion plainly contrary to the intention of the statute as a whole. Presumably another example would be where a relevant decision of the House of Lords was

---

[15] Cross. *op. cit.* n. 13 above, 134. In *R.* v. *National Insce Comr, ex p. Hudson* [1972] A.C. 944 their lordships announced that they would not normally reconsider their own decisions on the construction of a statute. A Procedure Direction in [1971] 1 W.L.R. 534 requires advance warning to be given by a party to an appeal who wishes to ask the House to depart from its own precedent, presumably in order to enable the House to sit in extra strength. See M.D.A. Freeman in 121 N.L.J. 551.

[16] The arguments for the autolimitation rule are ably demolished by Rickett in 43 M.L.R. 136.

[17] *Young* v. *Bristol Aeroplane Co. Ltd.* [1944] K.B. 718.

not considered.[18] (4) A special rule applies to the Criminal Division of the Court of Appeal. The court (in practice sitting as a "full court" of five judges instead of the usual three) can refuse to follow and in effect overrule its own prior decision rendered *against* the defendant in the precedent case (or the similar decision of the older courts that this court has superseded).[19] (In practice, however, it almost never does so.) The court is supposed to be bound by its own decisions rendered *in favour of* the defendant on a point of substantive law.

In addition to these four main exceptions, the court has shown a disposition to add to them whenever it feels a strong need to throw off the authority of its own precedent. So the court has held that it need not follow its own decision when it was inconsistent with a later pronouncement of the Privy Council,[20] or when it was the decision of a court of two relating to an interlocutory matter (a point of procedure arising before trial).[21] These pronouncements were not the result of any logical compulsion; they were merely ways of getting rid of particular precedents that now irked the court.

For several years Lord Denning M.R. has spoken in the Court of Appeal (Civil Division) in favour of a general freedom from the court's own past decisions when they now appear to be clearly wrong. These expressions of opinion culminated in *Davis* v. *Johnson*,[22] where the court had to consider two of its own previous decisions restrictively interpreting a recent statute passed for the purpose of protecting a woman who was attacked by the man with whom she was living, whether or not she was married to him. The restrictive interpretations had been severely criticised in the Press, and the Court of Appeal, sitting as a court of five, was evidently anxious to disembarrass itself of them. A bare majority of the court decided that it was free to do so. Lord Denning gave his accustomed reason that the court was not bound by its own decisions. Sir George Baker, President of the

---

[18] *Dixon* v. *B.B.C.* [1979] Q.B. 546. See generally on *per incuriam* Wesley-Smith in 15 Journal of the Society of Public Teachers of Law 58.

[19] *R.* v. *Gould* [1968] 2 Q.B.65. See Zellick in [1974] Crim.L.R. 222.

[20] Cross, *op. cit.,* 107 n. 2, 145.

[21] *Boys* v. *Chaplin* [1968] 2 Q.B. 1.

[22] [1979] A.C. 264.

Family Division, concurred in the result but assigned a narrower reason. "The court is not bound to follow a previous decision of its own if satisfied that that decision was clearly wrong and cannot stand in the face of the will and intention of Parliament expressed in simple language in a recent statute passed to remedy a serious mischief or abuse, and further adherence to the previous decision must lead to injustice in the particular case and unduly restrict the proper development of the law with injustice to others." Shaw L.J., the third member of the majority, tentatively drafted the exception in an even more limited way. "It would be in some such terms as that the principle of *stare decisis*[23] should be relaxed where its application would have the effect of depriving actual and potential victims of violence of a vital protection which an Act of Parliament was plainly designed to afford to them, especially where, as in the context of domestic violence, that deprivation must inevitably give rise to an irremediable detriment to such victims and create in regard to them an injustice irreversible by a later decision of the House of Lords." These words are so tightly related to the facts of the case that Lord Diplock in the House of Lords racily but justly characterised them as creating a "one-off" exception, applicable to the facts of the instant case but probably not to any other. Judges who make up exceptions in this way are in effect throwing off the compulsive force of precedent, and it would be more convenient to say so. In form, however, the decision of the Court of Appeal merely adds one more exception to the general rule, though there was no agreement on its wording. On further appeal, all the Law Lords expressed the decided opinion that the Court of Appeal was (exceptions apart) bound by its own decisions, but they did not state any convincing reasons why this should be so. The practical effect of denying the Court of Appeal the power to correct its own errors is to force a further appeal to the Lords, with its attendant delay and expense. However, two points should be noticed. First, their lordships did not enter into the question whether the Court of Appeal could properly create fresh exceptions. Secondly, Lord Salmon said that Lord Denning's views could not prevail "until such time, if ever, as his colleagues in the Court of Appeal agree with those views." He

---

[23] "Stand by the decided cases."

thus recognised that the question whether the present practice of the Court of Appeal should continue is entirely a matter for that court, which is surely right. This is for either of two reasons. One is that when the House of Lords is considering an appeal its function is to decide the case between the parties, not to consider whether the lower court was bound by precedent. Any pronouncement it makes on the latter point can be regarded as *obiter*. Alternatively, and preferably, the view may be taken that the rules of precedent stand outside the doctrine of precedent. To support the doctrine of precedent by reference to precedent would be to try to pull it up by its own bootstraps. *Stare decisis* is, in fact, merely the practice of the particular court, and a court can announce a change for the future in its intended practice notwithstanding what it may have said in the past and notwithstanding what a higher court may say.[24]

When counsel wishes to ask the Court of Appeal not to follow its own previous decision on one of these grounds, he may outline the point to the court, which may then arrange to sit with five or more members (the so-calleld "full court") instead of the usual three.[25]

The exceptional rules freeing the Court of Appeal from the authority of its own previous decisions do not operate to free it from the authority of the House of Lords—at any rate, in the opinion of that House. Their lordships take it amiss if the Court of Appeal announces that a decision of the House was *per incuriam*. On one occasion when the Court of Appeal did this and a further appeal was taken to the House of Lords, their lordships expressed strong disapproval. They regarded the action of the lower court, in the words of Lord Denning (speaking subsequently in the Court of Appeal), "as a piece of *lèse-majesté*. The House of Lords never does anything *per incuriam*."[26] In consequence of the unpleasantness on that occasion the position now is that if the House decides a case in ignorance of a previous decision of its own going the other way,

---

[24] See Goldstein in [1979] C.L.J. 386-391; Rickett, *loc. cit.*

[25] But this is not essential. For example, *Gould* (n. 19 *above*) was decided by a court of three, which declined to follow an earlier decision of the Court of Criminal Appeal rendered against the defendant.

[26] *Fellowes & Son* v. *Fisher* [1976] Q.B. 132 E.

the Court of Appeal will nevertheless regard itself as bound to follow the later of the two decisions.[27] So the law will remain uncertain until a litigant who has ample private means or who can call on the legal aid fund takes the point to the House of Lords for reconsideration.

Turning to Divisional Courts, their decisions are binding precedents for magistrates' courts in other cases. Also, Divisional Courts bind themselves,[28] except that they will presumably exercise the same freedom in criminal cases as the Court of Appeal. Presumably Divisional Courts bind judges and recorders when the latter hear appeals from magistrates' courts, because Divisional Courts are superior in the hierarchy—as was said before, a further appeal can be brought from the Crown Court to the Divisional Court.

However, the Divisional Court does not bind Crown Court judges who try cases with juries, because they do not form part of the same judicial hierarchy.[29] The Crown Court is a branch of the Supreme Court having equal status with the High Court,[30] and therefore with a Divisional Court of the High Court. It makes no difference that only one judge sits in the Crown Court while two or more sit in the Divisional Court.[31]

Single judges of the High Court trying civil cases bind inferior courts (county courts, and magistrates' courts in their civil jurisdiction), but they do not absolutely bind other High Court judges. One such judge may, if he feels strongly enough, refuse to follow another judge, and the result will be a conflict of authority that will one day have to be settled by the Court of Appeal. In other words, a High Court judge cannot overrule one of his brethren, he can only "disapprove" his decision and "not follow" him. Refusal to follow is, however, rare.

Decisions of courts inferior to the High Court do not bind anybody, not even themselves.

In legal theory decisions of the Judicial Committee of the

---

[27] *Ibid.* See also *Miliangos* v. *Frank (Textiles) Ltd.* [1976] A.C. at 476–479.

[28] *Huddersfield Police Authority* v. *Watson* [1947] K.B. 842.

[29] *Colyer* [1974] Crim.L.R. 243.

[30] Courts Act 1971 s.1.

[31] For other problems relating to the Crown Court see Ashworth in [1980] Crim.L.R. 402.

Privy Council do not bind English courts, nor even the Judicial Committee itself. But they have great "persuasive" authority.

My suggestion is that the student should try to remember when a case belongs to the House of Lords, the Court of Appeal (or its predecessors the Court of Exchequer Chamber, the Court of Appeal in Chancery, the Court for Crown Cases Reserved, and the Court of Criminal Appeal), or the Privy Council. Since he cannot remember everything, he can usually permit himself to forget the exact court that decided cases of authority inferior to these. Nothing is gained by trying to distinguish between the three common law courts (King's Bench, Common Pleas, Exchequer) before 1875, or the various branches of the High Court today. He should, however, remember whether a particular rule was established by the common law courts or by the Court of Chancery, *i.e.* whether it is a rule of common law or one of equity, for on that, important questions sometimes depend (see Chapter 2). Also, he should remember if a particular decision was simply that of a judge given by way of direction to a jury. Such decisions are of inferior authority, largely because in a jury trial questions of law are unlikely to have been fully debated. It is no longer usual to report these directions to a jury, though, as Pollock says, "many of the older ones have become good authority by subsequent approval, and some of them are the only definite reported authority for points of law now received as not only settled but elementary."[32] It may be added that directions to a jury have been more important in criminal than in civil law, because there used to be no appeal from a jury verdict of not guilty, and thus if on a particular point of law judges were in the habit of directing the jury in the defendant's favour the appeal court may have had no opportunity to pronounce upon it. Since 1972 the Attorney-General may refer an acquittal for the opinion of the appellate courts, but this does not affect the particular defendant.[33]

A word may be said about international law. In studying this subject the student will be expected to know the more important decisions of international and municipal (*i.e.* national) tribunals.

---

[32] *First Book of Jurisprudence*, 6th ed., 348. The old *nisi prius* cases are reprinted in Vols. 170-176 of the English Reports.

[33] Criminal Justice Act 1972 s. 36.

Always distinguish between the two, for the pronouncement of an international court is generally more authoritative for other international tribunals on a matter of internatonal law than that of a merely national body. (But the decision of a municipal court may be more authoritative for other courts of the same State).

CIRCUMSTANCES AFFECTING THE WEIGHT OF A DECISION

The good lawyer will often make a mental note of some circumstances that go to increase or diminish the authority of a case. Among the circumstances adding to its authority are: the eminence of the particular judge or judges who decided it; the large number of judges who took part in it; and the fact that the judgment was a "reserved" one, *i.e.* not delivered on the spur of the moment. (This last is indicated in the report, at the end of the arguments of counsel, by the words *C.A.V., Curia advisari vult.*) Naturally, a case is reinforced if it has been frequently followed, or has created expectations in commercial or proprietary matters. Some say that any decision of long standing is unlikely to be disturbed[34]; on the other hand, it may be hard to persuade a court to depart from its own precedent established only a few years before, for that would look like vacillation![35] So this will often be "Catch 22" for a party seeking to challenge a decision. Among the circumstances detracting from the authority of a case are: the presence of strong dissenting judgments; the fact that the majority do not agree in their reasoning but only in their result; the failure of counsel to cite an inconsistent case in argument; the disapproval of the profession; and the fact that the case was taken on appeal and that the appeal went off on another point.

These circumstances have no importance if the case is absolutely binding on the court before which it is cited and if it is incapable of being distinguished. But they are of great importance if the case is not absolutely binding, or if on the facts of the later case it is capable of being distinguished or extended at the pleasure of the court.

---

[34] *Per* Lord Simon in *Farrell* v. *Alexander* [1977] A.C. at 90G.
[35] Cp. *Nock* [1978] A.C. at 997E.

JUDICIAL LAW-MAKING

Rules of precedent instruct judges that they are or are not bound to decide the case before them in a particular way. The rules do not tell the judge on what principles he should act when he is free, for example when he is faced by a precedent in a lower court which is not binding on him. He then has to choose between notions of justice, convenience, public policy, morality, analogy, and so on, perhaps taking into account the opinions of other judges (in American, Canadian, Australian and Scottish[36] cases, for instance) or of writers. The various considerations may not point in the same direction, but may conflict with each other.

Judges do not generally admit that they make law; they cherish the "fairy tale" (as Lord Reid once termed it) that the common law is a miraculous something existing from eternity and not made by anyone. One consequence is that the judges do not explicitly consider the principles on which they should act in deciding whether or not to introduce a change. And since they pretend that they are merely declaring the law, they assume that what they say must be retrospective (applying to the past as well as the future), unlike legislation proper, which generally applies only to the future.

One generalisation can be made. The judge has to balance two opposing needs in the law: the need for stability and certainty, and the need for change. It would obviously be going too far to say that he can scrap or alter any established rule whenever he disagrees with it. The judge, even when free from binding authority, must take account of people's understanding of what the law is—as when they make contracts, or insure against liability. But not all judicial legislation defeats expectations. For example, a judgment *restricting* the area of liability does not do so (except to the extent that it defeats the plaintiff/prosecutor's expectation of succeeding in the particular proceedings, which is a matter of no great importance). Again, the law of procedure and evidence does not create expectations in the ordinary

---

[36] Generally, Scottish decisions are only of persuasive (*i.e.* non-binding) authority in English courts; but they are accorded binding force on points common to English and Scots law. See Bentil in 35 M.L.R. 537.

citizen. It can be said that in these areas the judges exercise their power to alter course too little rather than too much.

Some textbooks state a proposition of law and follow it by a case in small type in a separate paragraph. Do not adopt this practice. It is a good teaching method, but you are not teaching the examiner the law: you are showing him that you can use authorities like a lawyer. Therefore, introduce cases into your answer in literary form.

Remember that the citation of cases is not an end in itself; it is a means to the establishing of legal principle. For this reason you should try to avoid making your written work look like a mere bundle of cases. As a matter of style, an essay that sets out the principle involved in the case before mentioning the case is preferable to one that merely blurts out one case after another without introduction. Here are two answers to the same examination question in constitutional law: both are made out of the same raw material, but observe how much more intelligible the second is than the first.

Q.—To what extent is Act of State a defence in respect of acts done on behalf of the British Government which would otherwise be torts?

Answer 1.—"In *Buron* v. *Denman*[37] the defendant, a British naval commander, had set fire to Spanish slave barracoons[38] on the coast of Africa (not British soil), and his act was ratified by the Crown. It was held that the aggrieved Spaniard, being a foreigner, had no action in England, Act of State being a defence.

"In *Walker* v. *Baird*[39] the defendant, again a British naval officer, had trespassed upon the plaintiff's lobster fishery in Newfoundland. In doing so he acted under the orders of the Crown. The Privy Council held that Act of State was no defence, the reason evidently being that the plaintiff was a British subject and that the act was done on British soil. A similar conclusion was reached in *Nissan* v. *Attorney-General*,[40] where the plaintiff was a British subject and the act was done in the Republic of Cyprus.

"In *Johnstone* v. *Pedlar*[41] the plaintiff was an alien resident in

---

[37] (1848) 2 Ex. 167, 154 E.R. 450.
[38] Sheds
[39] [1892] A.C. 491.
[40] [1970] A.C. 179.
[41] [1921] 2 A.C. 262.

England. His property was seized by the police with the ratification of the Crown. The House of Lords held that Act of State was no defence."

The foregoing answer sets out the authorities but it does not clearly extract the principles from them.

Answer 2.—"Act of State is a good defence where the tort was committed by a State servant against a foreigner outside British soil, and the act was authorised or ratified[42] by the Crown. In *Buron* v. *Denman* all these conditions were satisfied. The facts were that a British naval commander fired Spanish slave barracoons on the coast of Africa (not British soil), and his act was ratified by the Crown. The defence availed.

"The law has, however, been thrown into doubt by the decision of the House of Lords in *Nissan* v. *Attorney-General*.[43] According to Lord Wilberforce, Acts of State are confined to 'acts committed abroad in the conduct, under the prerogative, of foreign relations with other states.' It seems that not every act authorised by the Crown will fall under this definition. Could it even be applied to the act done in *Buron* v. *Denman*?

"Discordant views were expressed in *Nissan's* case on whether the defence availed in respect of a tort committed to a British subject on foreign soil. It seems that British subjects (or, at any rate, citizens of the United Kingdom and colonies) are fully protected where the act is done on British soil: see *Walker* v. *Baird,* where the Privy Council held that Act of State did not excuse a trespass committed on a British subject's lobster fishery in Newfoundland.

"Equally the defence cannot be set up in respect of a tort committed against a person resident on British soil, even though that person is an alien: *Johnstone* v. *Pedlar,* H.L. (property of alien in England seized by the police with ratification of Crown; Act of State no defence)."

In writing down the name of a case it is a good habit to underline the proper names of the parties. It is because lawyers do this that the names of cases come out in italics in print. For the student the practice has two advantages. It helps him in revising, because it makes the names of the cases stand out to the eye; and it makes his examination-script easier for the examiner to read.

[42] The difference between authorisation and ratification is that the first comes before the act, and the second after it.
[43] It has been said that this decision was "a disaster for students of the law. The decision of the House of Lords lacks any clear *ratio decidendi.* . . . Important questions of law were raised but left half-answered or unanswered, and points that once seemed clear were left shrouded in obscurity." S.A. de Smith, *Constitutional and Administrative Law,* 3rd ed., 133.

THE SUCCINCT WAY OF STATING CASES

A difficulty that is likely to press upon the better student in dealing with cases in the examination room is that of lack of time. If a single question demands the citation of (say) a dozen cases, how can these be adequately dealt with in the time allowed? The answer is as follows: If at all possible, each case should be dealt with fully, giving in due order the principle involved in the case, its name, its facts, (possibly) the argument of counsel, or the losing argument, (possibly) the court before which the case came, the decision, (possibly) the reasons for the decision, and the *obiter dicta* (if any). If time does not allow of this there is another method. This is to state the rule of law contained in the case, and then to put a full colon, followed by the name of the case, (possibly) the court that decided it, and (in brackets) some outstanding fact or facts. This method was used for *Johnstone* v. *Pedlar* in Answer 2 above. As another instance, the case of *Callow* v. *Tillstone*, [44] on participation in crime, could be stated as follows: "Strict liability in crime does not extend to accessories, who are not liable unless they know the facts: *Callow* v. *Tillstone* (vet who certified unsound meat negligently not an accessory to its exposure for sale, since he did not know it was unsound)." An example from contract would be: "Where it is reasonable to accept by letter, acceptance dates from the posting: *Household Fire Insurance Co.* v. *Grant*, [45] C.A. (lost letter of allotment; held, contract to take shares was complete)." This shows in a minimum of words that the student knows the rule of law contained in the case and also could state the facts more fully if he had the time. But the method should not be used if a more orthodox presentation of the case is possible. Stating the facts and decision in the ordinary way occupies little more time and looks much better.

"MAY I CRITICISE?"

Some lawyers assert that no case in an appellate court can be said to be "wrongly decided." It is the law, until reversed or departed from. This is a mere matter of words. Obviously one can say that

[44] (1880) L.R. 6 Q.B.D. 79.
[45] (1879) 4 Ex.D. 216.

the case was badly decided, or poorly reasoned, or unfortunate in its outcome, or inconsistent with other cases. And why not say that it was wrongly decided, thereby expressing the hope that it will be overruled? Anyway, in university and college examinations you may always criticise decided cases, and statutes as well if you think it profitable. In professional examinations the primary object is to test your knowledge of the present law. But criticism is often relevant to deciding whether a case will be followed or not. An objectionable precedent may be distinguished, or not followed, or overruled.

Lawyers are much too prone to assume that what has been decided cannot be upset. It often happens that a plainly wrong decision is given at first instance or even by the Court of Appeal, which is followed unquestioningly for many years because counsel do not advise their clients to take the point further on appeal. When, eventually, some counsel is found who has the courage and acumen to take the point, the precedent is reversed.[46] Now that the House of Lords has decided that it can question its own previous decisions, there is hardly any decided point that cannot be reopened if the arguments against it are strong enough.

FURTHER READING

On precedent and the judicial function, Michael Zander's *The Law-Making Process* (1980), Chaps. 3, 5 and 6 may be warmly recommended.

---

[46] *e.g. R.* v. *Gould* [1968] 2 Q.B. 65. In *R.* v. *Taylor* [1950] 2 K.B. 368 counsel had allowed his client to plead guilty on the strength of a decision in an earlier case notwithstanding that it was plainly erroneous. An appeal was taken against the sentence only, but, on being informed of the facts and of the earlier decision, the Court of Criminal Appeal was so surprised that it allowed the appeal to be converted into an appeal against conviction; it then allowed the appeal and overruled the precedent.

CHAPTER 7

THE INTERPRETATION OF STATUTES

The golden rule is that there are no golden rules.

—G.B. Shaw, *Man and Superman.*

THE subject of statutory interpretation is not usually taught in Law Schools, and you may perhaps not be examined upon it. An understanding of it is not so essential as that of the working of precedent. You may, therefore, postpone the reading of this chapter if you wish. But I hope that you will think, as I do, that because this basic subject is omitted in ordinary teaching syllabuses it is all the more important that law students should pick up something about it on their own. A practitioner with any pretension to legal learning should certainly know the lines of argument that may be open to him on a disputed point of interpretation.

THE CONTEXT RULE

In ordinary life, if someone says something that you do not understand, you ask him to explain himself more fully. This is impossible with the interpretation of statutes, because when Parliament has passed an Act the words of the Act are authoritative as words. It is only these words that have passed through the legal machinery of law-making, and individual Members of Parliament cannot be put into the witness-box to supplement or interpret what has been formally enacted. Hence the words of an Act carry a sort of disembodied or dehumanised meaning: not necessarily the meaning intended by any actual person in particular, but the meaning that is conventionally attached to such words. The point must not be pressed too far, since the statute obviously has a broad purpose (or, to speak more precisely, those who collaborated in framing and passing the statute had a broad purpose) which is expressed in the words.

The most important rules for the interpretation (otherwise called construction) of statutes are those suggested by common sense. The judge may look up the meaning of a word in a dictionary or technical work; but this ordinary meaning may be controlled by the particular context. As everyone knows who has translated from a foreign language, it is no excuse for a bad translation that the meaning chosen was found in the dictionary; for the document may be its own dictionary, showing an intention to use words in some special shade of meaning. This rule, requiring regard to be had to the context, is sometimes expressed in the Latin maxim *Noscitur a sociis,* which Henry Fielding translated: a word may be known by the company it keeps. One may look not only at the rest of the section in which the word appears but at the statute as a whole, and even at earlier legislation dealing with the same subject-matter—for it is assumed that when Parliament passed an Act, it probably had the earlier legislation in mind, and probably intended to use words with the same meaning as before.[1] Somewhat anomalously, reference may even be made to later statutes, to see the meaning that Parliament puts on the same words in a similar context. However, words need not always have a consistent meaning attributed to them: the context may show that the same word bears two different senses even when it is repeated in the same section.[2]

Formerly, the rule permitting recourse to earlier statutes was taken to allow the court to compare the wording of a consolidation Act with the Acts that it superseded, and to conclude that variation of wording indicated a change of meaning. But this tended to defeat the object of consolidation, which was to supersede a jumble of Acts of various dates by a single statute. Consolidation would be little help if one still had to look at the old repealed Acts in order to interpret the new one. Consequently, the rule now laid down by the House of Lords is that where in construing a consolidation Act

"the actual words are clear and unambiguous it is not permissible to have

---

[1] Maxwell, *Interpretation of Statutes*, 12th ed., 64 *et seq.*
[2] *R.* v. *Allen* (1872) 1 C.C.R. at 374; *West Midlands Joint Electricity Authority* v. *Pitt* [1932] 2 K.B. at 46.

recourse to the corresponding provisions in the earlier statute repealed by the consolidation Act and to treat any difference in their wording as capable of casting doubt upon what is clear and unambiguous language in the consolidation Act itself."[3]

In reading a statute, always look for a definition section, assigning special meanings to some of the words in the statute. Parliamentary counsel have the inconsiderate habit of not telling you (for example, in a footnote or marginal note) that a particular word in the section is defined somewhere else in the statute; you have to ferret out the information for yourself. In addition to the interpretation section in the statute, the Interpretation Act 1978 operates as a standing legal dictionary of some of the most important words used in legislation. This Act declares, among other things, that the plural includes the singular, and the singular the plural, unless a contrary intention appears. Also, by virtue of the Act, if not independently of it, "man" embraces "woman." These special meanings are duly noticed in the various annotations of statutes, such as Halsbury's *Statutes* and *Current Law Statutes*.

INTERPRETATION IN THE LIGHT OF POLICY: "FRINGE MEANING"

When interpreting statutes the courts often announce that they are trying to discover "the intention of the legislature." In actual fact, if a court finds it hard to know whether a particular situation comes within the words of a statute or not, the probability is the situation was not foreseen by the legislature, so that the Lords and Members of Parliament would be just as puzzled by it as the judges are. Here, the "intention of the legislature" is a fiction. Because of this difficulty, some deny that the courts are really concerned with the intention of Parliament.

"In the construction of written documents including statutes, what the court is concerned to ascertain is, not what the promulgators of the instruments meant to say, but the meaning of what they have said."[4]

Others, however, think it proper to speak of the intention of

---

[3] *Per* Lord Diplock in *Curran* [1976] 1 W.L.R. at 90H–91A, [1976] 1 All E.R. at 165*b*, reaffirmed by a majority of the lords in *Farrell* v. *Alexander* [1977] A.C. 59. See the reservations by Lord Simon at p. 84.

[4] *Per* Lord Simon in *Farrell* v. *Alexander* [1977] A.C. at 81G.

Parliament, in the sense of "the meaning which Parliament must have intended the words to convey."[5] In case of doubt the court has to guess what meaning Parliament would have picked on if it had thought of the point. The intention is not actual but hypothetical.[6] There is, of course, a limit to what a court can do by way of filling out a statute, but to some extent this is possible.

An illustration is the familiar legal problem of "fringe meaning." The words we use, though they have a central core of meaning that is relatively fixed, have a fringe of uncertainty when applied to the infinitely variable facts of experience. For example, the general notion of a "building" is clear, but a judge may not find it easy to decide whether a temporary wooden hut, or a telephone kiosk, or a wall, or a tent, is a "building." In problems like this, the process of interpretation is indistinguishable from legislation: the judge is, whether he likes it or not, a legislator. For, if he decides that the wooden hut is a building, he is in effect adding an interpretation clause to the statute which gives "building" an extended application; whereas if he decides that the hut is not a building, he adds a clause to the statute which gives it a narrower meaning. The words of the statute, as they stand, do not give an answer to the question before the judge; and the question is therefore legislative rather than interpretative. This simple truth is rarely perceived or admitted: almost always the judge pretends to get his solution out of the words of the Act, though he may confess in so doing to be guided by its general policy. The rational approach would be to say candidly that the question, being legislative, must be settled with the help of the policy implicit in the Act, or by reference to convenience or social requirements or generally accepted principles of fairness.

This kind of "interpretation" may be legally and socially sound although it reaches results that would surprise the lexicographer. Thus it has actually been held that murder can be

---

[5] *Per* Lord Edmund-Davies, *ibid.* at 95B.

[6] Even this formulation of the judge's task has an element of unreality, as Professor Dworkin has pointed out (64 Proc.Brit.Ac. 259). Even if the legislature had thought of the point, it might have preferred to leave it unresolved—for example, because to resolve it would arouse the opposition of some group or other and imperil the whole measure, or because it would encumber the Act with too much detail.

an "accident."[7] The word "accident" was being interpreted in the context of the Workmen's Compensation Act, and the result of the decision was that the widow of the deceased workman was entitled to compensation from the employer,[8] because the murder in question arose out of and in the course of the employment. The court admitted that it was giving an unusual meaning to the word, for a historian who described the end of Rizzio by saying that he met with a fatal accident in Holyrood Palace would fairly be charged with a misleading statement of fact. Similarly, Farwell L.J. remarked that one would not in ordinary parlance say that Desdemona died by accident, because "the horror of the crime dominates the imagination and compels the expression of the situation in terms related to the crime and the criminal alone." Yet, if one looks at the situation from the point of view of the victim, it is an accident, in the sense that it was not expected or intended by the victim himself. In preferring this wider meaning of the term "accident" the court looked to the general purpose of the Act.

THE "MISCHIEF" RULE

As can be seen from the illustration just given, the task of interpreting statutes gives judges the chance of expressing their own opinions as to social policy; and, inevitably, their opinions do not always command universal assent. However, the judges are on fairly safe ground if they apply the "mischief" rule, otherwise known as the rule in *Heydon's* case.[9] This bids them to look at the common law (*i.e.* the legal position) before the Act, and the mischief that the statute was intended to remedy; the Act is then to be construed in such a way as to suppress the mischief and advance the remedy.

The practical utility of the rule depends to some extent upon the means that the courts are entitled to employ in order to ascertain what mischief the Act was intended to remedy. A true historical investigation would take account of press agitation, party conferences, Government pronouncements, and debates

---

[7] *Nisbet* v. *Rayne & Burn* [1910] 2 K.B. 689.

[8] Now turned into industrial injuries benefit as part of the national insurance scheme (Social Security Acts 1975 to 1977).

[9] (1584) 3 Co.Rep. at 7b, 76 E.R. at 638.

in Parliament; but all these are ignored as the result of a rule
excluding evidence of the political history of a statute. The rule is
justified by the burden that would be placed upon legal advisers
and the uncertainty that would be introduced into the law if such
historical materials had to be consulted.[10] In practice, therefore,
the judge generally divines the object of a statute merely from
perusal of its language, in the light of his knowledge of the
previous law and general knowledge of social conditions.[11]

Many statutes are the result of recommendations made by the
Royal Commissions and departmental committees. Can the
reports of these commissions and committees be looked at as an
aid to construction? The rule as now settled is that they are
inadmissible in order to show what the committee thought its
proposals meant, but admissible under the rule in *Heydon's* case
to the extent that they show the mischief against which the Act
was directed. It may be expected that the practice of referring to
these reports will extend itself in the future, because they often
supply the best commentary upon the wording of an Act.[12]

THE LITERAL RULE

Granted that words have a certain elasticity of meaning, the
general rule remains that the judges regard themselves as bound
by the words of a statute when these words clearly govern the

[10] Although the reason is convincing, the rule sometimes has unhappy
consequences. On one occasion, when a section was included in an
Act for the avowed purpose of getting rid of a certain decision, a
Divisional Court, not realising this, followed the decision, whittling
down the section by applying rules of interpretation, and saying that
Parliament could not have intended to change the law. See Cretney in
119 N.L.J. 301.

Exceptionally, where a statute is passed to give effect to an
international treaty (convention), the courts will apply the Continen-
tal rule that the discussions leading to the treaty may be looked at:
Fothergill v. *Monarch Airlines Ltd.* [1981] A.C. 251. But Lord
Scarman said that such *traveaux préparatoires* should be used only
where the text is ambiguous or where a literal construction appears to
conflict with the purpose of the treaty.

[11] See e.g. *Davis* v. *Johnson* [1979] A.C. at 338F.

[12] See the close vote on this subject in *Black-Clawson International Ltd.*
v. *Papierwerke Waldhof-Aschaffenburg A.G.* [1975] A.C. 591, discussed by Sir Rupert Cross, *Statutory Interpretation* (1976), 136 *et seq.*

situation before the court. The words must be applied with nothing added and nothing taken away. More precisely, the general principle is that the court can neither extend the statute to a case not within its terms though perhaps within its purpose (the *casus omissus*) nor curtail it by leaving out a case that the statute literally includes, though it should not have. (There is no accepted name for the latter, but it may be called the *casus male inclusus*). Lord Diplock expressed the point as follows.

"At a time when more and more cases involve the application of legislation which gives effect to policies that are the subject of bitter public and parliamentary controversy, it cannot be too strongly emphasised that the British constitution, though largely unwritten, is firmly based upon the separation of powers; Parliament makes the laws, the judiciary interpret them. When Parliament legislates to remedy what the majority of its members at the time perceive to be a defect or a lacuna in the existing law (whether it be the written law enacted by existing statutes or the unwritten common law as it has been expounded by the judges in decided cases), the role of the judiciary is confined to ascertaining from the words that Parliament has approved as expressing its intention what that intention was, and to giving effect to it. Where the meaning of the statutory words is plain and unambiguous it is not for the judges to invent fancied ambiguities as an excuse for failing to give effect to its plain meaning because they themselves consider that the consequences of doing so would be inexpedient, or even unjust or immoral. In controversial matters such as are involved in industrial relations there is room for differences of opinion as to what is expedient, what is just and what is morally justifiable. Under our constitution it is Parliament's opinion on these matters that is paramount."[13]

Lord Diplock went on to say that the principle applies even though there is reason to think that if Parliament had foreseen the situation before the court it would have modified the words it used. "If this be the case it is for Parliament, not for the judiciary, to decide whether any changes should be made to the law as stated in the Acts."

According to this, courts should not use the "mischief" rule when the statute is "plain and unambiguous." They can use the mischief rule if the statute is ambiguous, but must not "invent fancied ambiguities" in order to do so.

---

[13] *Duport Steels Ltd.* v. *Sirs* [1980] 1 W.L.R. at 157, 1 All E.R. 529. For earlier pronouncements to the same effect see *Magor and St. Mellons* v. *Newport Corpn* [1952] A.C. 189; *Stock* v. *Frank Jones (Tipton) Ltd.* [1978] 1 W.L.R. 231, 1 All E.R. 948.

It is, nevertheless, difficult to reconcile the literal rule with the "context" rule. We understand the meaning of words from their context, and in ordinary life the context includes not only other words used at the same time but the whole human or social situation in which the words are used. Professor Zander gives the example of parents asking a child-minder to keep the children amused by teaching them a card game. In the parents' absence the child-minder teaches the children to play strip poker. There is no doubt that strip poker is a card game, and no doubt that it was not the sort of card game intended by the instructions given. One knows this not from anything the parents have said but from customary ideas as to the proper behaviour and upbringing of children. On its face, the literal rule seems to forbid this common sense approach to statutory interpretation.

The rule has often been criticised by writers. What is a real ambiguity, and what is a fancied ambiguity? Consider the following case decided by the House of Lords on the construction of the Factories Act.[14] This Act requires dangerous parts of machines to be constantly fenced while they are *in motion*. A workman adjusting a machine removed the fence and turned the machine by hand in order to do the job. Unfortunately he crushed his finger. Whether the employers were in breach of the statute depended on whether the machine was "in motion." In the primary or literal sense of the words it was, but since the machine was not working under power and was only in temporary motion for necessary adjustment, the House of Lords chose to give the words the secondary meaning of "mechanical propulsion."[15] Since the machine was not being mechanically propelled it was not in motion.

This was a decision of the House of Lords 25 years before the pronouncement of Lord Diplock previously quoted, and no doubt has been cast upon it. Is the provision in the Factories Act ambiguous or not? "Motion" primarily means movement; the machine was in movement, and therefore, in the ordinary meaning of the phrase, was in motion. The reason why the House of Lords cut down the meaning of the phrase must have

---

[14] Currently the Factories Act 1961.

[15] *Richard Thomas & Baldwins Ltd.* v. *Cummings* [1955] A.C. 321. For a fuller discussion see Cross, *op. cit.* 29–31, 74–84.

ɔeen because the House did not believe that Parliament intended to cover the particular situation. According to Lord Diplock it is improper to do this if the meaning of the statute is plain. So the decision in the Factories Act case was justifiable only if the Act was regarded as not plain. But in what way was it not plain? "In motion" is on its face a perfectly plain phrase. Was not the reason why the House thought it not plain that their lordships believed that Parliament did not have this situation in mind and would have cut down the wording if it had? Yet it seems that according to Lord Diplock such reasoning is merely the invention of a fancied ambiguity, which is no reason for denying the "plain" meaning of a statute.

The literal rule is a rule against using intelligence in understanding language. Anyone who in ordinary life interpreted words literally, being indifferent to what the speaker or writer meant, would be regarded as a pedant, a mischief-maker or an idiot.

One practical reason for the literal rule is that judges are now deeply afraid of being accused of making political judgments at variance with the purpose of Parliament when it passed the Act. This fear is sometimes understandable, but not all statutes divide Parliament on party lines.

Other reasons advanced for the literal rule may be briefly answered.[16] "Many statutes are passed by political bargaining and snap judgments of expediency; the courts can rarely be sure that Parliament would have altered the wording if it had foreseen the situation." This may be true, but is it any reason why the courts should not do justice as best they can, leaving it to Parliament to intervene again if the decision does not meet with Parliament's approval? "If courts habitually rewrote statutes in order to effect supposed improvements, this might cause statutes to become more complex in order to exclude judicial rewriting in a way that was politically unacceptable." This supposes that the court misjudges what Parliament would wish it to do, whereas in fact the decision may win general approval. A court that tries to decide as Parliament would have wished is more likely to be right than a court that follows the words believing it was not what

[16] Some of these reasons are given by Lord Simon in *Stock* v. *Frank Jones (Tipton) Ltd.* [1978] 1 W.L.R. at 236–237, 1 All E.R. at 953–954, but the above paragraph does not represent direct quotation.

Parliament intended. "People are entitled to follow statutes as they are; they should not have to speculate as to Parliament's intention." This is a strong reason against the extensive construction of prohibitory legislation, but not in other cases. "If the courts undertook to rewrite statutes this would tend to foment litigation, because it would encourage people who objected to the legislation to try their luck with the courts." To suggest that the courts will ever completely rewrite a statute is a great exaggeration; and even judges who accept the literal rule in words will depart from it when the circumstances press them hard enough.

Lord Diplock says that there may be differences of opinion as to what is expedient, just and moral, and that Parliament's opinion on these questions is paramount. This is obviously true, once Parliament's opinion is established. It is also true that Parliament's opinion is ascertained primarily from the words it has used. Nevertheless, the facts of the case may be such as to raise serious doubts whether Parliament intended its words to apply. The decision by a court that a particular situation was not intended to come within the ambit of a statute, though within its words in what may be their most obvious meaning, does not deny the supremacy of Parliament, for if Parliament disagrees with the decision it can pass another Act dealing specifically with the type of case. However, the hard truth is that Parliament generally pays little attention to the working of the law. It is not merely that Parliament fails to keep old law under continuous revision; it loses interest in its new creations as soon as they are on the statute book.

INTERPRETATIONS TO AVOID ABSURDITY: THE "GOLDEN RULE"

As the Factories Act case illustrates, the courts sometimes allow themselves to construe a statute in such a way as to produce a reasonable result, even though this involves departing from the *prima facie* meaning of the words. The rule that a statute may be construed to avoid absurdity is conveniently called the "golden rule."[17] It is by no means unlimited, and seems to apply only in three types of case.

---

[17] *Mattison* v. *Hart* (1854) 14 C.B. at 385, 139 E.R. at 159. The general statement of the golden rule is that (1) the literal (primary) meaning

In its first application, the golden rule allows the court to prefer a sensible meaning to an absurd meaning, where both are linguistically possible. It does not matter that the absurd meaning is the more natural and obvious meaning of the words. Lord Reid:

"Where a statutory provision on one interpretation brings about a startling and inequitable result, this may lead the court to seek another possible interpretation which will do better justice."[18]

On another occasion Lord Reid put the point more strongly.

"It is only where the words are absolutely incapable of a construction which will accord with the apparent intention of the provision and will avoid a wholly unreasonable result that the words of the enactment must prevail."[19]

This application of the golden rule does not contradict the literal rule, *provided* that the absurdity of the particular proposed application of the statute is conceded to be a reason for finding an ambiguity in it. If one accepts the golden rule, this involves rejecting Lord Diplock's opinion that the inexpediency, injustice or immorality of the proposed application of the statute cannot in itself be a reason for finding an ambiguity in the statute. According to the golden rule it can be a powerful motivating force leading the court to detect such an ambiguity.

It is frequently said that the question of absurdity cannot influence a decision in any type of case except the one just stated. Nevertheless, the courts sometimes act on a second principle, stated by Cross as follows.

"The judge may read in words which he considers to be necessarily implied by words which are already in the statute, and he has a limited power to add to, alter or ignore statutory words in order to prevent a provision from being unintelligible or absurd or totally unreasonable, unworkable or totally irreconcilable with the rest of the statute."[20]

Acting on this principle judges have occasionally corrected a statute that foolishly said "and" when it meant "or," or that

must be adopted unless (2) this results in absurdity. It is convenient to take the "golden rule" as meaning (2) alone, since this is what it adds to the literal rule; but some judges use the phrase to refer to meaning (1) alone.

[18] *Coutts & Co.* v. *I.R.C.* [1953] A.C. at 281.

[19] *Luke* v. *I.R.C.* [1963] A.C. at 577.

[20] Cross, *op.cit.* 84–98.

foolishly said "or" when it meant "and." However, the argument must be very strong to induce the court to meddle with a statute. Instances occur where the courts feel obliged to construe a statute in a way that they themselves acknowledge creates outrageous injustice.[21]

PRESUMPTIONS

A third principle may be regarded as an application of the second but is best stated on its own. In interpreting statutes, various presumptions may be applied, all of which are of a negative or restrictive character. They are the background of legal principles against which the Act is viewed, and in the light of which Parliament is assumed to have legislated, without being expected to express them. Some embody traditional notions of justice, such as the rule that a statute is presumed not to be retrospective (except in procedural matters). Others reflect what was almost certainly the intention of Parliament, as that an Act applies only to the United Kingdom unless the contrary is expressed. The most controversial presumptions are those enshrining the values of a capitalist society—the presumption against interference with vested rights, the presumption against the taking of property without compensation, and the presumption against interference with contract. The last of these now has few followers; but the first two still retain vitality. Even so, the judges are hampered by the thought that they must not run counter to political trends, for example by implying a right to full compensation for the appropriation of property when a socialist legislature did not in terms provide for such compensation. The traditional presumption upon which a clear consensus still exists is that against interference with personal liberty.

Presumptions may be regarded as instances of the proposition that the duty of judges goes beyond the automatic enforcement of the dictates of Parliament. The judges' function is also to do justice in accordance with certain settled principles of law in a free society; and they are entitled to assume that Parliament

---

[21] As in the case instanced by Cross, *op. cit.* 75. Professor Cross approved this decision as a matter of law, but I continue to find the reasons given by the ·House of Lords for reversing the C.A. unconvincing.

does not intend to subvert these principles, unless there is a clear statement that it does. For this reason, the courts apply the rule that when Parliament has conferred a judicial or quasi-judicial power upon a person, he must act in accordance with the rules of natural justice. When Parliament creates a new crime, this is presumed to be subject to certain defences at common law, such as self-defence and duress, and also (very frequently) to the requirement of a state of mind (intention, knowledge or recklessness). These are judge-made principles required by our ideas of justice and grafted on the statute by "implication" although there may be no words in the statute to suggest them.

The common law provides quite an armoury of such principles, and new applications can be found for them by a bold judge. A striking example is *Re Sigsworth*.[22] Under legislation now contained in the Intestates' Estates Act 1952, a child has certain rights of succession on the death of the parent intestate. For the purpose of his decision in *Re Sigsworth,* the trial judge assumed it to have been proved that the deceased, Mary Ann Sigsworth, had been murdered by her son; and the question was whether the son was entitled to her estate as "issue" under the Act. The learned judge held not, for the reason that no one is entitled to profit from his own wrong. The decision was rendered somewhat easier by the fact that a similar conclusion had already been arrived at in the law of wills: a murderer cannot take under his victim's will. Long before that—at least as early as 1775—the courts had laid down the general principle of law that a person cannot bring an action based on his own wrong (*ex turpi causa non oritur actio*).[23] In *Re Sigsworth*, the judge applied this principle to the interpretation of the intestacy statute which made no mention of it. Even statutes may be read as subject to certain fundamental principles of justice which are to be discovered in the common law.

Incidentally, *Re Sigsworth* is enough to disprove the oft-repeated assertion that "where the words of an Act of Parliament are clear, there is no room for applying any principles of interpretation."[24] This proposition may have a useful applica-

---

[22] [1935] Ch. 89.
[23] See Broom's *Legal Maxims*, 10th ed., 497.
[24] *Per* Scott L.J. in *Croxford* v. *Universal Insce. Co.* [1936] 2 K.B. at 280.

tion in limiting some of the more pedantic rules of interpretation, but it does not exclude the application of a presumption or certain common-sense principles. Although *Re Sigsworth* was only the decision of a puisne judge it has been approved by the Court of Appeal and extended to other statutes raising a similar question.[25] One can therefore say that the courts retain the power to read statutes in the light of general principles, the only question being whether the particular court will be able to find or invent a general principle that will enable it to give a sensible effect to the statute. Much will depend on the legal knowledge and ingenuity of counsel and the court, as well as on the readiness of the court to take a liberal view.

A liberal interpretation to prevent the statute operating upon a *casus male inclusus* may sometimes be comparatively easy, as it was in *Re Sigsworth*. Although the courts have not expressly said so, it may be more difficult to do anything for the *casus omissus*. To extend a statute to a regrettably omitted case looks like legislation, whereas refusing to extend it to a *casus male inclusus* is more like imposing a provisional fetter on legislation (provisional, because Parliament can always come back and include the case expressly if it wants to).[26] Even so, it is possible for a court to interpret a statute as covering what looks at first sight as a *casus omissus* if it can find or invent some plausible general principle of interpretation, an exercise that may call for a little ingenuity.

Consider, for example, *Adler* v. *George*.[27] The Official Secrets Act 1920 section 3 prohibits persons "in the vicinity of" any prohibited place from impeding sentries. The defendant impeded a sentry when he was inside a prohibited place. The argument for the defence was that the defendant, being inside, was not "in the vicinity of" the place, which meant outside. The court rejected the argument, holding that the statute was to be read as if it were "in or in the vicinity of." Obviously, the case was stronger than the one actually provided for, so it could be regarded as *a fortiori*.[28] Just as the greater includes the less, so a

[25] *R.* v. *Chief National Insce. Commr., ex p. O'Connor* [1981] 2 W.L.R. 412; *R.* v. *Home Secretary, ex p. Puttick, ibid.* 440.

[26] But the distinction is to some extent arbitrary. A *casus omissus* from an exception to a rule is a *casus male inclusus* in the rule.

[27] [1964] 2 Q.B.7.

[28] "With stronger reason"—generally anglicised as "ay forsheeory."

provision for the marginal case must include the central case. *Adler* v. *George* shows that statutes may be read not only against the background of notions of justice and settled legal principle (which tend to limit their operation) but also against the background of notions of ordinary common sense (which may extend their operation). The disquieting feature of the pronouncements of the House of Lords is that by flatly insisting upon the literal rule without expressing any qualifications, they tend to repress the use of the traditional tools by which the judges have in the past introduced rationality into the statute law.

The modern movement for the legislative recognition of "human rights" is in fact a movement for the increased control of legislatures by the judiciary, because the human rights that are claimed are couched in such broad terms, and involve so much balancing of one consideration with another, that they inevitably call for much judicial "interpretation." The European Convention on Human Rights[29] has not been made part of our law by statute, so it does not in itself create rights enforceable in our courts; but having been ratified by this country it is binding on us as a matter of international law.[29] There is a long-standing presumption that Acts of Parliament are not intended to derogate from the requirements of international law. This line of reasoning enables the courts to use the Convention as a means of restricting the operation of statutes.[30] However, no occasion has yet arisen on which the courts have had an opportunity to demonstrate the Convention as having practical effect in this aspect.

These few words are perhaps sufficient to enable the student to understand what is involved in the interpretation of statutes. For an enlargement upon the theme see Michael Zander, *The Law-Making Process* (1980), Chap. 2. A fuller account of the technical rules will be found in Sir Rupert Cross's *Statutory Interpretation*. The practitioner's work is by Maxwell.

[29] For the convention see Francis G. Jacobs, *The European Convention on Human Rights* (Oxford, 1975). The text of the convention and protocols can be obtained free of charge from the Council of Europe, Strasbourg, France.

[30] See Lord Reid in *Miah* [1974] 1 W.L.R. at 694, 2 All E.R. at 379; Lord Denning in *R.* v. *Home Secretary, ex p. Bhajan Singh* [1976] 1 Q.B. at 207; Scarman L.J. in *Ahmad* v. *I.L.E.A.* [1978] Q.B. at 48.

CHAPTER 8

WORKING OUT PROBLEMS

> I scarce think it is harder to resolve very difficult cases in law, than it is to direct a young gentleman what course he should take to enable himself so to do.
>
> —Sir Roger North, *On the Study of the Laws.*

[Since much of the value of this chapter must depend upon the concrete illustrations it gives, I have been forced to assume the reader's knowledge of a certain amount of elementary law. He should postpone reading it until he has made a start with the study of a case-law subject like Constitutional Law, Criminal Law, Contract or Tort.]

THE object of including problems in the examination paper is to discover legal ability. But it is not easy even for an intelligent candidate in the heat of the examination to show the calm judgment that a problem requires. It is, therefore, most important to train oneself in problem answering beforehand. In doing so the student will not merely be preparing in the best possible way for his examination: he will also be developing his mind as a working instrument and preparing himself for legal practice. The technique of solving academic problems is almost the same as the technique of writing a legal opinion upon a practical point. The chief difference is that in practical problems the material facts often lie buried in a much larger mass of immaterial detail, while the examination problem contains comparatively little beyond the material facts.

If the student is studying under a tutor or supervisor an adequate number of problems will be supplied to him. If not, he will have to buy or otherwise get sight of copies of past examination papers.

Perhaps the most important piece of advice with problems, as with all examination questions, is to *read every word of the problem.* Almost every word has been put in for a purpose and needs to be commented upon. In the law of contract, for instance, the word "orally" or "verbally" or "on the telephone," in describing the formation of a contract for the sale of land, will invite discussion of section 40 of the Law of Property Act 1925. Even if you are of opinion that a fact stated in the problem is immaterial, you should not (in general) pass it by in silence but should express your opinion that it is immaterial, and, if possible, give reasons. However, there is no need to deal in this way with an argument that, if raised, would not receive a moment's serious consideration from the court.

FACTS STATED IN THE PROBLEM ARE CONCLUSIVE

A common query on the part of the novice when he reads an examination problem is: "How could such facts ever be proved?" The teacher's answer is that the student must assume this proof. (Actually, it is surprising how facts often can be proved in practice that at first sight seem to be unprovable if the defendant is prepared to contradict them. But in any case the student is not concerned with this question.)

The student should not assume facts *contrary* to those stated in the problem for the purpose of giving the examiner a piece of information for which he did not ask. Also, there is generally no need to assume facts that go clean beyond those given in the problem: had the examiner wanted a discussion of such facts he would have inserted them himself. Here is an example of a problem in criminal law where the examiner clearly wanted to confine the facts to a narrow compass.

X and Y, discovering that Z intended to commit a burglary in A's house, arranged together to persuade him to steal therefrom certain articles for them. Have X, Y or Z committed an offence?

The fact that the question is thrown into the perfect tense shows beyond doubt that no other facts than those stated in the first sentence are to be assumed. The question is: have they *on those facts alone* committed an offence? An answer that assumes that X and Y have persuaded Z to steal, or that Z has stolen, will therefore miss the mark. The correct answer to the question is that X and Y are guilty of conspiring to incite (or, indeed, of conspiring to commit) burglary or theft. (There are technical points relating to the charge that need not be considered here.)

OMITTED FACTS

Although supplementary facts should not, in general, be added to a problem, the case is different with what may be called omitted facts. One of the marks of a competent lawyer is his ability to know what gaps there are in the facts of his case. The solicitor, for example, when interviewing a client has to draw from him by questions many legally relevant facts that the client has not thought of disclosing. The barrister, too, may find that such facts are missing from his brief, and have to extract them from his instructing solicitor in conference. In order to test the candidate's perspicacity a problem may deliberately omit something that is important. Always look for such omissions and state how your answer will be affected by the presence or absence of the fact in question. Here is a simple illustration from the law of tort.

> B is A's employee. Discuss A's liability for an accident caused by B's negligence in the following cases:
> (i) B, when driving A's van, picks up his friend C and gives him a lift to the station. An accident happens by B's negligence.
> (ii) [etc.]

Two vital facts are omitted from this casually stated problem. First, we are not told who was injured. We are to understand that owing to B's negligence an injury was sustained either by C or by some other user of the highway. But the answer may differ according as the person injured was C or some other user of the highway. This distinction should therefore be taken, and each of the two possibilities discussed separately.

Secondly, we are not told whether the station lay on or near B's proper route, or whether it was so much off the route that every yard he went was a yard away from his employment and not to it. This distinction, coupled with the previous one, yields four possible combinations of fact, each needing discussion.

Another example of an economically worded problem, this time taken from criminal law:

> A killed his baby thinking that it was a rabbit. Discuss A's criminal responsibility.

Here A's mistake is so extraordinary that we are justified in wondering whether he was not insane at the time of the deed, his insanity being an omitted fact. On the other hand we are not positively told that he was insane, and so we must also consider the unlikely hypothesis that the mistake was merely an act of folly. (As a matter of fact, nature imitates not only art but examination questions; not long ago a man of my acquaintance shot his wife in the leg, in the shrubbery, thinking she was a rabbit.) Or there is the possibility that A killed his baby in the course of a dream.[1] The answer, then, again falls into two parts: (i) on the assumption that A was sane, (ii) on the assumption that he was insane. However, it is not justifiable to discuss a problem from the angle of insanity if there is no indication of insanity in the facts of the problem.

One more example, again from criminal law:

> A, a mountaineer, roped to his fellows, cut the rope in order to prevent them from dragging the leader of the party to death. Discuss.

Presumably A is being prosecuted for murder; but the question does not actually say that A's fellows were killed as a result of what he did. We must assume that they were killed, or at least injured, in order to create a legal problem. Presumably, too, A sets up the defence of necessity; we are not expressly told that there was (or that A thought there was) no other way of saving the leader's life, but this is a fair inference from the question. Finally, the question tells us that A's object was to save the leader; it does not tell us whether his object was also to save himself. In other words it does not tell us whether he cut the rope above or below himself. If he cut it below himself his object was presumably to save himself as well as his leader. If he cut it above himself he presumably fell, and in that case his life was evidently saved by something approaching a miracle—at any rate, we know that he was saved because otherwise he would be beyond the jurisdiction and the question would have no legal interest. Perhaps this last doubt is irrelevant; it may not matter whether A's object was entirely altruistic or partially self-interested. But on the other hand it may, and so the point ought to be taken.

Having thus discussed the interpretation of this problem, you would, of course, go on to consider the law relating to it.

If, as in the last illustration, you decide that a fact can be

---

[1] As in *H.M. Advocate* v. *Fraser* (1878) 4 Couper 70.

inferred from what is given, though not explicitly stated, it is wise to guard yourself by stating expressly that you assume the fact to exist. For the examiner may not agree that the fact is implied in the question; but he will not mind about this if he sees that your assumption is not the result of carelessness but is your considered interpretation of the question. If you are in any doubt whether a fact is implied you should "play safe" and take the problem each way, that is, first on the assumption that the fact exists and then on the assumption that it does not exist.

Even if all the relevant facts (in one sense of the word "facts") are stated, what is legally called a "question of fact" may still arise on the problem—*e.g.* a question whether the defendant has, on the facts, been negligent, or whether a lapse of time is "reasonable." In a real case these would be questions for the jury (if the case were tried with a jury), although the judge might withdraw the issue from the jury if satisfied that there was no evidence of negligence or unreasonableness. On such a problem, although you may venture an opinion as to the proper verdict on the point, and argue your opinion to the best of your ability, you should not, in the last resort, usurp the function of the jury (or of the judge when there is no jury). The most you should say is that on these facts there is evidence of negligence (or unreasonableness), and that a finding to that effect would clearly be right (or conversely). If the point is at all doubtful, take the facts each way and state the legal result following on each possible finding. The following problem in the law of contract illustrates the importance of this.

A telegraphed an offer to sell his library to D for £1,000. B telegraphed in reply: "Will give £900. B." A day elapsed in which nothing further occurred. Then at 9 a.m. A handed to the post office a telegram to B: "You can have the library for £900.   A." At exactly the same moment B handed to the post office a telegram to A: "Cancel my first telegram. I will take the library for £1,000. B." A received B's telegram at 9.30 a.m. B received A's telegram at 9.40 a.m. What contract, if any, exists?

Everything in this problem turns on the unobtrusive sentence: "A day elapsed. . . . " The question is whether this was an unreasonable delay on the part of A in replying to B's counter-offer of £900. If it was unreasonable, the offer (*i.e.* B's counter-offer) has lapsed, and there is no contract. If it was not unreasonable, the offer was still alive when A handed in at the post office his telegram of acceptance, and the contract was therefore completed at that moment.[2] Now it is not possible to give a confident answer to the question whether the delay was unreasonable. The only rule of law is that an offer by telegram raises a presumption that a speedy reply is expected (*Quenerduaine* v. *Cole*[3]), and therefore the lapse of a whole day would normally be too long. But it is to be noticed that in our problem the telegraphing business was started not by B but by A. B may have sent his counter-offer by telegram simply out of politeness, and not because *he* was in any hurry. It is not certain, therefore, whether the rule in *Quenerduaine* v. *Cole* would apply, though on the whole I think it would, because I do not think that a court would speculate on the reasons that moved B to telegraph rather than write.

There is more to say about this problem, but the essence of it is this question of fact. (Although telegrams are now little used in business matters, the question could arise in connection with international cables.)

It may be added that where facts are given from which the negligence or unreasonableness (or absence of it) may be inferred, you should argue from these facts in much the same way as if you were addressing a jury. But, as I have said, your opinion on this should not (except in a completely unarguable case) deter you from taking the problem each way.

TWO POINTS OF TECHNIQUE

Some examiners conclude the statement of facts in a problem with the direction to discuss it: others adopt the mannerism of requesting you to advise one of the parties. This second form of question does not mean that you are expected to bias your answer in favour of the particular party; the legal advice you give in your answer will generally be the same whichever party you are supposed to be advising. However, there may be some practical advice to be given to the party you are supposed to be advising, and you should certainly comply with the examiner's direction as far as you are able. By the way, do not use the

---

[2] *Cowan* v. *O'Connor* (1888) 20 Q.B.D. 640. Distinguish the Telex case, *Entores Ltd.* v. *Miles Far East Corporation* [1955] 2 Q.B. 327.
[3] (1883) 32 W.R. 185.

second person in your answer—make the answer impersonal, thus you should say "X is liable," not "You are liable."

If the examiner has exercised his fancy by using fictitious names, like Tomkins, you are perfectly entitled to abbreviate them to the initial letter—unless, of course, two parties in the same problem have the same initial letter.

RULES AND AUTHORITIES

Next, a few remarks upon the giving of reasons and authorities for an opinion. A bald answer to a problem, even though correct, will not earn many (perhaps not any) marks, because the examiner cannot tell whether the student has knowledge or is just guessing. Reasons and authorities should, therefore, always be given. Pretend to yourself that the examiner will disagree with your point of view, and set yourself to win him over by argument.

One of the most important of a lawyer's accomplishments is the ability to resolve facts into their legal categories. The student should therefore take pains to argue in terms of legal rules and concepts. It is a common fault, particularly in criminal law, to give the impression that the answer is based wholly upon common sense and a few gleanings from the Sunday newspapers. The following illustration of a question and answer in criminal law may show this.

Q.—A fire-engine driven at full speed to a fire knocks down and kills somebody. Discuss the criminal responsibility of the driver.

Student's answer.—"If the driver has been careful he is not responsible. (1) It is a well known custom that as soon as the siren of a fire engine is heard, other vehicles should pull up at the side of the road, in order to afford free passage. It is therefore safe for a fire-engine driver to proceed at a higher speed than would be possible for other drivers. Further (2) it is reasonable for a fire-engine to proceed quickly to a fire, for life and property may be in danger. But I do not put much weight on this second ground, for great as may be the importance of putting out a fire, it is not sufficiently great to justify the driver in leaving a trail of destruction behind him."

Upon reading this answer the examiner may well comment: "A commendable effort by an intelligent student who has not read the textbook and knows no criminal law." The answer, to be complete, should have stated the crimes for which the driver may be prosecuted (manslaughter, causing death by reckless driving, or, in the magistrates' court, driving without due care and attention); it should have stated the requirements of each crime, so far as relevant; and it should have pointed out that the burden of proving these requirements beyond reasonable doubt lies on the prosecution. It should also have discussed the possible defence of necessity, referring to it expressly by that name, not vaguely as the last two sentences of the answer do. Put into this legal setting the answer would have been first-class.[4]

It is bad style to begin an answer to a problem by citing a string of cases. Begin by addressing yourself to the problem. If the law is clear, first state the law and *then* give the authorities for your statement. If the law is not clear, first pose the legal question and *then* set out the authorities bearing on it.

When citing cases, the mere giving of the name is of little use. What is wanted is not only the name but a statement of the legal points involved in the decision, and perhaps also a consideration of its standing—*i.e.* whether it has been approved or criticised. This is so even though the case directly covers the problem. Still more is it so when the case is not on all fours with the problem. New points often occur in the law, and the lawyer in advising his client must, in effect, predict the probable decision of the court. So also in examinations: a problem is often set upon some point of law that is not covered exactly by authority. No candidate who fails to see this point can get a first class on that question. The late Dr. Coulton, in his autobiography, told a tale of a great mathematical teacher at Cambridge who met a candidate in the College court just after the Tripos. "That was a d— good answer of yours, A, to the sixteenth question." Yes, sir, but it was a b— good question, wasn't it?" In order to create this relationship of mutual esteem between yourself and your examiner, pay him the compliment of searching for the point of his problem. Ask yourself what is the point it raises that is not precisely covered by authority.

Failure to follow this common-sense rule is a frequent error of the tyro. Take again, for instance, the "mountaineering" problem already given (p.115). Most raw beginners think that

---

[4] The point may also be made that firemen are by statute exempt from speed limits.

they have adequately solved this problem if they quote *R.* v. *Dudley and Stephens*[5] and declare that necessity is no defence. But if they paused to reflect, they would discover several differences between *R.* v. *Dudley and Stephens* and the facts of their problem. It cannot be asserted with confidence that every, or even any, of these distinctions would find favour with a judge, but at any rate they are possible distinctions which would certainly be made much of by an experienced counsel for the defence. They are as follows:

(1) In *Dudley and Stephens* there was a choice as to who was to die. It will be remembered that *Dudley and Stephens* was the case where three men and a cabin-boy were compelled to take to an open boat after the wreck of their yacht *Mignonette*. On the twentieth day after the wreck two of the men killed the boy for food; four days later they were rescued. The two men were convicted of murder. It may be said that these facts are materially different from those in our problem, for in our problem there seems to be no choice as to who is to die: it is simply (one supposes) a question of some or all. It is true that in *Dudley and Stephens* the jury found that the boy was in a much weaker condition than the others and was likely to have died before them. But the jury did not find that the boy might not have been revived had one of the others been killed to provide food for him. So long as the boy was alive and had a chance of survival he was as much entitled to retain that chance as the others; whereas in our problem it may be that the men who are cut away have no chance of survival at all.

(2) It is not certain on the facts of *Dudley and Stephens* that the two defendants would have died had they not killed the boy. All that the jury found was that had they not done so they would *probably* not have survived to be rescued. It may be that on the facts of our problem the death of the leader is certain, not merely probable, if the rope is not cut. But it must be admitted that this is not a very strong distinction, for in *Dudley and Stephens* the jury also found that "at the time of the act there was no sail in sight, nor any reasonable prospect of relief"; and it would seem that if the law recognises necessity as a defence it should proceed upon the facts as they appeared to the defendant at the time.

[5] (1884) 14 Q.B.D. 273.

(3) In *Dudley and Stephens* the cabin-boy was not by his own conduct, voluntary or involuntary, bringing the others nearer to death. In our problem the men whom the defendant presumably sends to death are themselves dragging the leader to what will otherwise be his death. It is true that they cannot help it; but does that matter? If a lunatic attacks me, I am surely entitled to defend myself, even though he is not criminally responsible for his conduct. Also, I am entitled to defend another. Is not our problem a case of defending another?

Another illustration, this time from the law of contract, is as follows:

A writes to B offering to sell him his horse Phineas for £100. B posts a letter accepting, but he misdirects it and in consequence it is a week late in being delivered to A. Meanwhile A has sold Phineas to C. Discuss.

The ordinary beginner answers this problem simply by quoting *Household Fire Insurance Co.* v. *Grant,*[6] or some other authority to the same effect, and saying that by our law an offeror can be landed with a contract even though he never receives an acceptance, since the contract is held to be complete on the posting of the letter of acceptance. But the whole point of the question is whether *Grant's* case applies to a misdirected letter of acceptance. I cannot help thinking that the booby who so completely misses the point of the question is often actuated by some hidden (and mistaken) motive of self-preservation. He really scents the difficulty but thinks it too hard for discussion and so conveniently pretends that he has not seen it. If this ostrich only knew, he would gain more marks *by posing the legal difficulty,* even though he suggested no solution, than he ever could by blinking it completely. If, in addition to posing the difficulty, he could say that there is no authority in point and that *Grant's* case is distinguishable, and could also suggest some reasons why on these facts it ought to be distinguished, he would get a first class on that question instead of a very doubtful pass.

One of the techniques of argument is to take an extreme case. " 'I took an extreme case,' was Alice's tearful reply. 'My excellent preceptress always used to say, When in doubt take an extreme case. And I was in doubt.' " The technique need not always result in tears. Let us make our problem into a more

[6] (1879) 4 Ex.D. 216.

extreme case. A week's delay in a letter does not sound inordinately long, but to isolate the question of principle let us make it longer. Suppose that the misdirected letter of acceptance had taken two months on its way, or had never arrived. Had it been properly directed there would have been a good contract and A would have been liable in damages to B for not delivering the horse. That is a harsh rule from A's point of view (I think a stupid rule, and I hope that if you are the reader of this book who is destined to become Lord Chancellor you will get it changed), but it would be even worse if the same rule were applied where B has carelessly misdirected his letter, resulting in gross delay or loss. The rule in *Grant's* case cannot possibly apply to such circumstances. If this be conceded, the next question is . . . what? Close your eyes and think deeply. If you have done that, compare your answer with mine. The next question is whether B's letter is to be regarded as an acceptance from the time when A receives it. If that is the rule, then there will be a good contract if the lapse of a week before acceptance is not thought to be an unreasonable time; and, on these assumptions, A not having revoked his offer before acceptance is liable to B for breach of contract if he does not deliver the horse. If the lapse of time is held to be unreasonable, there is no contract.

But an alternative rule is possible. This is that B's letter is a nullity even if it arrives on time. When A posts the offer to B he impliedly authorises B to conclude the contract by posting a letter of acceptance, but only on the assumption that the acceptance is properly addressed; if it is not, there is no acceptance even though the Post Office cleverly delivers it on time. I do not myself think that this alternative is correct, but it would be worth putting forward in court.

The general lesson from this is: in all legal problems use your brain and *have the courage to argue.*

If a case falls midway between two authorities, this may indicate that there is a fundamental conflict of principle between the two authorities, and that it is necessary to hold that one of them was wrongly decided. Alternatively, you may come to the conclusion that there is a real distinction between the authorities, and in this event the problem must be looked at from the point of view of general legal principle or public policy to decide whether it should be brought under the one head or the other. The situation was characterised by Paley, an eighteenth-century divine, as the "competition of opposite analogies."[7]

To sum up, when the problem is possibly distinguishable from the authority or authorities nearest in point, a careful analysis of the possible distinction or distinctions should always be given. This is particularly important if the authority in question has been doubted by judges or criticised by legal writers. It may be that the student does not feel competent to discuss the various distinctions, but even so the existence of the possible distinctions should be pointed out in the answer. Moreover, distinctions should be pointed out even though in the opinion of the student they are not material, if it could conceivably be argued that they are material: of course the student should express his own opinion that they are not material.

If there is a possibility of the authority in question being overruled, it is more important than ever to mention its status in the judicial hierarchy, as well as stating any objections that have been urged against it.

When you have a number of cases to quote, it is generally best to quote the nearest authority first and to allot it the most space; the other cases can be brought more casually into the discussion, as you have time. When you have read a case in the reports or in a case book, do your best to convey this fact by referring to some apposite passage in the judgment or some other relevant detail of the report which will indicate that you have not merely relied on a textbook.

If you know that there is no case bearing directly upon the problem, say so. The fact that the problem is not covered by authority is in itself a valuable piece of information. If the authority for a proposition is a statute, say this also, even though you have forgotten the name of the statute.

DOUBT

Where the law is doubtful, a categorical statement that the rule is one way or the other will earn few, if any, marks. This is

---

[7] *Moral and Political Philosophy*, vi. VIII. The classical discussion of Paley's remarks is in Austin's *Jurisprudence*, 5th ed., ii, 632-633.

particularly important in answering problems. If the answer to the problem is doubtful, say so, and then suggest what the answer ought to be. It is a mistake to simulate confidence where you have no certain knowledge.

After discussing a "mooty" problem, try to avoid the weak conclusion that "A is perhaps liable." Your conclusion may be that if the facts are so-and-so, he is liable; if they are such and such, he is not. Or, if the court follows *Smith* v. *Jones,* then A will be liable, but if it follows *Robinson* v. *Edwards,* which is to be preferred for reasons previously given, then A will not be liable.

A point can often be scored by demonstrating that the law applicable to a problem may depend upon the court before which the case comes. For example, there are some decisions of the Court of Appeal, like that in *Musgrove* v. *Pandelis,*[8] that would probably be reluctantly followed by the Court of Appeal but would almost certainly be overruled by the House of Lords. Consequently, the "law" on the subject of *Musgrove* v. *Pandelis* (strict liability for petrol in the tank of a car) may depend upon the number of appeals that the client is prepared to take.

PROBLEMS ON STATUTES

A problem may be set on a statute as well as on a case. You must then recall the words of the statute as best you can, apply them to the problem and, as in all problems, look for the "catch." Here is an illustration from constitutional law:

Aikenhead J., a judge of the High Court, is convicted of driving under the influence of drink. Can he be dismissed from his judicial office, and if so by whom?

The attitude of students towards a problem like this varies. Some, though knowing the terms of the Act of Settlement, or of the similar statute now in force, steer clear of the problem because they are afraid of it. Others write down simply:

By the Act of Settlement 1701, "Judges' Commissions [shall] be made *quamdiu se bene gesserint,*[9] but upon the Address of both Houses of

---

[8] [1919] 2 K.B. 43.
[9] "For as long as they behave themselves."

Parliament it may be lawful to remove them."[10] Aikenhead J. can be removed under this provision.

This is not a bad answer and would win a pass. Had the candidate added that dismissal was actually effected by the Crown he might have risen to a second. To obtain a first class, one needs to do a little thinking. Aikenhead J. was appointed "during good behaviour." He has been convicted of crime, and we shall assume for the moment that he has not behaved himself within the meaning of these words. Clearly he can be dismissed if both Houses present an Address to that effect. But can he not, in this case, be dismissed even without an Address? What the examiner is evidently after is the correct interpretation of the words of the Act of Settlement, or rather of the Act now in force replacing the Act of Settlement. Do these words mean that judges can be dismissed by the Crown *only* upon an Address of both Houses (with a direction to the Houses that they are not to present an Address unless the judge has misbehaved himself)? Or do the words mean that judges can be dismissed by the Crown *either* if they have not behaved themselves (*e.g.* been convicted of crime) *or* on an Address of both Houses? In other words, are the Houses the sole judges of the correctness of the judges' behaviour, or not? The second interpretation can be arrived at by reading the provision in two parts: (1) judges' commissions are to be made for as long as they behave themselves, implying that if they misbehave they may be dismissed by the Crown; (2) they may be removed by the Crown on an Address of both Houses, even though they have not misbehaved themselves. The first interpretation can be arrived at by reading the provision as a whole (judges are appointed during good behaviour, and the two Houses are the sole judges of bad behaviour).

A good lawyer, who reads carefully, ponders meanings and is prepared to discuss difficulties, might be able to see this point in the problem even though he had read nothing upon it. When one studies the literature one finds that, surprising as it may seem, the weight of legal opinion is in favour of the second view; and it is not even clear what is the proper legal means that the Crown

[10] See now Supreme Court of Judicature (Consolidation) Act 1925 s 12 (1).

should use to establish misbehaviour before dismissing a judge.[11] A further question that arises (and that might be perceived on the face of this problem) is whether dismissal by the Crown can only be for misbehaviour in office or whether it can be for an offence not related to judicial office or affecting judicial ability. If the latter, can it be for any offence or only for a serious one, and is the offence in the problem sufficiently serious? In practice the Crown would now be unlikely to dismiss a judge without an Address, and it would be for the two Houses to decide whether the misbehaviour justified dismissal.

This example shows how it is possible to display the qualities of a good lawyer without knowing much law. Here is another problem in constitutional law to reinforce the point.

A statute is passed giving power to make Orders in Council for the public safety and defence of the realm. Would it be a valid objection to an Order made under this statute that it imposes a tax?

The type of answer to be expected from the Painful Plodder would be as follows:

"A statute similar in terms to that in the problem was DORA,[12] passed in the First World War. By Regulations under this statute the Food Controller was empowered to regulate dealings in any article. Under these powers the Food Controller ordered that no milk should be sold within certain counties except under licence. In *Att.-Gen.* v. *Wilts United Dairies*[13] the question arose whether the Food Controller was entitled to charge for the granting of a licence under this Order. It was held by the H.L. that he was not. This case was approved by the Court of Appeal in *Congreve* v. *Home Office.*[14] The answer to the question is therefore 'Yes.' "

This answer exhibits a common defect: it cites a case without explaining the legal principle involved in it, *i.e.* the legal ground on which the case was decided. Plodder says that in *Att.-Gen.* v. *Wilts U.D.* it was held that the Food Controller could not charge for the licence. This is true, but we need to know why. The facts of the case contained three elements: (1) DORA, giving power

[11] Anson, *Law and Custom of the Constitution,* 4th ed. ii 234–235; Sir K. Roberts-Wray, *Commonwealth and Colonial Law* (London 1966) 486 *et seq.*; W.P.M. Kennedy in 6 U. of Tor. L.J. 464-465.
[12] The Defence of the Realm Consolidation Act 1914.
[13] (1922) 91 L.J.K.B. 897.
[14] [1976] Q.B. 629.

to make Regulations for the public safety and defence of the realm; (2) the "daughter" Regulations made under DORA, allowing the Food Controller to regulate dealings in any article; and (3) the Food Controller's Order ("granddaughter" of DORA) that no milk should be sold without licence, coupled with his grant of a licence on condition of receiving payment. Now the decision was that the money promised by the dairy company could not be recovered by the Crown, for the reason that (*a*) any prerogative power to tax had been taken away by the Bill of Rights 1689, and that (*b*) as for the statutory powers of DORA, the Regulations under which the Food Controller was acting did not on their wording enable him to impose a tax. The Regulations enabled him to regulate dealings in an article, but regulation of dealings is one thing, taxing another. Order (3) was therefore *ultra vires*[15] the Regulations (2). Had the candidate understood these reasons he would at once have seen that the decision in *Att.-Gen.* v. *Wilts U.D.* did not conclude the question he was asked. All that the case decided was that the Food Controller was acting outside the *Regulations* since the Regulations did not give the power to tax. The question whether a Regulation that expressly gave the power to tax would itself be *ultra vires* DORA was not decided.

Now here is the answer of a gentleman who may be called the Discerning Dilettante. He knows nothing about the Bill of Rights or the decision in *Att.-Gen.* v. *Wilts U.D.,* but he addresses himself to the question and uses his intelligence.

"It may be that the Order is *intra vires*[16] the statute. The statute gives power to make Orders for the public safety and defence of the realm: in other words for the waging of war. Obviously you cannot wage war without taxing. Money, it is said, makes the sinews of war.

"To this it may be objected that although it is necessary to tax in order to wage war, it is not necessary for the Executive to tax without a statute. Parliament is still in being; why not leave taxation to Parliament?

"I think that a valid reply to this objection would be that it is a political objection to the passing of a statute worded in this wide way, not a legal objection to the validity of the Order, if a statute worded so widely has been passed. If the objection were legally valid it could be used to defeat almost all Orders made under this statute, which would be absurd. Suppose that under this defence statute the Government makes an Order

[15] *i.e.* "outside the powers" conferred by the enabling provision.
[16] "Within the powers [of]."

requisitioning land for anti-aircraft missile sites. It would obviously be no valid objection to such an Order that the Order is not necessary for public safety because Parliament could have passed it. The object of the defence statute is to delegate to the Executive what in peacetime would be the function of Parliament. Surely the question whether Parliament could have passed the particular legislation is logically irrelevant to the question whether the legislation is for the public safety and defence of the realm.

"At the same time I do not suppose that a court would take the view that I am here expressing. The English tradition that it is for Parliament to do the taxing is so deep-seated that the court would probably assert a legal presumption, as a matter of statute interpretation, that powers of taxation are not included in a statutory delegation of power unless clear words are used, and that a general formula like that in the statute stated in the question is not sufficient."

Or, as Atkin L.J. (as he then was) put it in *Att.-Gen.* v. *Wilts U.D.* in the Court of Appeal, "in view of the historic struggle of the legislature to secure for itself the sole power to levy money upon the subject, its complete success in that struggle, the elaborate means adopted by the representative House to control the amount, the conditions and the purpose of the levy, the circumstances would be remarkable indeed whch would induce the court to believe that the legislature had sacrificed all the well-known checks and precautions, and, not in express words, but merely by implication, had entrusted a Minister of the Crown with undefined and unlimited powers of imposing charges upon the subject for purposes connected with his department."[17] The point is reinforced by *Congreve's* case (above), where the Court of Appeal assumed that *Att.-Gen.* v. *Wilts U.D.* was an authority on the application of the Bill of Rights.

In thus unfavourably contrasting Plodder's answer with Dilettante's, I am not, of course, suggesting that book work is useless. As I have already said, book knowledge should always be used to provide a starting-point. Dilettante's answer would have been better if he could have shown that the *Wilts* case, though apparently relevant, was not conclusive on the question. The point is that although book knowledge is in itself a good thing, it is useless and worse than useless if it deflects your attention from the question that you are being asked.

---

[17] (1921) 37 T.L.R. 884 at 886.

RELEVANCY

When answering a problem, never preface your answer with a general disquisition on the department of law relating to the problem. Start straight away to answer the problem. Problems are set chiefly to test your ability to *apply* the law you know, and the examiner will speedily tire of reading an account of the law that is not brought into direct relation to the problem. Where the problem contains several persons, say A and B as possible plaintiffs and C and D as possible defendants, the best course is to begin your answer by writing down the heading: *A.* v. *C.* When you have dealt with this, write (say) *B* v. *C,* referring back to your previous answer for any points that do not need to be repeated. Then you will deal with *A* v. *D* and *B* v. *D.*

The advice to plunge into the specific problem, on the model of counsel's opinion, applies even where the problem is divided into several parts, all of which are on the same general department of law. For instance, suppose that in criminal law a question consists of a chain of short problems on insanity numbered (i), (ii), (iii), etc. In my opinion it is not advisable to preface the answer with a discussion of *McNaghten's* case,[18] even though *McNaghten's* case is relevant to each of the numbered problems. The examiner is impatient to see you answering the problems, and he may even ignore altogether anything you write before writing down figure (i). You should therefore write the figure (i) at the very beginning of your answer, and begin to tackle problem (i). In the course of doing so you can, of course, set out and discuss *McNaghten's* case. When you come to (ii), (iii) and the rest, it will be easy enough to put a back reference, if necessary, to your previous discussion of the case.

Although a problem is not an invitation to launch out into a general disquisition on the department of law on which the problem is set, it is important in working out the problem to state all the rules of law that are really relevant to it. A frequent blemish upon an otherwise good answer is that the relevant rule of law is not expressly stated but is left to be implied from the candidate's conclusion. Much the better practice is first to state the rule of law and then to apply it to the facts. Do not write: "D

---

[18] (1843) 10 Cl. & F. 200, 8 E.R. 718.

is liable on the contract because he did not communicate his revocation of his offer." It is better style to write: "An uncommunicated revocation of an offer is ineffective. Here D's revocation did not come to the notice of the offeree, so the offeree's acceptance of the offer was valid, and D is liable on the contract." Here is another illustration of the point, from the law of tort.

Q.—A, finding B, a stranger of rough appearance, in his shed, locks the door in order to keep B there while he fetches the police. Can B sue A?

Student's answer.—"B can sue A for false imprisonment because no 'arrestable offence' has been committed by anyone."

The answer reveals some knowledge of the law, and would be correct in many cases. But the law is not fully stated (not even the important provision in the Criminal Law Act), and some facts can be imagined that would make the arrest lawful. To earn marks you must state the law and imagine variations of fact. Here is a model:

There is no power to arrest for trespass. But under the Criminal Law Act 1967[19] anyone can arrest on reasonable suspicion of an arrestable offence, save that where the arrest is by a private person (as here) he must show *either* (1) that the arrested person was in fact *in the act of committing* the offence for which he was arrested, or he reasonably suspected the arrested person to be *in the act of committing* it, *or* (2) the arrested person *had in fact committed* the offence, or he reasonably suspected the arrested person of *having committed* the offence *and* (in this last case) *the offence had in fact been committed by someone.* An arrestable offence is defined as one for which a person may by virtue of any statute be sentenced to imprisonment for at least five years, or an attempt to commit such an offence. Theft comes within the definition.

A will have the statutory power of arrest if B was in fact attempting to steal something in the shed, or if A reasonably suspected him of being in the act of attempting to steal something in the shed. A's defence on the latter ground would of course be assisted if there was something in the shed worth stealing. If there was not, A might still believe that B was looking for something to steal, which could constitute an attempt to steal under the Criminal Attempts Act 1981 notwithstanding that there was nothing there that B would have stolen.

Suppose, now, that the shed was clearly bare of everything and A's suspicions did not relate to theft in the shed. A might still suspect B of having stolen something from him elsewhere (*e.g.* if he has just discovered that a bunch of keys is missing from the hall table). The arrest

[19] Section 2 (2), (3).

could then be lawful if B had in fact stolen the thing in question or if A reasonably suspected B of having stolen it, provided (in the last case) that the thing had in fact been stolen by someone. If it turned out that Mrs A had gathered up the keys, the arrest would be unlawful. This is obviously a trap for private arresters.

Even if A has the power of arrest, he must ordinarily inform the person arrested that he is being arrested and the reason for it, *i.e.* the act for which arrest is made: *Christie* v. *Leachinsky*[20] [facts]. So A must shout to tell B that he is under arrest and why.

Not one candidate in a hundred gives an answer comparable with this; students regularly fail to consider what it is exactly that A suspects. The Vagrancy Act 1824 section 4 could also be referred to, but those taking an examination in the law of tort would not be expected to know it.

The question just considered asked: "Can B sue A?" This formula, very common in law examinations, means "Can B sue A *successfully?*" Examinees sometimes answer it by saying: "B can sue A but he will fail." This displays the writer's common sense but also his lack of knowledge of legal phraseology. It is true that there is virtually no restriction upon the bringing of actions: for instance, I can at this moment sue the Prime Minister for assault—though I shall fail in the action. But when a lawyer asserts that A can sue B, what he means is that A can sue B, successfully; if he meant his words to be taken literally, they would not have been worth the uttering.

For much the same reason, you should never write a sentence like: "B can argue that...but the argument will fail," or "B has committed such-and-such a crime, but he has a good defence." The proper way to put the last sentence would be to say: "If B is charged with such-and-such a crime, he will have a good defence."

When a problem is based on a rule—*e.g.* the rule in *Derry* v. *Peek*[21] or *Rylands* v. *Fletcher*[22]—it is usually advisable to state the whole rule in a sentence or two, even though some parts of the rule are not material to the problem. No further details should be given of parts of the rule that are not material.

Where the problem turns on an exception to a rule (*e.g.* an exception to the rule in *Rylands* v. *Fletcher*), there is usually no

---

[20] [1947] A.C. 573.
[21] (1889) 14 App.Cas. 337
[22] (1868) L.R. 3 H.L. 330.

need to state any exceptions other than the one that is relevant.

Questions are frequently divided into two or more parts, and this division raises difficulties of its own for the inexpert candidate.

Sometimes the problem begins with a common opening part before branching out into its subdivisions. The following is an example:

> A writes to B offering to sell him his horse Phineas for £100.
>
> (i) B posts a letter accepting, but he misdirects it and in consequence it is a week late in being delivered to A. Meanwhile A has sold Phineas to C.
>
> (ii) B, after posting a letter of acceptance to A, sends A a telegram cancelling "my letter now in the post." The telegram is delivered to A before B's letter.
>
> Discuss.

It should be obvious that in this type of problem (i) and (ii) are alternative possibilities, to be dealt with separately; (ii) is not meant to follow upon and include the facts of (i). Yet I have known students to suppose that this is all a single problem, to be disposed of in a single breath.

Another mistake that one student made with this particular problem was to suppose that the opening sentence was itself a question, inviting a general disquisition on the legal nature of an offer. This, of course, is not so.

A different type of two-part problem is one in which the second part commences: "Would it make any difference to your answer if . . . ?" This means that the second part of the question is the same as the first part, except for the variation expressly stated. An illustration is as follows:

> (i) A is firing with an air gun in his garden at a target on a tree. The shot glances off the tree and hits A's gardener, B. Can B sue A?
>
> (ii) Would your answer be different if the shot had been fired by A's son, C?

Most students assume that (ii) is a question as to the liability of C. Clearly on its wording the question is the same as in (i), namely, as to the liability of A.

Sometimes a problem is so worded as to involve two successive questions, but the second question logically arises only if the first is answered in a certain way. Suppose that the student has answered the first question in the *other* way; is he now to answer the second? The answer is "Yes." For the purpose of answering the second part of the question he should state that he is assuming that he is wrong in his answer to the first. An example from the law of contract:

> Pickwick, who manufactures cricket bats, affixed a signboard on the boundary of the field belonging to the Dingley Dell Cricket Club, stating that if any batsman hit the signboard with a batted ball during the course of a match Pickwick would pay him the sum of £5. Podder hit the board whilst batting in a match between Dingley Dell and Muggleton, and afterwards orally requested Pickwick to pay £5 to Mrs Jingle, to whom Podder was indebted for board and lodging. Mrs Jingle demands payment of the £5 from Pickwick but is refused. Discuss the rights of the parties.

This problem involves two issues: (i) whether there is a contract between Pickwick and Podder, resulting in a debt owed by Pickwick to Podder; (ii) whether Podder has validly assigned the debt to Mrs Jingle. Issue (i) turns on the difficult distinction between consideration and the performance of a condition precedent to a gratuitous promise,[23] or if you like on the equally difficult question of intent to contract. It may well happen that the student in considering this comes to the conclusion that there is no contract between Pickwick and Podder. If this view is correct, issue (ii) does not really arise. All the same, it should be dealt with. It may be that the examiner disagrees with the candidate in his answer to (i), and although that may not affect the candidate's marks on (i), the candidate will lose the marks on (ii) if he does not deal with it. Even if the examiner agrees with the candidate in his answer to (i), the examiner must have meant (ii) to be dealt with, or else he would not have troubled to put it in.

A fourth kind of two-part question consists of a book-work question followed by a problem. The difficulty here is often that it is not clear whether the problem is meant to bear a relation to the book-work question or not. No universal rule can be stated, because examiners differ in their practice, but nearly always there is meant to be a connection, at least if the two parts of the

[23] See Salmond and Williams, *Contracts* (1945), 100 *et seq.*; Cheshire and Fifoot, *The Law of Contract,* 9th ed., 80-81.

question are not subdivided by numbers or letters. I am conscious that this may not sound very helpful advice. But some examinees fail to search for a connection between the book-work question and the rider, thus missing the point intended by the examiner, while other examinees, finding no connection between the two (in fact there being none), avoid the question altogether. The student must be left to steer his own course between this Scylla and Charybdis.

THE OVERLAPPING OF SUBJECTS

In a problem on criminal law, make no statement as to the law of tort, unless of course the question whether a crime has been committed involves a question of tort. Similarly, in a problem on tort make no statement as to the law of crime, unless again the existence of a tort depends on the law of crime.[24]

This mutual exclusiveness of subjects does not hold between tort and contract. Where a problem is set in a tort paper or in a contract paper involving both a possible tort and a possible breach of contract, both aspects of the matter should be discussed. This is because a tort and a breach of contract can be proceeded upon in the same action, whereas the distinction between criminal and civil law is more deeply marked. The overlap between tort and contract should be looked for particularly in problems involving the negligent carriage of passengers by rail, road or sea, and the sale (or repair) of goods or houses that turn out not to be of merchantable quality or reasonably fit and that cause physical injury to the buyer (or owner).

In problems on tort and criminal law the student is expected to enumerate and discuss all the possible torts or crimes that may have been committed on the facts given in the problem, and also all the possible defences that may be raised. In this respect the answering of an examination question differs somewhat from the giving of an opinion in legal practice. A practitioner will not argue legal points unnecessarily. He will not, for example, argue the question whether there exists a tort of offensive invasion of

---

[24] As in a problem of false imprisonment (above p.130), or on the rule that the imputation of a crime punishable by imprisonment is actionable without proof of damage.

privacy, if his client has a clear remedy in defamation. But an examiner will usually be disappointed if, in an appropriate problem, both points are not discussed. In other words, if a point is *relevant,* discuss it, even though it be not necessary.

THE ANSWERING OF PROBLEMS IN CRIMINAL LAW

Always consider all the possible crimes that have been committed, by all possible persons,[25] and all the possible defences open to them. By "possible" I mean "seemingly possible to an ignorant person." If you consider that such-and-such crime has not been committed, or that such-and-such defence is not available (though an ignorant person might think it is), do not pass it by in silence but state your opinion expressly. You should also give the reason for your opinion as shortly as the importance of the point seems to require. The reason for this advice is that quite possibly the question was set as a trap, and if you refrain from commenting upon the trap the examiner may think that you have avoided it by good luck rather than good management.

Never come to the defences until you have stated the crime for which the defendant is in your opinion being charged. Start with the responsibility of the perpetrator (principal), taking accessories afterwards.

If you think that the problem leaves open some question of fact, state the law according as the fact is present or absent.

If the outcome is clear you can say so—*e.g.* "D is guilty of murder." But if the application of law to fact is not clear, you need not state a definite opinion or even "submit" that the position is so-and-so. For example, the question may state that the defendant shot at a burglar when a bystander was standing dangerously close, and hit the bystander. It is not for you to say that the defendant foresaw the possibility of hitting the bystander: that is for the jury. Never assume that the defendant had a particular state of mind unless the question states that he had it. Instead, consider whether there is any evidence for the jury (sufficient to require the judge to leave the case to the jury); if there is, explain how the judge would direct the jury, and state

---

[25] Unless, of course, the problem specifically asks for the criminal responsibility of some only of the *dramatis personae.*

whether a verdict of guilty would be likely to be upheld or upset on appeal. It is at these points in a jury trial that the legal opinion is important: a lawyer is not *directly* concerned with the work of the jury.

Often the problem will be found to fall short of one of the major crimes. In such a case it will very frequently involve a lesser or lesser-known crime. The student should note these lesser or narrower crimes very carefully when they are mentioned in his book. Here is a short list of them.

An act that falls short of:	may be:
Manslaughter	Assault and battery (O.A.P.A. 1861, s. 47). Offences under Road Traffic Act 1972 as amended: section 1, causing death by reckless driving; section 2, reckless driving; section 3, careless driving; section 5, driving "under the influence." Excessive speed (Road Traffic Regulation Act 1967, s. 78A, inserted by Act of 1972, s. 203).
Murder	Abortion (O.A.P.A. 1861 s. 58). Child destruction (Act of 1929). Concealment of birth (O.A.P.A. 1861 s. 60). Infanticide (Act of 1938). Manslaughter (O.A.P.A. 1861 s. 5). Manslaughter on account of diminished responsibility (Homicide Act 1957 s. 2).
Attempted murder (Criminal Law Act 1981, ss. 1,4)	Assault and battery. Wounding, etc., with intent (O.A.P.A. 1861 s. 18 as amended). Malicious poisoning resulting in danger to life, etc. (O.A.P.A. 1861 s. 23). Malicious wounding, etc. (O.A.P.A. 1861 s. 20). Occasioning actual bodily harm by an assault (O.A.P.A. 1861 s. 47). Malicious poisoning with intent to injure, etc. (O.A.P.A. 1861 s. 24). Robbery (Theft Act 1968 s. 8). Offence under Prevention of Crime Act 1953 or Firearms Act 1968. Possessing an article with intent to commit an indictable offence against the person (O.A.P.A. 1861 s. 64, as amended by C.L.A. 1967 Sched. 2).

Criminal damage (Criminal Damage Act 1971)	Cruelty to animals (Protection of Animals Act 1911). Theft (Theft Act 1968). Using threat (Criminal Damage Act 1971 s. 2). Having custody of article with intent (*ibid.* s. 3).
Theft (Theft Act 1968 s. 1)	Taking articles on public display (Theft Act 1968 s. 11). Taking motor-vehicle or other conveyance (Theft Act 1968 s. 12). Obtaining property by deception (Theft Act 1968 s. 15). Obtaining services by deception (Theft Act 1978 s. 1). Making off without paying (Theft Act 1978 s. 3). False accounting (Theft Act 1968 s. 17). Corruption (Prevention of Corruption Act 1906 as amended). Being found on private premises for an unlawful purpose (Vagrancy Act 1824 s., 4). Going equipped for stealing etc. (Theft Act 1968 s. 25).
Robbery (Theft Act 1968 s. 8)	Assault and battery: aggravated assaults; carrying weapons. Blackmail (Theft Act 1968 s. 21). Threatening letters (O.A.P.A. 1861 s. 16).
Obtaining property by deception (Theft Act 1968 ss. 15, 16)	Obtaining services by deception (Theft Act 1978 s. 1). Deception in relation to liabilities (Theft Act 1978 s. 2). False accounting (Theft Act 1968 s. 17). Offences under Trade Descriptions Act 1968. Obtaining making of valuable security (Theft Act 1968 s. 20(2)). False document to mislead principal (Prevention of Corruption Act 1906 s. 1(1)).
Forgery Coining (Forgery and Counterfeiting Act 1981)	Theft; obtaining property by deception. False trade description (Trade Descriptions Act 1968 s. 1).

When several crimes appear to emerge from the facts of a problem, it is best to start your answer with the gravest crime that seems clearly to have been committed. For it would be absurd to open your answer by considering some summary offence of which the defendant is guilty, and then to wind up with the conclusion that he has also committed, say, murder! The murder should come first, and the summary offence as a rather casual postscript. If the defendant is clearly guilty of a crime like wounding with intent, and only doubtfully guilty of murder, it is sensible to start with the clear crime before coming to the doubtful one.

Problems in criminal law often start with an inchoate crime—conspiracy, attempt or incitement. Even though the problem shows that the full crime was consummated, the culprits may be convicted of attempt or incitement, so that it may be relevant to mention these crimes—though normally, of course, the indictment would be for the completed crime, not for a mere attempt or incitement. If you mention the possibility of a conspiracy charge, it would be wise to add that the addition of conspiracy counts when the crime is consummated must be specially justified. As for incitement, if the crime is actually committed the inciter becomes an accessory to it. In other words, the difference between (i) incitement and (ii) being a participant in a crime as one who has counselled or procured it is that in (i) the main crime has not been (or need not have been) committed by the person so incited, and in (ii) it has.

THE ANSWERING OF PROBLEMS IN TORT

As in criminal law, look for all the possible torts that may have been committed, and consider whether their essentials have been satisfied. Draw into your net all possible defendants, and then turn round and consider all the possible defences open to them on the facts given.

There are not so many "obscure" torts as there are obscure crimes, but a considerable overlap occurs between some of the leading torts. The following are the chief examples:

Nuisance.
Rylands v. *Fletcher*.
Negligence.

Negligence.
Contractual duty to use care.

Negligence.
Breach of statutory duty.

Defamation.
Offensive invasion of privacy
  [—at present non-existent.]
Slander of title.
Malicious falsehood.

Conversion
Trespass to goods.

In the tort of negligence, it is frequently necessary to consider the machinery as to proof of negligence—the burden of proof, functions of judge and jury, *res ipsa loquitur*. Questions of negligence, contributory negligence and remoteness of damage are frequently wrapped up together, and so are questions of contributory negligence and *volenti non fit injuria,* and of necessity and private defence.

If the problem appears to be a novel one, it may raise the theory of general liability in tort.

CHAPTER 9

ANSWERING BOOK-WORK QUESTIONS

> He that knows, and knows not that he knows,
> is asleep—wake him.
>
> —Anon.

THIS chapter is chiefly concerned with the answering of questions other than problems, though some of the remarks apply also to the answering of problems. Like the last chapter it is not meant for hasty consumption immediately before the fray. The wise student will at the outset of his course look at the examination papers for the past few years, and, whether compelled to or not, will write out the answers to some questions (even though only in brief note form) in order to gain practice in self-expression. Past examination papers will also show him the probable lay-out of the paper that he will be expected to answer, and the amount of time likely to be allowed on each question.

SUBDIVIDED QUESTIONS

If your question is expressly divided into several sub-questions, answer each sub-question separately; and if the sub-questions are numbered (i,ii,iii) or lettered (*a,b,c*) number or letter them in the same way in your answer. A question may be divided into parts even though numbers or letters are not used. For instance, the question—

Summarise the provisions of, and the changes introduced by, the Unfair Contract Terms Act 1977, Part 1.

—invites an answer in two parts: (1) the provisions of the Act; (2) its impact on the previous law. It would be wise to write your answer under these two headings (though there would be no objection to applying the double answer to the Act section by section). Always model your answer to conform to the question: do not, for instance, on this particular question adopt the chronological order of (1) the pre-Act law, and (2) the Act. The reason is that if the examiner is reading your script quickly (and he may have hundreds of scripts to mark) he may be puzzled and annoyed by your departure from the order of his question. Besides, he may have set the question like that with the object of seeing whether your mind is sufficiently adaptable to vary the order of what you have learnt.

RELEVANCY

In answering a question you should, of course, give as much detail as you can within the limits of the question. It is sometimes possible to answer a question literally in a couple of sentences, but this will not always impress the examiner. The extreme example of this kind of answer is the story told by Mark Twain, in his *Life on the Mississippi*, of his piloting lesson.

"Presently Mr. Bixby turned on me and said: 'What is the name of the first point above New Orleans?'

"I was gratified to be able to answer promptly, and I did. I said I didn't know."

Not many candidates would attempt this frankness in the examination room, but they often do suppose that an accurate answer directed to the very words of the question is all that is required. This is frequently a mistake. For instance, in the law of contract the question, "What is the difference between void and voidable contracts?" can be accurately answered by saying that a void contract is an apparent contract that is in truth no contract at all, while a voidable contract is a contract that is capable of being avoided at the option of one party. This, though correct, would not score many marks. It is an accurate statement of the difference of *definition* between void and voidable contracts, but it says nothing of their different *effects*. The candidate should, therefore, add, as a minimum, a discussion of such cases as *Cundy* v. *Lindsay*[1] and *Lewis* v. *Averay*[2] in order to illustrate the effect of each kind of contract (or apparent contract) upon

[1] (1878) 3 App.Cas. 459.
[2] [1972] 1 Q.B. 198.

third-party rights. To put this advice generally, if you are asked to distinguish between two legal concepts or institutions, you should give not only the difference of definition but also the difference of legal effect.

It need hardly be added that the examiner *always* wants reasons and authorities for the answer, even though he does not expressly ask for them.

To say that a question should be answered fully is not to say that irrelevant matter should be introduced into the answer. Questions are often worded to cover only a fragment of a particular subject; in that case the examiner does *not* want the whole of it.

This question of relevancy is often the examinee's greatest headache. Often he has to interpret a badly worded question, with no hope of redress if his guess as to the examiner's meaning should turn out to be wrong. My advice is this. If the question is reasonably clear do not wander outside it. If there is a doubt as to its meaning, the question will usually have at least a central kernel of meaning that is relatively clear. Answer this to begin with. Then, as to the doubtful "shell" of the question, if you still have time to write on the question, you should expressly point out the doubt in your mind as to what you are being asked, and proceed to write on the doubtful part of the question for the rest of the allotted time. If, on the other hand, you have no time left for the doubtful part of the question, declare your doubt whether the question was intended to have any further scope, and leave it there. The fact that you have been able to spend your whole time on the core of the question is itself some indication that the question was not intended to have any wider scope.

For instance, suppose that a question in the law of contract is:

Discuss the maxim, *In pari delicto potior est conditio defendentis.*

Clearly this invites a discussion of the general rule preventing recovery of money paid or property transferred under an illegal contract, and this rule, with its exceptions and quasi-exceptions, should therefore be discussed first. The problem then arises: does the question cover also the general rule against suing for damages for breach of an illegal contract? However you decide this conundrum, you should state your decision in the answer. If you rule this second topic out of order, and the examiner wished it to be included, the examiner will at least see that you have had the point present in your mind, and will probably also be brought to see that he was at fault in his wording of the question. In any case, the proper limits of time for the question should not be exceeded.

If in doubt whether a particular matter is relevant, a good test is to ask yourself whether, if the examiner had wished you to discuss it, he would naturally have framed an extra question upon it.

Once the limits of the question are settled, do not canter beyond them. The examiner cannot give credit for irrelevancy, because that would be unfair to others who have answered only the question that they were asked. There is, however, a clever way in which matters otherwise irrelevant may be lightly introduced. This is by the method of comparison. For instance, if in constitutional law you are directed to write a note on the "kangeroo" (a method of curtailing discussion in the House of Commons), a discussion of the closure and guillotine (two other methods of curtailing discussion) would generally be out of order. But a comparison of the kangeroo with the closure and the guillotine would be admissible, and credit would be given for it.

Many students begin an answer with a prologue. Cut it out. In particular, do not start with the historical background if you are not asked for it, unless you have some special reason for doing this—and if so, state the reason. Sometimes the historical background makes the law more intelligible, or supports one interpretation of the law rather than another. But if you are asked the history of the action of *assumpsit*, do not begin with a paragraph on the medieval precursors of *assumpsit*—debt, detinue and account. If the questioner had wanted these he would have said so. If you are asked to discuss, say, *Nordenfelt's* case,[3] begin by setting out the facts and decision—do not start in the Middle Ages. Having stated the case you may legitimately put it into its historical setting in order to show what advance it made on the previous law; and you may also indicate the trend of development that it started. But all this depends on the time you have left after giving your attention to the centre of the question.

[3] [1894] A.C. 535.

Students (particularly advanced students) are frequently vexed by doubts as to the amount of detail that they should put into their answer. The best advice is: aim at concentrating all your intelligence on the specific question, and bring in your knowledge only so far as it is relevant. If you show that you are a master of the *relevant* knowledge, the examiner will readily give you credit for knowing the rest of the subject. An example would be the question: " 'The jury is a historical anachronism.' Discuss." This is not an invitation to give the whole history of the jury system: the question is whether the jury *is* a historical anachronism. Are there any features of the modern jury that can be explained only as historical survivals, which are out of place in modern society, or has the jury been so adapted that it is a truly modern institution?

Again, should you assume that your examiner is an ignoramus and explain everything to him, or can you assume that he is a lawyer so that a hint is sufficient?

The answer lies somewhere between these two extremes. On the one hand, the examiner wants to be told *nothing* that is irrelevant to the question. On the other hand, he is suspicious of nutshell knowledge and footnote knowledge, and he wants as full an explanation of everything that *is* relevant as is possible in the time allowed. More specifically, the following rules may be laid down.

(a) If a legal concept is mentioned in the question, do not attempt a full explanation of it unless explanation is requested or necessitated by the question. For instance, on a question involving the law of wagers, there is generally no need to discuss what is a wager. Had the examiner wanted such a discussion he would have asked for it in a separate part of the question. On the other hand, a question in the form of a quotation with a request for discussion normally requires an explanation of everything in the quotation. Thus the question—

"The use of impeachment at law as a method of control of the Executive by the Commons has been replaced by the convention of ministerial responsibility to Parliament." Comment.

—demands a detailed explanation of impeachment as well as of the convention of ministerial responsibility and of the reasons why the second replaced the first.

(b) If the legal concept is not mentioned in the question but is first introduced by the candidate in his answer, it should be explained. Take, for instance, the question: "When will the right to avoid a voidable contract be lost?" It is not enough, in the course of answering this question, to mention that the right will be lost if *restitutio in integrum* ceases to be possible. You must not assume that the examiner knows what *restitutio in integrum* means. Tell him what it means, and when such *restitutio* ceases to be possible.

GETTING AT THE POINT

Before unmuzzling your wisdom on any question, ponder the question carefully. Very often the examiner will have worded it in a particular way in order to enable you to show a little originality of treatment. Take, for example, the following question in criminal law.

Discuss the decision in *R. v. Dudley and Stephens* from the standpoint of the purposes of criminal punishment.

This is not simply a question on the decision in *R. v. Dudley and Stephens*, as most students seem to think, nor even is it simply a question on the defence of necessity in general. It is a question, primarily, on the purposes of criminal punishment. You are requested to set out the different theories of the purposes of criminal punishment (general and particular deterrence, incapacitation, reformation, ethical retribution) and to consider whether any of these theories can be used to support the conviction in *R. v. Dudley and Stephens*.

Another "angle" question, this time from constitutional law:

What parallels may be drawn between royal prerogative and parliamentary privilege? Examine, in particular, the attitude of the court in questions concerning (a) their exercise, and (b) their extent.

I have marked hundreds of scripts in which the answer offered to this question was a formless mass of cases and propositions concerning prerogative and privilege. These candidates simply vomited over the page everything they knew upon the two topics; they made no attempt to bring their knowledge into relation with the question, and did not even divide off their answer by the (a) and (b) of the question. The following is a skeleton of the answer that an examiner wants. It should be within the competence of everyone of moderate ability who has worked properly and who directs his mind to what he is being asked.

Prerogative and privilege are somewhat similar in definition. Prerogative may be defined as the exceptional position of the king at common law. Privilege is the exceptional position of the two Houses of Parliament and of their members at common law *and by statute*. There is, of course, a difference of content between prerogative and privilege.

Turning to (a) in the question, the traditional rule is that the court will *not* inquire into the *mode of user* of an undoubted prerogative or privilege. [Demonstration of this by decided or hypothetical cases.] Some recent developments suggest that the exercise of the prerogative can sometimes be questioned. [Demonstration[4].]

As to (b), the rule is that the court *will* inquire into the *limits* of both prerogative and privilege. [Similar demonstration of this.]

Both prerogative and privilege are subject to statute.[Demonstration.]

Another example.

"The legal sovereignty of Parliament has not been affected by the European Communities Act." Discuss.

This does not invite a discussion of the basic principles of sovereignty; still less is it an invitation to write a general essay on Parliamentary sovereignty. It is a question on the consequences of the Act.

It may seem unnecessary to add: if given a choice, do not attempt to answer a question that you do not understand (unless, of course, your plight is such that there is no other you can do instead). This may seem obvious advice, but it is often ignored. The following, taken from a constitutional law paper, is a good example of the "wrapped-up" question.

"Much of the structure of the Constitution is now mere form; it is tolerated only because in practice its form is no indication of the way it functions." Comment.

What does this question mean? If it conveys no clear meaning to you, avoid it. For if you attempt to answer it and miss the point, the examiner may not be able to give you any marks, because you will not have answered his question. Actually the question is on our old friends, the conventions of the constitu-

[4] See H.W.R. Wade, *Administrative Law*, 4th ed., 335–336.

tion. It is an invitation to enumerate the conventions and to contrast them with the law. Once the meaning is penetrated, the writing of the answer is easy.

Often the answer to a fearsome-looking question can be divined by a little patient thought. Here is another specimen from constitutional law.

What is the constitutional importance of the power to dissolve Parliament?

Very probably you have never given a moment's thought to this question. But that does not mean that you must stand mute to it. Just ponder for a moment. Probably you know that, under the Parliament Act, Parliament lasts for five years unless sooner dissolved by the Crown, and that the Crown acts on the advice of the Government of the day. We are asked to state the constitutional importance of this power possessed by the Government. Very well: to find the importance of x, the obvious thing to do is to consider what would happen if x were not present. Let us consider what would happen if the power to dissolve did not exist. Clearly Parliament would last its full five years and the Government could not bring it to a premature end. One result would be that the Government could not time a general election to its own advantage, going to the country at the moment when it feels most popular; so general elections might result in a change of Government more often. But this is not the main point: more important would be the effect on private members. Suppose that within the five-year term the Government were defeated in the Commons on a topic so important that it regarded it as a matter of confidence in itself. As things are the Government has the choice of either (a) resigning or (b) advising a dissolution—*i.e.* going to the country. If there were no power to dissolve it could only resign, and a new Government would have to be formed from the ranks of the existing House of Commons. What would be the consequence of that? A moment's reflection will show that it would make private members more independent. Government back-benchers do not like elections; they prefer a quiet life. It is the fear of an election that at present prevents them in many instances from disobeying their party whip. If they knew for certain that a vote of censure could not result in a general election, but would simply bring about a reshuffle in the Government, their conduct would become more robust. Governments would have to give way more often to the opinions of back-benchers, and not force every measure through as a matter of confidence. But it might occasionally happen that, rather than give way, the Government might prefer to recon-struct itself as a Coalition Government with the support of some middle-of-the-road members of the Opposition. This might cause a realignment of the parties.

If you happen to know that it is the Prime Minister personally who advises the Queen to dissolve Parliament, you will realise that this gives him the whip hand over other members of the Cabinet— who fear the cataclysm of an untimely election as much as back-benchers do. Without power to dissolve Parlia-ment, the Prime Minister could only resign, probably to be replaced by a rival within his own party. So we should have more changes of leadership.

Is it too imaginative to suppose that all these consequences would follow an abolition of the power to dissolve? If they would, we have demonstrated the importance of the power. It is the existence of the power that ensures the supremacy of the Cabinet and of the Prime Minister within the Cabinet. Whether they are *too* supreme is another question.

Knowledge of recent political history may enable you to correct these generalisations to some extent. When the parties are evenly balanced in the Commons or when the Government has to depend for support upon minority parties, the Prime Minister may well let it be understood that he will not resign or call an election on an adverse vote in the Commons except on an explicit issue of confidence. This sometimes emboldens back-benchers belonging to the Government party to vote against the Government on issues on which they feel strongly.

CRITICISM

When the question quotes a statement and asks for a discussion of it, do not be afraid to criticise the statement if you think it is open to criticism. As often as not the examiner will have disagreed with the statement himself; that is why he thought of setting it.

THE USE OF FORENSIC MANNERISMS

It was said in the last chapter that doubtful law should not be represented as if it were well establised. Conversely, to state the law as doubtful when it is not doubtful will also be penalised in marks. Excessive caution is therefore as much to be avoided as excessive dogmatism. This may seem obvious, but I have known students repeatedly use the phrase "I respectfully submit" before some trite proposition or other, purely out of affectation. Even words like "seemingly" or "probably" are out of place if the law is clear.

Strictly, a submission ("I submit that . . . ") is an argument advanced in court. Counsel will use deferential language in court, particularly in respect of a decision that he submits was mistaken; the worse the error, the deeper will be the respect that he expresses for the judges he is criticising. He will venture to suggest, with the greatest possible respect to Mr. Justice Blank, that his lordship perhaps did not intend his words to be understood in their widest acceptation. Or counsel may suggest, again with the very greatest respect, that a certain decision may perhaps be reconsidered if the point arises again before a court having power to overrule it; meanwhile, it can be distinguished on the facts before the present court.[5] Counsel will, in the time-honoured phrase, "wrap it up." Similarly, a court that feels impelled to depart from its predecessor's decision will do so not only "with the deepest respect" but "with great regret." These punctilios, which help to moderate tempers and maintain the dignity of the courts, are admirable if not carried too far[6]; but legal writings need not be encumbered in this way.

[5] In *Broome* v. *Cassell & Co.* [1972] A.C. 1027 a decision in the House of Lords was characterised by the Court of Appeal as being "unworkable" and as having been rendered *per incuriam*; on appeal, the House waxed indignant, but accepted that the Court of Appeal might properly have suggested that the precedent might be reconsidered by the House.

[6] As they can be. Norman Birkett (afterwards Lord Birkett) as an undergraduate used "I submit" in debating. An undergraduate journal took him to task for usng this "tiresome formula," and after becoming a judge Birkett commented: "I have paid handsomely for this piece of folly, for I now have to listen every day of my life to a more tiresome formula—'in my respectful submission'—and I confess I weep secret tears of remorse and contrition. "(Hyde, *Norman Birkett* 43).

Some writers express humility in a particularly strange way: when they wish to express an opinion but feel that the first person singular is too assertive, they use the plural ("we submit"). It is not proposed to discuss the aesthetics of this usage for the text writer[7]; all that I wish to say is that it should not be copied by the student, for in his mouth it sounds too grandiloquent. Naturally, one desires to suppress the personal element so far as possible, but if one has an opinion to express there is nothing to offend anybody in a straightforward "in my opinion." Alternatively, expressions like "it is thought that" or "there are good grounds for saying that" or "it follows from the authorities that" can be used. Or you can say "the better opinion is that" (since your opinion is inevitably the better opinion—in your opinion).

THE ARRANGEMENT AND WORDING OF THE ANSWER

Try to make your answer attractive. Examiners are human beings, and they are easily bored. If a question is capable of being answered in a sentence, answer it immediately in that sentence and proceed to explanation afterwards. Within limits, it is permissible (and often desirable) to divide up the answer into numbered "points," with subheadings underlined. This both saves your time and enables the examiner to see without effort how you have treated the subject. But the process of subdivision should not be pushed too far. An answer that is excessively divided and subdivided gives an unpleasant impression that the candidate has simply learned a crambook or correspondence course by heart.

Lecturers and text writers often indulge in what R.L. Stevenson called "a little judicious levity." The student, who usually cannot distinguish between the judicious and the injudicious sorts, should avoid levity altogether. He should likewise shun all colloquialisms and colloquial abbreviations ("it's," "isn't," etc.). In short, the student should write his script upon the model of a counsel's opinion or judge's judgment, with gravity and decorum.

A few remarks may be made about citing authorities. Never

---

[7] But I cannot forbear to record the observation that the use of "we" should be confined to kings, editors and women in the family way.

quote the textbook for an established principle of law. A sentence like "Every simple contract needs consideration to support it, as Treitel points out," is infantile. Textbooks should be quoted only if they express an individual opinion, and the lecturer (*qua* lecturer) not at all. When quoting authors, if the author is dead he may be referred to by his surname only, but if he is still with us it is polite to give him a handle—Sir or Prof. or Dr or Mr. As regards judges the customary J., etc., should be used irrespective of whether they are alive or dead.

If you cross out some words and subsequently wish to restore them, the accepted way of doing it is to put dots underneath the words so deleted and to write *"stet"*[8] in the margin.

The commonest grammatical error (if it is an error) is the split infinitive. Fowler divided the English-speaking world into (1) those who neither know nor care what a split infinitive is; (2) those who do not know, but care very much; (3) those who know and condemn; (4) those who know and approve; and (5) those who know and distinguish. Most examinees belong to the first class, most examiners to the third. Whatever the merits of the dispute, the safe course for the student, as for every writer who does not wish to risk offending the susceptibilities of his readers, is to avoid splitting infinitives. A split infinitive occurs when a word (usually an adverb) is placed between the word "to" and a following verb, as in "to really understand." On grammar and style in general, Fowler's *Dictionary of Modern English Usage* is an invaluable guide; a more recent competitor is Eric Partridge's *Usage and Abusage*. Other useful works are H.W. and F.G. Fowler's *The Kings's English*, 3rd ed. (£2.50), *The Hamlyn Guide to English Usage* (£1), and *Good English* by G.H. Vallins.

HANDWRITING AND ORTHOGRAPHY

Some people write atrociously. If you feel apprehensive on this, give a page of your notes to a friend and ask him to tell you which letters or words in your handwriting gave him difficulty in reading. Make a special effort to improve them.

Some people cannot spell and do not care about it. This may be all very well for those who have no ambitions that involve writing. But if you want to make a good impression or

---

[8] "Let it stand."

examiners, prospective employers or clients, the mastery of our unreasonable orthography is a necessity. Test yourself with the following passage, which contains misspelt words taken from examination scripts. Some of the words are correctly spelt, others incorrectly. Pick out the words that you think are misspelt and write your own version. Compare your effort with the key at the end of this chapter.

"The Homocide Act does not effect this problem, for the Act has not superceded the common law on the point. The question that ocurrs here is whether responsibility is deminished because there is a likelyhood that the provokation would have lead a reasonable man to loose his self-control and inflict this grievious harm. The affect of provocation in cases of this catagory is always difficult to gauge. An analagus case is *Brown*, where something like these facts occured. The acussed alledged that he could not forsee the harm he would do, and proceeded to argue that since he acted inavertently, he did not committ the offence. The prosecution tried to rebutt this defence by offering evidence of a statement made by the defendant to the police in which he inferred that he wanted to get rid of the person he attacked. After legal arguement the confession was ajudged to be admissable. The defendent appealed, argueing that he had been lead to make his statement by being promised bail, and had been mislead by being falsely told that his companion had confessed; but the judgment of the court was against him. On the principle question in the case, the concensus of the judges was that the authorities against the existance of the defence were irresistable, but perhaps this payed too little regard to the paralell rule for the priviledge of self-defence. I believe it would be indefensable to assert that the court leant it's authority to the test of reasonableness. In any case, it is permissable to observe that one cannot regard the same problem as occuring here. As to the wife, she is now treated seperately from her husband, and her responsability is independant of his. Her ommission to help the victim definately does not mean that she abetts the crime, or is an accessary to it. In the absense of other facts, she is not guilty."

The proper spelling is "homicide". The word comes from the Latin *homo* (stem, *homin-*), a man, or rather a human being of either sex, + *cidium*, killing. Contrast the word *homosexual*, where the prefix comes from the Greek *homos*, meaning "the same": a homosexual is a person who is sexually attracted within his or her own sex. Classically, the first *o* in both words was short, but both are sometimes lengthened in English.

Effect is wrongly used in the first sentence of the passage. The Homicide Act can affect (have an influence or bearing upon) a problem, or it can effect (bring about) a result, but we would not speak of "effecting" a problem. If these two words bother you, try to remember that *affect* is always a verb (something affects something else), while *effect* is nearly always a noun "the effect of X was disastrous").

The rule for verbs ending in the sound *-er*, such as *offer, prefer, occur,* is to double the *r* for the *-ed* and *-ing* endings if the accent is on the *-er* syllable, but not otherwise. Thus *prefer, occur, transfer,* make *preferred, preferring, occurred, occurring, transferred, transferring,* but *offer* makes *offered, offering.*

The spelling of words derived from *appeal* is confusing. Whereas *appellant* and *appellate* have two *l*s, *appealed, appealing* are like *sealed, sealing, peeled, peeling,* and have only one.

The "seed" words are also troublesome. Some are spelt "cede," as in *accede, concede, precede, intercede, recede.* Others are spelt "ceed": *exceed, proceed, succeed.* So you must write *preceding, proceeding*; yet *procedure* is so spelt. *Supersede* is exceptional, being derived not from *cedere* but from *sedere,* and means to "sit upon"; remember this, and you will remember the spelling.

The word *consensus* (agreement) is spelt with an *s* because it is derived in the same way as *consent,* from the Latin *sentire,* to feel. *(Census* is spelt with a *c* at the beginning because it is derived from the Latin *censere,* to rate.)

To express the sound *ee,* the rule is: *i* before *e,* except after *c.* So: *achieve, believe, grievous;* but *deceive, receive.*

The word *foresee* takes an *e* in the middle, but you can write either *forgo* or *forego*[9]. *Judgment* is spelt correctly in the above test, but an alternative spelling is *judgement.* The rule generally followed in dictionaries is that mute *e* is dropped before suffixes beginning with a vowel *(e.g. deplorable, desirable, likable, movable, notably, ratable, sizable, unusable, milage, suing),* but not before suffixes beginning with a consonant *(statement).* Statutes do not altogether follow the former rule: "rateable value" is an established statutory spelling. Mute *e* is generally retained after soft *c* or *g (e.g. unenforceable, changeable);* so *judgement* should really be the preferred spelling.

English has no clear rule on the *-ent* and *-ant* endings, but the former is the commoner. All you can do is to notice the spelling when you read. One special peculiarity: the adjectives *dependent* and *independent* take an *e* in the final syllable, but the noun *dependant* (meaning one who is dependent on another for his bread and butter) takes an *a.* The difference of spelling in the endings of *appellant, respondent,* derives from Latin.

---

[9] But "foregoing" in the sense of "preceding" must be so spelt.

The word *inferred* in the passage is correctly spelt but wrongly used. The correct word in the context is *implied*. *Inference* is what Sherlock Holmes did: one fact is deduced from others. A person may *imply* something in what he says, without actually expressing it.[10] Implication is an indirect way of conveying one's own meaning; inference is a process of discovering a fact outside oneself. Dr Watson implies what he means, and Sherlock Holmes infers what Dr Watson means. It is nonsense to speak of a person inferring what he himself means.

Note that *criteria, data* and *dicta* are plural words: the singulars are *criterion, datum* and *dictum*. Say "this dictum," not "this dicta." Treating *data* as singular (as people are coming to do) makes it difficult to speak clearly of "this particular datum" as opposed to "the rest of the data."

If the test has convinced you that you are weak on spelling, a useful reference book is Cassell's *New Spelling Dictionary* (£1.95). This gives the spelling of words not always included in other dictionaries, *e.g.* *kidnapped*.

> *Key to spelling test.* Homicide affect superseded occurs diminished likelihood provocation led lose grievous effect category ["gauge" is correct] analogous occurred accused alleged foresee ["proceeded" is correct] inadvertently commit ["offence" is correct] rebut offering argument adjudged admissible defendant ["appealed" is correct] arguing led misled principal consensus existence irresistible paid parallel privilege believe indefensible lent its permissible occurring separately responsibility independent omission definitely abets accessory absence.

---

[10] There is also legal implication, where one statement is deemed by law to include another (whatever the person making the statement may have meant). A contract of sale, for example, contains certain terms implied by law, even though the parties knew nothing about them.

CHAPTER 10

THE EXAMINATION

Examinations are formidable even to the best prepared; for the greatest fool may ask more than the wisest man can answer.

—C.C. Colton, *Lacon*.

PREVIOUS chapters gave advice that you can act on when practising writing answers before the examination. Now some further words of wisdom as to the event itself.

Examinations usually start at 9 a.m., so make sure that you are physically attuned to that time by keeping regular hours and rising sufficiently early for at least a week before.

You may find it helps to form a "revision syndicate" with two or three friends. Each member revises a different portion of the syllabus, and there is a meeting at which each teaches the others. The process of interchange helps to fix the memory for both sides.

Some students suffer from excessive anxiety, which produces sleeplessness which in turn aggravates the anxiety. If you know from experience that you are the over-anxious type you must take yourself firmly in hand and allot a fixed ration of time for revision, the rest of the day being spent in healthy exercise. Another way of reducing end-of-session flap is to spread the task of memorising over the whole year. Spend some time each week revising the week's material.

FIRST READ THE PAPER

Before starting to write, read through the whole of the examination paper and jot down in the margin the names of plaintiffs (or criminal defendants) in any relevant cases you remember, the dates of statutes and any other details that are likely to elude you when you come to write out the question.

You thus give your memory two chances of recalling the elusive details. Also, if during the examination you think of any fresh authorities that you do not propose to incorporate at once in your script, make a similar note of them on your question paper. Some candidates leave the examination room complaining that at one stage they remembered a case, but later forgot to cite it. The practice above suggested should obviate this.

The most important general piece of advice on examinations is that every question in the paper that the student is expected to and can answer should be answered. He should not spend all his time on a few only of the questions. There is nothing more tedious for the teacher than to hear one of his best students saying, after the examination: "Oh, I did very well, but I only had time to answer half the paper." In nearly all examinations the scripts are not judged simply on the questions that the student has answered, where he has not answered all he was expected to answer. On the contrary, the total possible marks are divided equally among all the questions, and no answer can earn more than the appropriate marks for that question. The result is that a student may have answered half the paper in a manner worthy of a Law Lord, and yet obtain a third class because he has not answered the other half. Another point to be remembered in this connection is that an examiner is much more willing to give the first 50 per cent. of marks on a question than the second 50 per cent., and full marks are practically never given. A candidate may, therefore, get 50 per cent. on the whole paper if he answers all the questions moderately well, whereas he certainly will not get 50 per cent. if he answers half the questions almost perfectly. For the good student, therefore, there is nothing more important in examination technique than dividing up his time as equally as may be between all the questions.

The same remark applies to questions containing two or more distinct parts. Here the examiner will probably have divided up the possible marks in his mind among the component parts, and an answer to one part, be it ever so brilliant, can earn only the appropriate total for that part. It is, therefore, most important to search for all the possible angles to a question, and this involves reading the question with meticulous care.

THE CHOICE OF QUESTIONS

All law examinations give a certain choice of questions.

Sometimes questions of enormous width are found in the paper. They are meant for the pass man. If a first class student attempts them, he will usually find that the answer required is so long that it will throw his whole script out of balance.

Where a choice is given between problems and book-work questions, there are two reasons why the better candidate should prefer the problems. First, they are usually shorter to answer, and so save time. Secondly, an examiner tends to be grudging in his marks for book-work questions, which he knows do not require much intelligence in the answering. A good answer to a problem, on the other hand, at once evokes his admiration.

There is, it is true, a certain danger in problems, for if the point of the problem is completely missed the result may be catastrophe. But a good student should be able to sense whether he is getting the point of the problem or not. If the problem to his eyes appears "pointless," he had better exercise his choice elsewhere in the paper.

Perhaps I should add a corrective to the foregoing paragraph. I said that if the point of a problem is completely missed the result may be catastrophe. This is true, but on the other hand it must be said that to give the wrong answer to a problem is not necessarily to miss the point of it. If the point is seen and well argued, the fact that the examiner does not agree with your conclusion will not seriously affect your marks. In legal matters there is usually a certain room for difference of opinion, and even though there be positive authority against your view, the examiner is anxious not so much to test the details of your knowledge as to assess your ability to argue in a lawyer-like way. A safe course to adopt if in any doubt is to present the argument for both sides—to turn yourself successively into counsel for the plaintiff (prosecutor), counsel for the defendant, and finally the judge. If then the examiner disagrees with your judgment, it will hardly matter because you will have presented (even though you have also rejected) the argument for his point of view. Incidentally, you will have shown your ability to accept a brief on either side, or even to be promoted to the Bench.

THE PRESSURE OF TIME

Abbreviations of technical words and expressions should be used only very sparingly in an examination. If, however, you find that time has run short for the last answer, the best course is to reduce the answer to bare note form, using as many key headings as possible and abbreviating freely. You may head such an answer with the words: "(In note form)." This course should be adopted only in case of absolute necessity, and you should be able to plan out your time so that it is not necessary.

It is no use writing "unfinished" at the bottom of your answer. Some candidates send in meagre scripts in which every answer is carefully labelled "no time to finish." Let me assure them that the phrase has no mark-getting capacity whatever. There is all the difference between an *incomplete* answer labelled "no time to finish"—when marks can be given only for what is written down—and a *complete* though condensed answer labelled "in note form"—when the examiner may of his charity overlook defects of style, excessive abbreviation and lack of full detail.

The legitimate way to save time in an examination is normally not by extensive abbreviation but by omitting windy phrases, such as "first it is necessary to consider whether." Long before the examination the student should have practised and perfected a clear, incisive style in which every word is made to count.

SELF-CONTRADICTION

There is a story of a party of Americans who stood by the Porters' Lodge at King's College, Cambridge. One of them pointed north and said: "That's the chapel." They turned round and another pointed south. "No, that's the chapel." "No," said a third, pointing west, "that's the chapel." "Anyway," they said, as they turned to go, "we've seen the chapel." Many examination scripts are guided by the same philosophy. The candidate will start with one version of the law and then gradually veer round to a contradictory version—thus making sure that the right rule is there somewhere, even though he cannot pick it out. Perhaps he hopes by this means to get the best of both worlds; actually, of course, he gets the worst. If you find yourself changing your mind in the course of an answer, either cross out what you have written and start afresh, or, if there is no time for that, say frankly that you have changed your mind. You must show not only that you have seen the chapel, but that you can identify it.

CHAPTER 11

MOOTS AND MOCK TRIALS

"In my youth," said his father, "I took to the law,
And argued each case with my wife;
And the muscular strength which it gave to my jaw
Has lasted the rest of my life."

—Lewis Carroll, *Alice in Wonderland.*

MOOTS

MUCH stress is laid by educationalists on literacy and numeracy, but we hear little about the importance of being articulate. Footballers practise passing and shooting; pianists, singers and clowns also practise assiduously. Why is it supposed that speaking comes naturally and needs no effort or concentration? Fluency and clear enunciation are particularly important for the lawyer, when our forensic practice is largely oral.

Taking part in moots will help you in these respects, and also give you experience in the art of persuasion, and of putting a case succinctly and intelligibly. Moots are legal problems in the form of imaginary cases, which are argued by two student "counsel" (a leader and a junior) on each side, with a "bench" of three "judges" (or perhaps only one) representing the Court of Appeal or sometimes the House of Lords. The arrangement of the moots is usually the responsibility of the students' law society,[1] though a law teacher or practising lawyer can usually be persuaded to set the moot and preside on the "bench." If no one else is arranging them, organise one yourself. Mooting not only gives you practice in court procedure but helps to develop the aplomb that every advocate should possess.

---

[1] Moots are held by students' law societies in the universities and Inns-of Court, by the Law Society (*i.e.* the official one) at its Hall in Chancery Lane, and by some provincial Law Societies.

The moot should ideally have two separate points for argument, one for each of the two pairs of counsel. Counsel should notify opposing counsel of the main propositions and of all the authorities on which they rely. (To exchange authorities before an appellate hearing[2] is a practice of the profession).The Master of Moots or other organiser should also be informed of the authorities to be cited, in order that he may arrange for such reports or case books as are available to be brought to the courtroom.

Since the moot is attended by an audience it is important to confine the proceedings to a reasonable length. Between half an hour and 40 minutes for each side (to be divided between leader and junior as they think fit) is enough time.

The presiding "judge" begins by referring to the case (he need not read it out if copies have been made available to the audience); then he says: "I call upon Mr/Miss X" (the leading counsel for the appellant, who sits upon the judge's left—that is to say, what the judge sees as his left). Junior counsel for the appellant is then invited to address the court, followed by the two counsel for the respondent (or Crown). The appellant is supposed to have a right of reply, but this may have to be sacrificed if it has grown too late. Alternatively, the speaking order can be: leading counsel for the appellant; both counsel for the respondent; junior counsel for the appellant (who thus has the last word).

Both counsel and judges follow the punctilios of court procedure and conduct, and a few words may be said on these. Counsel rise to their feet when addressing or being addressed by the court. If your opponent interrupts you, resume your seat while he is speaking. If you have occasion to refer to your colleague he is your "learned junior" or "learned leader," as the case may be, and your opponent is "my learned friend," or occasionally, informally, "my friend" (*not* "the opposition"!). "It has been argued on the other side that" is permissible.

Do not interrupt anyone, ever, if this can be avoided. If you must interrupt, do so as gently and courteously as possible.

Beginners sometimes get confused between the two polite

---

[2] And, generally, in the Chancery Division; less regularly in the Queen's Bench and Family Divisions.

ways of addressing a judge—"My Lord" and "Your lordship." The difference is that "My Lord" is the mode of addressing a judge in the vocative case, while "Your lordship" is the mode of referring to the judge in the course of a sentence, *i.e.* as a polite substitute for "you."[3] The formula for opening a case is: "May it please your lordship(s), I am appearing with Mr/Miss——for the plaintiff (prosecution) (appellant), and my learned friends Mr——and Mr——are for the defendant (respondent)(Crown). The claim (charge) is . . . ." Other counsel will begin by saying: "May it please your lordship(s)." Female judges are addressed as "my Lady," "your ladyship."[4]

In referring to the Queen as prosecutor in the course of a case one speaks not of "the Queen" but "the Crown."

The most common breach of etiquette committed by the enthusiastic beginner when arguing a moot case is the expression of a personal opinion on the merits of his case. Counsel may "submit" and "suggest" as strongly as he likes, and he may state propositions of law and fact, but he should not express his own belief or opinion. It is disrespectful to the Bench to say: "My Lords, in my opinion the law is so-and-so," still more to say: "My Lords, in my opinion this man is innocent." As an advocate you are paid to present your client's case, not to offer a sincere opinion on how you would decide if you were the judge. It is only by maintaining this rule that the advocate can be kept free from any possible charge of hypocrisy.

Begin your address to the court by stating quite briefly what you wish to show. Enumerate the points to be made, and state what part of the argument is being left to your junior (if you are acting as leader). This will enable the court, if it so wishes, to express particular interest in one point, in which case you should of course respond by devoting yourself chiefly to it. Take any hint the court drops: if the presiding judge indicates that as at

---

[3] As in Richard Bethell's famous piece of rudeness to the judge who, after hearing the argument, said he would reserve the point in order to turn it over in his mind—"May it please your lordship to turn it over in what your lordship is pleased to call your lordship's mind?" (It is said that the nearest approach Bethell ever made to politeness was in his reply to a judge who corrected him: "Your lordship is quite right, and I am quite wrong—as your lordship usually is.")

[4] For the modes of address of circuit judges, deputy circuit judges, and recorders, see below, p. 200.

present advised the court is with you on a particular matter, leave it alone—do not insist upon reading out your argument merely because you have come prepared upon it.

State your main point as impressively as you can. After stating it, pause to give time for it to sink in. Speak slowly, and get as soon as possible to the core of your case. Your time is much more limited than it would be in a real case, and you cannot afford to waste it; on the other hand, it is no use gabbling what you have to say, for then it will not be understood. Establish eye contact with the judge, and make sure that you can be heard. Do not read out your argument if you can possibly avoid it, but in any case do not mumble into your notes. While you must consistently keep your voice at a level at which it can be easily heard, you should try to put expression into it, avoiding a dull monotone. If you permit yourself a joke in arguing a moot you should not joke in court, at least until you are sufficiently experienced to know when one is allowable.

A frequent fault is to read out passages from textbooks as though they represented the last word on the law. Although textbooks and treatises are not taboo in court, they should be used sparingly and cautiously. What the judge principally wants to hear are the relevant cases (and, of course, statutes). It is always desirable, at least in the superior courts,[5] to refer the court to the cases cited by the writer for his propositions. When you read an authority, do so slowly, with proper periods and emphasis.

If possible, the reports of cases cited should be produced at the moot. If the reports are not available, case books should be used for the cases contained in them. Case books should also be available for the use of the bench. When citing cases the reference should always be given; and it should be pronounced in full, not in abbreviated form.[6] For instance, [1944] A.C. 200

---

[5] In magistrates' courts a treatise may be used as an authority in itself: *Boys* v. *Blenkinsop* [1968] Crim.L.R. 513.

[6] There is an old tale of a junior who cited the Law Reports to Lord Esher M.R. as "2 Q.B.D." "That is not the way you should address us," said Lord Esher. The learned counsel protested that he merely meant to use the brief and ordinary formula for the second volume of the Queen's Bench Division Reports. "I might as well," retorted his lordship "say to you, 'U.B.D.'"

is:"reported in the Appeal Cases for 1944 at page two hundred";
and 2 B. & Ald. 6 is: "in the second volume of Barnewall and
Alderson's Reports at page six." The facts of cases should be
read, unless the case is relied upon only for an *obiter dictum*.
Usually it is sufficient to read the headnote and the passage you
want; but if the case is an important part of your argument you
would, in court, read what you consider the essential facts in full.
Refer to judges by their full title (see pp. 64–65).

Citing cases, though usually a necessary part of the moot,
tends to take a long time and to be boring for the audience. Try,
therefore, to pick out the cases that are most apt for your
argument, and rely on them. In professional practice it is the
duty of the advocate to call the attention of the ourt to all
decisions that are in any way against the submissions he makes;
but this may not be possible in moot conditions. It is not a bad
plan to have a positive rule that not more than, say, six cases
shall be cited on each side. The object of a moot is to provide
practice in developing an argument, and while the reading out of
decided cases is often the necessary foundation of an argument,
it should not constitute the whole of it. Remember that your
primary object as an advocate is to persuade: the citing of cases
is only a means to this end.[7]

Just as you should not overload your argument with cases, you
should not load it with too many separate points of law.
"Mooty" as the case may be, it is unlikely that there are many
good points to be made for your side. All first-class advocates

---

[7] The observation of Lord Greene on this matter is worth quoting. If
one compares, he says, the student arguing a moot case with the
experienced practising lawyer arguing in court, "it will be found (at
least that is my own experience) that the student builds up his
argument on authorities which he refers to in great profusion, whereas
the experienced advocate builds up his argument out of his instinct for
legal principle and only uses his authorities to substantiate his points
or to convince a judge who declines to accept a proposition unless it is
supported by authority. Some of the best legal arguments which I have
heard on points of difficulty and complication have been conducted
with surprising economy of reference to authority. And the reason is
that the advocate's instinct for law and its principles has enabled him
to present in an attractive and logical way an argument which
convinces by its own inherent strength and does not require at every
point to be propped up by references to authority": [1936] J.S.P.T.L.
12.

concentrate on what they consider to be their good points; they do not run the risk of alienating the judge's affections by producing obviously bad ones. If you must add indifferent points to good ones, at least put the good ones first.

As will have appeared previously, judges do not take kindly to abbreviations in speech. Always use the official longhand. The Royal Air Force, for example, should be so referred to; and the Navy is the Royal Navy.

All moot court judges may and should give counsel a hot time by interjecting questions and objections to his argument. (In this they will not behave quite like real judges, who interrupt only occasionally.) The objection need not represent the judge's real opinion; he makes it in order to see how the student counsel responds.[8] If you are counsel and recognise that the judge's objection is valid, concede the point gracefully by saying: "I am obliged to your lordship." If you think you have an argument, stand up for yourself and say: "With great respect, my Lord," and so on. It does not matter how convinced or dogmatic the judge appears to be: keep at him as long as you think you have some hope of success and he is willing to listen to you.

When you think that the judge has got your point, do not go on repeating it. If you have presented your case to the best of your ability, and the judge is evidently unconvinced, accept defeat and sit down. All this advice applies equally to argument in real cases. If the judge intimates that you should take a certain course, say: "If your lordship pleases."

The judge may have tried to throw you with an interruption partly because you were reading your argument in a monotonous way. In answering the judge you will have had to abandon your notes. Try to continue your argument without them, referring to them only in order to read out an authority.

In a moot, you should keep punctiliously to your allotted time. In real life you will not have this limitation, but it will still be important not to ramble and repeat yourself.

After counsel have concluded their arguments the presiding judge may invite members of the audience to express their opinions upon the legal problem as *amici curiae*. The members

---

[8] If the student counsel fails to make an answer that was open to him, it is good training for the judge to suggest the answer to him.

of the court may then confer, and may deliver their judgments in turn. If there are two student members on the bench they may be asked to deliver their judgments before the senior member. (My own opinion is that, owing to the pressure of time, it is best if the senior member alone gives the judgment without consulting the other members. The main function of the other members of the court is to assist in putting possible objections to counsel.)

The organiser of a moot should consider its timing. Half an hour is the minimum for each side; so if the moot starts at 8.30 p.m., and if three judges each take ten minutes to give judgment, it is 10 p.m. even if not a minute has been lost—and this does not allow time for the presiding judge to invite the audience to comment before judgment is given. It would be much better to hold the moot, say, between 2 and 5 p.m. The presence of an audience is relatively unimportant. Far better have many moots with a small or even no audience than one moot with a large audience.

The moot competition provides a further element of rivalry. At the close of a moot the judge or judges declare which counsel or side performed best; he, she or they then go on to the next round.

Men cannot improve the beauty of their countenances, but almost all of us can, if we wish, add to the attractiveness of our speech. You will not be at ease speaking in court if you are conscious of defects in this respect. For all who have to speak regularly, money is well spent on lessons in elocution (speech training)[9]; but some blemishes can be cured by self-help. Many experienced speakers mar their conversations as well as their orations with a profusion of ums and ers which distract attention. Other bad habits are using "I mean" and "you know." The simplest way to cure these defects—which probably exist in your own speech, although you are unaware of them—is to tape-record your conversation with some other person on a serious subject in which you are both interested, and then listen to it critically. Probably you will be surprised at the imperfections in your own expression. Only by means of a tape-recorder can you hear yourself as others hear you. Try to eliminate all the "filled

[9] See "Schools—Dramatic Art" in the Yellow Pages.

pauses" in your speech: moments of silence are far more impressive than meaningless noises.

Poor, slurred speech is another common defect. As a Spanish observer caustically wrote: "To learn English you must begin by thrusting the jaw forward, almost clenching the teeth, and practically immobilising the lips" (José Ortega y Gasset). As things are going, the clarity and music of our language will remain only in the BBC sound archives. Good diction can still be heard occasionally, particularly on Radio 3, so that no one who wishes to improve himself need lack exemplars; yet many people are content to mumble and fumble their words. If your speech suffers from this defect, your teachers will not tell you of it. They have not the time for speech training, and are perhaps afraid to embarrass you, and by criticising your speech to add to your shyness in discussion. (They may themselves have fallen victims to the cult of mediocrity in articulation, as though slovenly speech is a way of expressing radical views.) Lawyers, above almost all others, should be able to express themselves clearly and pleasantly. Do you open your lips properly when speaking, or do you try to talk like a ventriloquist? (If you took singing lessons the first instruction would be to open your mouth, and the same applies to speech.)

Do you need to turn your volume control up? Quite a number of the people you speak to will be getting on in years and have lost their sharpness of hearing. Some people not only fail to speak up but talk with their hands wandering to cover their mouths.

Listen to that tape-recording again. Do you make distinct sounds for each of the vowels, or do you use pretty well one indeterminate noise for the whole lot? What I am aiming against is the indistinct mutter; it is not a question of regional idiom, which is often charming. Your aim should be to speak as educated people you admire speak, clearly and without affectation. Record a good speaker on the radio, play back a sentence and then record your own utterance of the same sentence. Compare. Repeat the effort until you feel that your own speech is as clear as his—and, if possible, as musical! Do not be afraid to mouth your words. And speak deliberately, not fast.

SPEAKING IN PUBLIC

It is an excellent thing to take part in debates. The skills involved in addressing a jury are common to the skills involved in public speaking. Here are a few hints for speech-making of any kind.

Plan your speech under a number of points so that it has a definite structure. Write it out in full, reflect on it overnight and polish it the next day. Then summarise the main headings on a small card or cards about the size of a postcard. Include in the card any figures, quotations, names, key phrases or other material which you wish to state exactly. Read through your full speech several times, preferably aloud and preferably into a tape-recorder, but do not try to memorise it word for word. You will probably not succeed in being word-perfect, and there is danger in reciting a memorised speech either of appearing unnatural or of forgetting a complete section or even coming to a dead halt. If you play back a recording of the rehearsal, consider whether you spoke at the right pace, and particularly whether you made an impressive pause at the right moment.

When on your feet before the audience, have the outline card or cards in your hand and, with this aid, speak naturally in the way you have planned.

The commonest fault among inexperienced speakers (and even many experienced ones) is to speak too fast. All good advocates speak with great deliberation and force. Tell yourself before you begin that you are going to speak slowly, and keep reminding yourself to do so.

Stand up: don't sit on an upturned seat. (And never do this in court, not even in a magistrates' court!) Don't hide behind any furniture if you can help it, and don't fold your arms or fiddle with your ears, your spectacles, or anything else.[10] Look at the audience as you speak, and turn to different sections of it. You may use your hands to emphasise points—not in too exaggerated a way, but sufficiently to show that you are putting your whole being into it. When you are not using your hands in this manner, keep them at your sides. Don't sidle around; keep your feet still. If you make a joke, pause before the punch line—and let the

---

[10] If you are sitting around a table in committee, on no account place your hand in front of your mouth when speaking. Don't even hold your chin!

audience know that humour is about to enliven the proceedings by enjoying it yourself beforehand.

If you are nervous, console yourself with the thought that the initially nervous speaker often performs far better than the stolid chap with no nerves. And remember that the audience are on your side. They want to be engrossed by your speech; they want the occasion to be a success. They are not there to criticise you, unless you force the criticism on them.

Ask a friend to observe your performance and to report to you on it with ruthless candour. Ask him particularly whether you have any irritating mannerisms: scratching yourself, adjusting your tie, pulling your clothes, waving your arms unduly, or swaying hypnotically.

MOCK TRIALS

A mock trial differs from a moot in that it is a mock jury-trial, with jury and witnesses, not an argument on law. The proceedings may be somewhat humorous; witnesses may dress themselves up, and court and counsel wear robes (if procurable). The audience may consist of non-lawyers, who, of course, come simply to be entertained. Since the trial is unrehearsed, it requires a high standard of forensic ability on the part of the student "counsel"; and the proceedings should either be leavened by humour or present an intellectual problem of the "whodunit" type.

There are two ways in which the "case" may be got up. It may have been enacted beforehand by the witnesses, so that they testify to what they have actually witnessed; alternatively, the organiser of the mock trial may simply have given to each witness a statement of his evidence, which he is expected to remember. The former method requires some effort, but it makes the case more realistic when it comes to cross-examination, and it enables the preliminary proceedings, including the interviewing of witnesses and briefing of counsel, to be done by student "solicitors." The actual trial is, of course, a valuable experience for budding advocates who take part in it as counsel.

It is a good plan to set the scene of the case (*e.g.* the murder) in some place known to the audience (*e.g.* the College or Law

School). Alternatively, the case can be modelled upon an actual case in one of the Trials Series (below, p.233). Try to depart from your model trial just sufficiently to prevent counsel using the same speeches and the same questions to witnesses. Keep the number of witnesses down to five or six. See that the legal participants have attended real trials in order to learn how things are done; the clerk of the court in particular should know his job. If you are at all doubtful about the success of the evening, do not advertise the event outside your Law Society.

As another diversion from the serious business of moots, the students' law society may like to try one evening the game of "Alibi." The gathering divides into groups of four, each group being composed of two prosecuting counsel and two defendants. It is assumed that the two defendants have committed some crime at a stated time—say between 10 and 11 p.m. last Wednesday—and have set up an alibi. They go out of the room for not more than ten minutes in order to prepare their story. They then return, one at a time, for cross-examination by the prosecuting counsel. Counsel's aim is to break down the alibi by asking unexpected questions and so getting contradictory answers from the two defendants. After the two cross-examinations, lasting perhaps ten or fifteen minutes in all, the two counsel put their heads together for a minute, and then one of them addresses the rest of the gathering, who have acted as jury, and submits that the alibi has been broken down because of this and that discrepancy. The jury signify their verdict by a show of hands, the opinion of the majority being taken.

A master of ceremonies is needed to dispatch successive pairs of defendants out of the room, in order to keep the game going continuously.

Would-be lawyers will find this game not at all a bad test of their powers of advocacy. No training for would-be defendants is intended.

A somewhat similar game is called "False Evidence." Three masked "defendants" are interrogated on their day-to-day lives by two counsel. One of these defendants has assumed a completely false name and occupation, and it is the jury's task to decide which. Each defendant must submit to counsel a week in advance a couple of hundred words summarising his life, and this enables counsel to prepare their questions. Each defendant calls a witness who has also submitted a statement with the facts of his or her life, particularly where that life crosses that of the defendant. In the case of the innocent parties they must have known each other for at least two years. The witness is not in court during the interrogation of the defendant, and counsel try to shake the evidence and establish discrepancies between the defendant and his witness. Each defendant and his witness are given a limited time—say fifteen minutes altogether—in the box. The judge sums up briefly to the jury, who consider and announce their verdict. The imposter then declares himself, and it is interesting to see if the judicial process has succeeded in ascertaining the truth of the matter. It may be mentioned that the written statements do not contain sufficiently specific information to enable counsel to identify who the person is. Two or three trials may be held on the same evening.

Yet another variant is "Third Degree." One member of the party is selected as the defendant: he is told the outline of an alibi defence and has to fill in the details impromptu under questioning. For example, he may be told that his alibi relates to a period between 2 and 5 p.m. last Thursday, when he left the refectory after lunch and took a train to a named neighbouring town and visited a friend in time for tea. The defendant on being told this alibi must immediately amplify it under questioning, and can be "gonged" for undue hesitation in answering or for any vagueness in answering (he must not say "I think so" or "That is probably what I would have done"). He can also be gonged for self-contradiction. The object of the rest of the company, who question him for fifteen minutes, is to establish a self-contradiction. Leading questions may be asked: for example, if the defendant says that he was not carrying a mackintosh, he can later be asked whether his host put his mackintosh on a peg in the hall or where else? If the defendant is gonged, or runs for the allotted time without mishap, another outline alibi can immediately be supplied to another volunteer defendant. A beauty of this game is that it can be played by two players only, and it may help you to bring out unsuspected ability as an implacable interrogator.

BIBLIOGRAPHY

Books on advocacy are referred to in Chapter 13 (p.201). For the procedure at a mock trial, consult any book on criminal or civil procedure. "Counsel" should make themselves acquainted not only with this procedure but with the main rules of evidence—*e.g.* those relating to leading questions.

CHAPTER 12

LEGAL RESEARCH

> First there's the Bible
> And then the Koran,
> Odgers on Libel,
> Pope's Essay on Man.
>
> —Mostyn T. Piggott, *The Hundred Best Books.*

GEORGE III is reputed to have said that lawyers do not know much more law than other people, but they know better where to find it. This chapter is written to help the reader to a more intimate knowledge of his law library, and also to guide the first steps of the research worker.

Whatever you write, remember that one of the prime qualities of a lawyer is accuracy. All your quotations must be verbatim; all your citations must follow accepted forms; all your statutes must be checked to make sure that they have not been amended or repealed; and if there be any doubt, your cases must be checked to make sure that they have not been reversed, overruled, or questioned.

LOOKING UP PRACTICAL POINTS

The only type of legal research that most practising lawyers want to do is research into the law relating to a case that they have on hand. A convenient place in which to start looking is frequently Halsbury's *Laws of England.* The 4th edition is in course of publication. If you know that your subject is in these volumes of the 4th edition, go straight to the volume and use the index at the end (there is a separate index for each title). When you have found the page, check the latest Cumulative Supplement, which is arranged alphabetically under the titles. There are annual abridgments of authorities since 1974, containing the headnotes of cases and summaries of legislation etc., arranged according to the titles of the main work. Also a Current Service Binder for the latest information.

If you do not know where your subject is located, use the index volumes 41–42 to the 3rd edition and the index to such of the volumes of the 4th edition as have been published. Use the Cumulative Supplement, etc., as before.

Often Halsbury will give the answer without further trouble, but if further detail is needed it may be necessary to turn to a specialised treatise. The experienced practitioner carries in his head the names of the best works on the subjects with which he usually deals, and the sooner the student gets to know some of them the better. Consult Raistrick and Rees, *Lawyers' Law Books* (1977) with supplement. A much larger and more widely-based list is the *Catalogue of the Institute of Advanced Legal Studies* (6 vols. 1978). A useful selective bibliography is A.G. Chloros, *A Biographical Guide to the Law of the United Kingdom, the Channel Islands and the Isle of Man.* An American counterpart is *Law Books in Print,* ed. J. Myron Jacobstein and Meira G. Pimsleur, which covers books in English published throughout the world. Recent books can be found in the catalogues published by Butterworth and Sweet and Maxwell.

If the question is one of common law, much assistance can be got from *The Digest* (formerly *English and Empire Digest*). This digests practically every reported case, and is well arranged and well indexed.

A valuable aid to the interpretation of legal expressions is *Words and Phrases Legally Defined.* This is a collection of words and phrases in statutes which have been interpreted by the judges, together with statutory definitions of terms and definitions advanced by legal writers. Another excellent work of the same type is Stroud's *Judicial Dictionary.*

CASES JUDICIALLY CONSIDERED

The method of tracing cases has been explained in Chapter 3. Cases on which you are relying should be checked in the list of cases judicially considered in the *Law Reports Indexes* (red and pink) or in *The Digest,* lest they have been overruled, not followed or doubted, or in the hope that they have been followed or approved. Alternatively, the *Current Law Citator* indexes all the cases, of whatever date, that have been judicially considered or affected by statute since 1947.

STATUTES

Many statutes can already be summoned up on a video screen at the touch of a few buttons, and complete coverage is in the offing; but, since the use of these computerised systems is expensive, the old-fashioned methods will long be with us. The most convenient place to find a statute that is still in force is in the official publication *Statutes in Force*. This is arranged in encyclopaedic form, in loose-leaf binders, some statutes being reprinted with amendments from time to time. If your statute obviously belongs to a particular title, like "Contract," take down that volume of the collection and open it at the title (known as the "group"). This begins with a blue divider; look at it first, to see if it contains the name of the statute you are after. Some groups are subdivided; here the blue divider states the subgroups, which are divided by yellow dividers, and the latter carry the names of the statutes in the particular subgroup. Each group is supposed to have a subject-index at the end, though some indexes are at present missing; there is also to be a general index to the whole work.

The divider will tell you the date up to which amendments have been included in the statute. Unless you are certain that the statute has not been amended since that date, take the cumulative supplement, which is arranged in the same way as the main work. Turn up the same group in the supplement, to see if your statute has been amended or repealed, or whether there are other relevant statutes on the point.[1] The divider sheets are not necessarily replaced when new statutes are added, so look for a recent statute in its proper chronological place, and if necessary check with the cumulative supplement before deciding that it is not included.

If you are not certain which group your statute falls under, turn it up in the tables provided. There is an alphabetical table,

[1] The vertical lines on the right-hand side of the page can be ignored; they merely indicate new entries.

and also a chronological table in case you know only the date of the statute. Unfortunately these tables are not kept up to date, so even if your statute is not in the table it may be found in the relevant group in the main work.

The only defect in *Statutes in Force,* apart from the fact that at the time of writing it is incomplete, is that it does not provide proper annotations to the statutes. For these you have to use Halsbury's *Statutes of England.* (This also gives the texts of the statutes, but they are often broken up between different titles in rather an inconvenient way, which is one of the reasons why the text in *Statutes in Force* is preferable.) The procedure for turning up Halsbury is much the same as for *Statutes in Force.* After volume 45 comes a volume entitled "Tables of Statutes and Index for Vols. 1–45;" this contains both an alphabetical and a chronological list. From this you can trace your statute in the main work, supposing it to be there. If the statute is later than about 1968 it will be found in the Continuation Volumes, which are all indexed in the latest Cumulative Supplement. This Supplement is a noter-up which lists amendments to the statutes; both the main work and the Supplement also note cases decided on the statutes. If your statute is later than the last Continuation Volume it will probably be in the Current Statutes Service, comprising loose-leaf binders containing the latest statutes, annotations and index.

To take an example, suppose that you wish to find the late annotations to a statute printed in the Continuation Volumes of Halsbury, such as the Children Act 1975. The index to the Continuation Volume for 1975 (or to the Cumulative Supplement) will tell you that it is in the 1975 volume (vol. 45) under the heading "Infants, Children and Young Persons," page 669. Therefore the annotations will be found in the Cumulative Supplement under the same heading. When you turn over the pages of the Supplement, pay no attention at first to the volume numbers at the top left-hand corner of the pages; look only at the headings at the top right-hand corner, which are in alphabetical order. The Acts are arranged in chronological order under the heading, so the Children Act 1975 is found near the end of the group. As you turn the pages, keep your eye on the volume numbers printed at the top left-hand corner till you see the number of the volume you are seeking (45); then go down the page-numbers in the left-hand margin till you see your page-number (p.669). This will be the annotation you are looking for, assuming that there is an annotation there. But you are not yet finished, because you must also check the annotation in the Noter-up binder of the Current Statutes Service. This gives the very latest annotation, and the mechanics of looking it up are the same.

Once you know the volume and page of your statute in the main work (or in the Continuation Volumes), it only takes a few minutes to find the annotations in the Cumulative Supplement and Current Statutes Service. Take this book into the library and follow the above routine for yourself.

A useful feature of Halsbury is the "Destination Table," which will be found at the end of some consolidating Acts and which enables the provisions of the Act to be traced back to earlier legislation.

For the names of statutes that have received the royal assent since the last supplement of *Statutes in Force* and Halsbury, consult the current numbers of *Current Law*.

There is also an official edition of the statutes in yearly volumes (called either *Public General Statutes* or *Law Reports— Statutes*). Before 1952 the only alphabetical index was at the end of the volume.

Until 1940 these volumes contained the statutes passed during a particular session. This has one tiresome consequence, that if one knows only the short title and calendar year, the statute may sometimes be in either of two volumes, and nothing but a process of trial and error can ascertain which. Since 1939 a very sensible change has been made: each volume contains the statutes passed during a single calendar year, and so the difficulty arises only for statutes passed before 1940.

Statutes since 1947 are better consulted in the annual volumes of *Current Law Statutes Annotated*[2] than in the official annual edition. This is published in parts which are subsequently bound into a volume for the year. Amendments, etc., can be traced through two *Current Law Statute Citators,* one for 1947–1971, and one for 1971 onwards. An excellent feature is the Table of

---

[2] These collections do not include Local and Personal Acts which are published separately.

Derivations showing sections in previous statutes now replaced.

An alternative to *Current Law Statutes* is Butterworth's *Annotated Legislation Service*. Both these publications are useful when the statute first appears, but both suffer from the defect that they are not regularly kept up to date by reprints or supplements. For this reason, *Statutes in Force* and Halsbury's *Statutes* are generally better.

There are two other methods of checking the legislative history of a statute. (1) By using the cumulative *Current Law Citator,* which is published annually; this can be brought up to date with the Statute Citator in *Current Law Statutes*—a table of the effect the statutes have on earlier legislation. These give only amendments and repeals since 1947 (the year when *Current Law* began), which is satisfactory if your main statute was passed after 1947, but otherwise not. It may be mentioned that the Statute Citator in *Current Law Statutes* includes statutory instruments issued under rule-making powers, cases decided on the construction of statutes, and legal literature dealing with statutes, as well as all statutes of any year that are affected by legislation during the years covered.

(2) The other method is to use the official work called *Chronological Table of Statutes*. This will show amendments and repeals up to the date of last publication; more recent changes are listed in an annual publication entitled *Annotations to the Acts*.

A very convenient source for some statutes is the Local Government Library, which publishes statutes and statutory instruments on certain topics in loose-leaf form with annotations and indexes. The subjects covered are: Health and Safety at Work; Highways; Housing; Planning; Compulsory Purchase and Compensation; Public Health; and Road Traffic. There are also the *British Tax Encyclopedia,* the *Encyclopedia of Value Added Tax;* the *Industrial Relations Encyclopedia,* and the *Encyclopedia of Social Security Law.* Criminal statutes can conveniently be consulted in Archbold or Stone.

STATUTORY INSTRUMENTS

Nearly all Government Orders made under statute are now

generically called Statutory Instruments.[3] They are cited by title, date and number, *e.g.* the County Court Fees (Amendment) Order 1981/898 (L.5).[4] (The last reference in brackets is added to instruments concerned with legal procedure.)

Such instruments can generally best be looked up in Halsbury's *Statutory Instruments*. The index volume 24 is arranged alphabetically by subject, with a supplementary index at the end. There is also a loose-leaf binder entitled *Service. Chronological List of Instruments*, which contains an annual supplement, monthly news sheets, and a chronological list. The work is updated by an *Additional Texts* binder.

An alternative source is the Stationery Office volumes. Orders in force in 1948 were reprinted under subject titles in a series of blue-bound volumes, continued in annual volumes (there are several to the year). There is an *Index to Government Orders* in force in 1979, arranged alphabetically under subject-headings, and continued by annual volumes. A *Table of Government Orders* lists all Orders, distinguishing between those repealed and those in force; continuation volumes are published annually, with monthly and daily Lists of Statutory Instruments in addition. The arrangement is chronological. Statutory instruments made under particular sections of statutes are listed under the section in front of the *Index of Government Orders,* and in the *Index to the Statutes in Force.*

RESEARCH PROPER

The ordinary practitioner will not need to dig any deeper than this—apart, of course from references to the statutes and law reports. I should, however, add a few words for the benefit of

[3] Statutory Instruments Act 1946.
[4] The following is the table of citation drawn up by Parliamentary Counsel and approved by the Editor of the *Revised Statutes*.

Instrument	First division	Second division	Third division
Statute	Section	Subsection	Paragraph
Bill	Clause	Subsection	Paragraph
Order in Council, or Order	Article	Paragraph	Sub-paragraph
Regulations	Regulation	Paragraph	Sub-paragraph
Rules	Rule	Paragraph	Sub-paragraph
Schedules	Paragraph	Sub-paragraph	(None)

any student who wishes to research more deeply. For periodical literature, consult the *Index to Legal Periodicals* and *Index to Foreign Legal Periodicals,* published for the American Association of Law Libraries. The *Current Law Index* is a similar publication started in 1980. There is also an *Index to Periodical Articles Relating to Law* which is supplementary to the *Index to Legal Periodicals*. A list of American and other periodicals in English libraries is published by the Institute of Advanced Legal Studies. See also W.A. Friend, *Anglo-American Legal Bibliographies* (1944).

The finding of an undated Command Paper may give trouble unless the following table is known. There are five series. From 1833 to 1869 they were numbered "1" to "4222." From 1870 to 1899 they were numbered "C.1" to "C.9550." From 1900 to 1918 they were numbered "Cd.1" to "Cd.9239." From 1919 to 1956 they were numbered "Cmd.1" to "Cmd.9889." The new series is numbered "Cmnd.1" consecutively. An extremely useful general guide is *British Official Publications* by John E. Pemberton (1971).

Much good work can be done by comparing legal development in the various common-law countries. Part II of the *Manual of Legal Citations,* referred to before, explains the mode of citation of Commonwealth material. Australian cases can be traced through the *Australian Digest,*[5] Canadian through the *Canadian Abridgement,* New Zealand through the *Abridgement of New Zealand Case Law*. There are various Irish Digests. The Institute of Advanced Legal Studies, 17 Russell Square, London, WC1B 5DR, publishes a Union List of Commonwealth legal literature in English libraries. See also Reynold Boult, *A Bibliography of Canadian Law* (1966), and Paul O'Higgins, *A Bibliography of Periodical Literature relating to Irish Law* (1966).

Turning to American material, the Middle Temple possesses an excellent collection of American reports, and a certain number of American textbooks. The libraries of the Inns of Court have a duplicated list showing which American reports are in which libraries. The Middle Temple has the American equivalent of Halsbury, the *Corpus Juris Secundum*. Copies of

---

[5] For Australian sources in general see Enid Campbell and Donald MacDougall, *Legal Research: Materials and Methods* (1967).

the American *Restatement* are fairly common. The Institute of Advanced Legal Studies, already mentioned, is also building up a library of American law. Useful guides to American law reports and digests arè Jackobstein and Mersky, *Fundamentals of Legal Research* (2nd ed. 1981), and the work by Beardsley and Orman already cited. There are an *Annual Survey of American Law,* an *Annual Survey of Commonwealth Law,* and an *Annual Survey of South African Law.*

The libraries mentioned above are, of course, private libraries, and non-members of the bodies to which they belong must obtain permission to use them. In addition the Libraries of the Commonwealth Relations Office, Downing Street, S.W.1, the Privy Council, Old County Hall, Spring Gardens, S.W.1, and the Colonial Office, Church House, Great Smith Street, S.W.1, possess some series of reports of other Commonwealth countries. Members of the public are permitted upon application to consult them.

Those reading French law may be helped by A. W. Dalrymple's *French-English Dictionary of Legal Words and Phrases* (2nd ed., 1948); there is also a companion English-French volume. Similar dictionaries for German have been compiled by Erdsiek, Dietl and Weil, and for Spanish by Louis A. Robb.

There is a *Directory of Law Libraries in the British Isles,* edited by Barbara Mangles (1977). Those working in London may be helped by Irwin and Staveley, *The Libraries of London* (2nd ed., 1961). Further information on law libraries and their use is given in Derek J. Way, *The Student's Guide to Law Libraries* (1967), the *Manual of Law Librarianship,* ed. Elizabeth M. Moys (1976), and Jean Dane and P. A. Thomas, *How to use a Law Library* (1979).

If the reader's research carries him beyond familiar legal fields into a large general library, he will find E.J. Dingwall's *How to Use a Large Library* a useful guide. Much the most important of general works of reference is the *British Museum Subject Index,* which classifies books according to their subject-matter. Where a book is not in a library, the librarian may be willing to apply to the National Central Library for a copy on loan.

Three hints may be given on the preparation of the finished script. (1) Frequently the date of decision of a case is a year before the date by which it is cited in the Law Reports. It is customary to take the date of the volume of the Law Reports as the date of the case. (2) If the case is reported in the Law Reports it may be thought sufficient to cite only the Law Reports; but if it is not in the Law Reports the main "collateral" reports should be cited in which the case appears. A list of references can be obtained from one of the Digests. (3) Useful advice on citations will be found in Part I of the *Manual of Legal Citations* published by the Institute of Advanced Legal Studies.

Those who are troubled by questions of style and grammar would be well advised to read *Complete Plain Words*, by Sir Ernest Gowers. A revised edition by Sir Bruce Fraser has been published by H.M.S.O. in elegant hardback at a very reasonable price.

CHAPTER 13

FROM LEARNING TO EARNING

No Wind makes for him that hath no intended port to sail unto.

—Montaigne.

MANY Arts graduates now find it impossible to obtain a post that matches their training and ability, unless they are willing to teach. The law offers better prospects; but the profession is crowded, and therefore competitive and tough. It is as difficult for beginners (except perhaps those of exceptional ability) as other professions are; many give up and leave it each year. If you have a career open to you in a family business you would probably be well advised to enter it; and in that case there is no point in obtaining a professional qualification. If you have specialised in Law in your University, Polytechnic or College, your knowledge will give you a useful background in many walks of life. It is always a help to know when precisely a contract is concluded, for example, and of possible legal liabilities against which it is advisable to insure. If you are reading this book before starting on your higher studies, the present chapter may cause you to decide not to study Law at all, or not to specialise in it. A more general course in Business Studies, which includes some Law, may be better for your career. For advice on institutions offering Business Studies courses, write to The Observer Student Service, Middlesex Polytechnic, 114 Chase Side, London N14 5PN, when the service restarts at the end of July, giving your examination record. The Observer carries helpful articles on careers during the late summer months; so do The Daily Telegraph and The Guardian.

These pages are written mostly for those who think they may wish to become qualified as a lawyer. An initial choice must be made between the Bar and the solicitor's profession, at a time when the aspirant will probably know little of the implications of the choice, or of his own potentialities. It would be sensible if we had a common system of training for the two sides of the profession (apart from specialist subjects),[1] so that the choice could be postponed until the last; but this has not been done. It is, nevertheless, pretty easy for a solicitor to transfer to the Bar: the most onerous requirement is that he must spend six months in pupillage. Barristers are specialist consultants and advocates, and are given exclusive rights of audience in the superior courts; this creates a class of specialists whose services are available to all solicitors. At the same time, an experienced solicitor may well be able to give a better legal opinion and be a far better advocate than a beginner at the Bar. It is, therefore, right that a solicitor who finds that his talents run to advocacy should be able to change to the Bar with a minimum of fuss. Any solicitor who proposes to do this can take inspiration from the example of Lord Lane C.J., and of his predecessor in office Lord Widgery C.J., both of whom were solicitors before turning to the Bar.

PRACTICE AT THE BAR

There are severe discouragements to new entrants for practice at the Bar. First, apart from certain transitional arrangements you will need an approved degree[1a] (not necessarily a law degree, though that gives you the advantage of providing you with examination exemptions[2]). Then you will have to pay fees, eat dinners, attend courses and pass the Bar examination. (If you have an approved degree but not in law, you will first need to study law for a year at the Polytechnic of Central London or the City University, and pass an appropriate examination). So far, it is only a matter of funds and conscientious work; and some financial assistance is available. After or shortly before taking your call, if you intend to practise, you will read in the chambers of a junior barrister. This is called pupillage, and arranging it may present a problem. But the end of pupillage is likely to be only the beginning of your real difficulty: "no room in the Inns." The practising barrister is a member of a group who share a set

---

[1] As the Ormrod Committee recommended. An editorial in the Justice of the Peace hardly went too far in saying that "the failure to implement the Ormrod recommendation in favour of a single system of education for both branches is nothing short of scandalous" (143 J.P.N. 631).

[1a] From 1984 a Class 1 or 2 will be required.

[2] Those who have a non-law degree will have greater difficulty in obtaining full local authority finance than others.

of chambers; one of these barristers, the head of chambers,[3]
appoints the clerk and secretaries. He may also allocate seats to
new entrants, but the decision on this is now generally taken on
the vote of all members of the chambers. In London your
pupil-master is unlikely to be able to arrange for an offer of a
seat (*i.e.* a room, or share of a room) to be made to you. A set of
chambers in London may have as many as twenty pupils and only
keep on two. The situation has arisen because of recent large
recruitments to the Bar, the traditional but constricting attach-
ment of the Bar to the Temple and Gray's and Lincoln's Inn, and
the natural reluctance of established practitioners to colonise
new chambers. Consequently, there are many "floaters"—
unhappy beginners who, having no local habitation, are gravely
handicapped in building up a practice. They live in perpetual
hope of persuading some head of chambers to take them in when
a vacancy occurs; meanwhile, to confer with a client they can
only occupy someone else's desk, by his good grace, when he is
not using it. Women and non-whites are likely to experience
particular difficulty.[4] You should think long and hard before
deciding to join the unhappy throng.

The chances of the new entrant will improve slightly as new
chambers are opened—by conversion from residences in the
Temple, or in Gray's Inn, or outside the ancient purlieus of the
law. But it is unlikely that this will keep pace with the flow of
new entrants. If you are considering pupillage or a seat in new
chambers, make careful enquiry into the status of the place and
the kind and amount of work coming in. Some do not offer good
prospects.

---

[3] By an ancient absurdity, the tenant of the (whole set of) chambers
must be a member of the Inn to which the chambers belong. But form
is one thing, reality another. The tenant need only be the nominal
tenant, and neither the head of chambers nor any of the other
members need be members of that Inn.

[4] As to women, the Bow Group in evidence to the Royal Commission
on Legal Services in 1977 said that many chambers limited the number
of tenancies given to women, on the ground that women tend to have
children and not to engage in full-time practice, and so cannot pay a
full proportion of the rent. For the same reason they are not
appreciated by the clerk, whose income depends directly on the
income of members. On the general question see Pearson and Sachs in
43 M.L.R. 400.

The position in the provinces is better, because the provincial Bar very sensibly controls its intake. If you obtain pupillage in provincial chambers, and perform satisfactorily, you are likely to be offered a place. This is a strong reason for starting in a provincial city rather than in London, especially as the provincial Bar is now as good as London, apart from specialist chambers.[5] Another argument in favour of the provinces is that the steady decentralisation of justice from London naturally increases the importance of the provincial Bar. In 1979 there were 3,080 barristers practising in central London and 1,283 spread over the rest of England and Wales; considering that most courts are now decentralised, this certainly seems to indicate an imbalance. We may well reach a situation in which all trials are held in the area in which they arise, and London retains special importance chiefly as the centre of appellate courts for the south of England. Solicitors in the north and west will no longer brief London barristers except in matters in which such barristers profess particular expertise. Unless local Bars are then strong enough to cope with the demand for advocacy, this will pass more and more to the solicitors.

Then there is the question of finance. During the first six months of pupillage the fledgling barrister is not allowed to accept briefs. During the second six months he can, and may get a little work; but until at least a year after the end of pupillage he will probably have to live on his parents or spouse. In addition to his living there will be professional expenses, including rent of chambers, clerk's commission, secretarial assistance, travel etc. The sum remaining from his fees will be subject to further deductions for income tax, national insurance and national insurance self-employed tax. Fees take months or years to come in, and quite a proportion are never recovered. In specialist chambers the time that must elapse before making a living is longer.

As to the volume of work available, crime is still a growth industry, and the constantly increasing complexity of many parts

[5] Local bars exist in Birmingham, Bradford, Brighton, Bristol, Cardiff, Chester, Colchester, Exeter, Hull, Leeds, Leicester, Liverpool, Manchester, Middlesbrough, Newcastle on Tyne, Norwich, Nottingham, Preston, Sheffield, Southampton, Stoke on Trent and Swansea; and others have more recently been instituted in other towns.

of the law inevitably creates a demand for skilled legal advice. The enlargement of the powers and pretensions of government gives administrative law great practical importance, while tax law creates continual problems for business and industry. For these and other reasons the Royal Commission on Legal Services expected "a long-term increase in the demand for the services of lawyers." However, legal work tends to rise and fall with the prosperity of the country: people avoid litigation in hard times. Owing to legal changes, young barristers can no longer earn easy money on undefended divorces, which are now done by solicitors. The Bar has lost by the gradual extension of county court jurisdiction (where solicitors have the right of audience); and the income limit for legal aid in civil cases has fallen well behind inflation, so that few people are now eligible for it. Account must also be taken of the degree of competition for the work. The Royal Commission on Legal Services reported in 1979 that "across the country as a whole there is now a surplus of barristers;" and the number has certainly not fallen since.

How does all this come out in actual figures? A survey of earnings in the tax year 1976–1977 made by the Bar for the purpose of its evidence to the Royal Commission on Legal Services showed that the net fees of junior barristers (before provision for pension, sickness insurance, indemnity insurance and national insurance contributions) averaged £7,319, but for barristers who had been only three years or less in practice were only £2,769. These were very modest incomes by then current standards. For leaders the average was £21,087.[6] Legal aid fees and the scales allowable on taxation have been improved since then. A friend at the Bar estimated to me in 1981 that a youngster of ability on the common law side can go up to eight or ten thousand pounds, but then tends to reach a plateau. The barristers who make a lot of money are those who are not dependent on fees allowed by the State—for example, those who practise in the fields of commerce, industry, insurance and banking.

As to the future, a good deal of personal injury litigation will disappear if State insurance is introduced as proposed by the

[6] Royal Commission on Legal Services, Cmnd. 7648–1, ii Table 18.19.

Pearson Commission. If we have a Family Court on the lines of the Crown Court, as seems inevitable eventually, it is unlikely that the Bar will have an exclusive right of audience. Finally, the gross overloading of the Crown Court, coupled with the great cost of criminal legal aid to the Exchequer, will probably bring about a further shift of criminal cases from the Crown Court to magistrates' courts, which will involve a reduction in the number of cases in which barristers are engaged. The same result will follow if solicitors are given the right of audience in the Crown Court, as is by no means impossible. The present arrangements, under which a defending barrister will often not see his client until the morning of the trial, is unsatisfactory in the extreme. To allow the solicitor who has prepared the case to take it in court would not be a perfect solution, but might be some improvement.[7]

Having done my best to put you off the Bar, I must add that the public interest strongly requires that the profession should continue to attract a flow of top quality recruits. Great success at the Bar leads to a very considerable income and the strong possibility of a judgeship. Those who do not reach this level but are pretty good can aspire to a circuit judgeship eventually, but the chances of rising beyond that are problematical. For those in this upper-middle range of ability employment in the civil service may well offer better rewards. You may make a switch of this kind after starting at the Bar. Many barristers who fail in practice, or who do not find it congenial, obtain employment in salaried posts, as will be explained later.

Let me assume that you would like to enter for practice at the Bar and are prepared to brave all hazards. Have you the right qualities? For advocacy, obviously, the prime need is the ability to communicate by speech. Judges confess in private that there are counsel now practising whom they cannot understand. If you mumble or burble, give up all thought of advocacy. Not only must you be able to speak up loud and clear, but you should be able to put a case relevantly, neatly, succinctly, and generally in a way pleasing to the tribunal before which you are appearing. The last means that good manners are important.

Quickness of thought is a considerable asset. Cases on the

[7] Michael Zander, *Legal Services for the Community* (1978) 185.

common law side are usually won not through counsel's address to the court, which there is usually a little time to prepare in advance, but through the effective examination of witnesses. Now cross-examinations cannot be prepared, because you can never be quite sure what the other side's witnesses are going to say until they are actually in the box. A certain nimbleness of wit is therefore essential. Some people are very sound but can formulate opinions only after prolonged consideration. That type of mind is no use for advocacy.

A good barrister must also be able to assimilate facts quickly. He may have a brief with correspondence numbering two or three hundred letters delivered to him the night, or two nights, before the case begins, and all the facts must be mastered before he goes into court. The best advocates have had prodigious memories, enabling them to retain the details of one complicated case after another for presentation in court. Lord Alverstone recorded that when at the Bar he was able to read the sheets of correspondence almost as fast as he could turn them over, and he never required to read them twice. Hawkins, one of the most powerful leaders of the common law Bar in the nineteenth century, used to give the following advice. "Never examine or cross-examine from your brief. Know your brief and examine from your head." The student can best test and foster his powers of advocacy by making full use of his debating society.

A sound constitution is another requirement, as can be realised from the following passage from Gilchrist Alexander's *The Temple of the Nineties*. Anyone who has seen a busy barrister at work will bear out the truth of the picture.

"Few people realise under what pressure successful barristers live. . . . The busy barrister is on the *qui vive* all the time. In court he has to be on the alert every moment and is watched by a highly trained expert on the other side who pounces upon his slightest mistake. Out of court he has to work far into the night, night after night, working hard and continuously at a mass of detail. He cannot, like the head of a big business, delegate to subordinates the actual carrying out of his work. His 'devils' prepare for him notes of his material but once he has gone into court he has to take entire responsibility on his own shoulders."

The advocate needs a sound knowledge of the law, especially that of evidence and procedure. If evidence and procedure are among the subjects available to you at the University, you should either include them in your course or, at least, attend the lectures as an extra.

Then again the advocate, like every kind of lawyer, needs accuracy. Your ability to write and argue is of little avail if you get your facts wrong, fail to find the relevant authorities, rely on a statute that has been superseded or a case that has been overruled, or simply misunderstand the authorities. All these mistakes are only too easy to make, and it takes constant effort to keep oneself up to the mark.

On the Chancery side the chief qualifications are, I think, patience and thoroughness. There is not so much advocacy to be done; much of the work is non-litigious (such as drafting documents and advising on title), and the cases that do get into court tend to turn upon technicalities of company law, taxation, property and wills, or upon questions of company finance, rather than upon controversial questions of fact. Also, a good deal of litigious work is disposed of not in open court but before a judge or master in chambers. To some types of mind work at the Chancery Bar appears dull and repellent, because it tends to lack human interest. On the other hand, existence is more placid than on the common law side. It is better remunerated, too, since the continual rise in property values helps to keep incomes not too far behind inflation. At the time of writing the Chancery Bar offers considerably better prospects than the common law; there is reported to be a shortage of good applicants for tenancies.

It is hardly necessary to emphasise the necessity of probity for all members of the Bar. A barrister must have the confidence of the Bench. Any kind of sharp practice or dishonest dealing will infallibly ruin his career. Make up your mind that whatever the short-term temptations may be, you will never deviate from the highest standards of honour. This remark applies to solicitors as well, of course.

A sound lawyer who has found a seat in chambers on the common law side can expect at least some work. Even indifferent lawyers may be kept going by their clerk arranging for briefs to be passed to them from dud solicitors. This is, of course, a criticism of the system. One of the deficiencies of our arrangements is that no provision is made for young barristers obtaining a salaried position in chambers, allowing them to do minor work under supervision. Since even the neophyte practises on his own, there is no senior partner to keep an eye on him and to clamp down upon him if he is incompetent.[8]

In specialist chambers (such as taxation, family law, employment law, company law, local government law, town and country planning, rating, commercial law, shipping, restrictive practices, libel law, and patent), it is harder for the beginner to get a start and less likely that the incompetent can make headway. There may be virtually no briefs for a year or more, and it will be longer still before the young barrister pays his way. However, his prospects then are better than in general practice. His life is likely to be less hectic, and his income distinctly greater. There is no official limit to the fees chargeable to clients who are not legally aided, so that when practitioners in a particular speciality are in short supply, their fees rise. For those who have an eye to practise eventually at the Parliamentary Bar[9] a scientific qualification is a help, and in patent work it is a necessity.

---

[8] In 1979 the legal correspondent of The Times, disquieted by reports from judges and senior lawyers that standards among young barristers were declining, attended magistrates' courts and the Crown Courts in the London area in order to find out for himself. He reported as follows. "I was appalled. It was not just that so many young barristers seemed incapable of forming a grammatically correct English sentence (and I am not talking about 'immigrant' lawyers). Much more distressing was the poor, sometimes inexcusable, standard of presentation of the lay client's case. I was present on two occasions when counsel managed to forget the crime with which his client had been charged. I saw more than one example of counsel clearly being unaware of the leading relevant case or the relevant piece of legislation. Mistakes about the detail and circumstances of the crime and, in pleas in mitigation, about the defendant's age, occupation and personal circumstances were common-place. I did not try to ascertain the reasons for the incompetence, but it could not all have been the result of late briefs:" 129 N.L.J. 1117. One reason for present incompetence is that the great increase of work at the Bar through criminal legal aid, at a time when there were not many established practitioners, meant that many incompetent youngsters survived when they would otherwise have failed. It seems that no disciplinary proceedings have ever been taken for professional incompetence.

[9] Members of the Parliamentary Bar are concerned with the passage of private Bills through Parliament. Planning inquiries are now of greater importance than Parliamentary work, and practitioners (as at most of the specialised Bars) are doing very well.

Apart from the fees he earns, a practising barrister is not feather-bedded in any way. There is no pension (except the national insurance pension and any voluntary pension, both of which have to be paid for), no goodwill to sell, no partner to help earn your money if you are ill. Even if you succeed in building up a good practice as a junior your troubles will not be at an end, because at that point in your career you will have to decide whether to apply for silk. These expressions need a word of explanation. A "junior" means any barrister who has not taken silk; and some highly successful barristers (especially on the Chancery side) remain juniors all their lives. "Taking silk" means obtaining the right to wear a silk gown by becoming a Q.C. or (to use the language of lawyers) a leader. Whereas a junior does both advocacy and the preliminary paper work, a leader confines himself to advocacy (apart from the giving of oral and written opinions, an activity common to both grades).

One of the many indefensible anomalies of practice at the Bar is that the grant of silk is entirely in the discretion of political officer, the Lord Chancellor; but he canvasses the views of various legal eminences including the heads of the judicial divisions. Only about a quarter of the applicants survive the rigorous screening and obtain silk. Certainly the Lord Chancellor weighs the needs of the various circuits and branches of law. But the result of this restrictive attitude to the grant of silk is that successful leaders are in such short supply, and consequently are able to charge such high fees, that the cost of fighting an important case in the High Court is a public scandal. One day the whole silk system may be reconsidered.[10] Why should it not be left to individual members of the Bar to decide whether they wish to specialise in advocacy?

Anyway, the position now is that if you do not take silk at the right moment, it may mean that you have to continue working much too hard for your time of life; on the other hand some barristers who take silk repent it, for they find too late that their services in the more expensive class of advocacy are not in demand. Once you have taken silk there is no going back to a

[10] See Thorold in 129 N.L.J. 555; Zander, *op. cit.* 174. The procedure for awarding silk was fully described by Lord Elwyn-Jones L.C. in evidence to the Royal Commission on Legal Services published on November 27, 1978.

junior's practice. It seems a perverse arrangement to add this hazard to a profession that is already too full of risks for our comfortable age.

Assuming that you decide to take the plunge, you should if possible determine at the same time whether you are going to practise on the common law or on the Chancery side. For the latter you will probably join Lincoln's Inn, for the former one of the three other Inns. (This is the usual course, but there is nothing to prevent a member of any Inn from practising on either side of the profession.) As between the three common law Inns the choice does not really matter: you can quite well be a member of one Inn, become a pupil in chambers belonging to a second, and in due course attain a seat in chambers belonging to a third. Apart from the difficulty of chambers, the ordinary person who has no special connections normally finds it easier to get some kind of start on the common law side, where there is a great deal of small work, in county courts and the criminal courts; on the Chancery side there is no criminal work and all the civil work tends to be fairly important. The Chancery side is much more concentrated in London than the common law side, though some Chancery chambers have now been established in the provinces.

The Bar student must, according to the quaint custom, eat dinners at his Inn of Court as well as passing the Bar examinations before he can be called. In general the dinners must extend over two years, but there are certain exemptions, and in particular students who are exempted from the "academic" stage of the Bar examinations (as most are) can cut their dining period down to one year by double dining, *i.e.* by dining 24 times that year instead of the usual 12.

There is no need to enter further into the details of dinners, examinations and fees. The Consolidated Regulations of the Inns of Court, together with the particulars of the scholarships and prizes available, can be had by applying to the Sub-Treasurer at the Inner Temple or to the Under-Treasurer at the other three Inns. The total fees up to and including call (including the cost of dinners) are about £670. Attendance at the course at the Inns of Court School of Law, including the practical exercises, is compulsory for those who intend to practise in England and Wales; so including living expenses in London and books the law graduate can reckon on expenses of at least £2,300 for the eight months of the course, with another £180 for robe and wig.[11] Many local authorities award grants to students reading for the Bar on the same basis as University awards. Some discriminate against University graduates.

A year's pupillage is (in general) compulsory for those who intend to practise in England and Wales. Certain limited exemptions are allowed. Generally, no fee is charged for pupillage, but local authorities do not give grants for maintenance, which has the unfortunate result that students without adequate parental means may find it impossible to establish themselves at the Bar. You have to reckon not only on the cost of living in London or some other city but also the expense of accompanying your master when he travels. The Inns of Court and Senate have modest funds for the purpose of alleviating hardship.

How does one find a barrister who will accept one as a pupil? There is no fully organised system. A few chambers have set a shining example by stating that they will grant pupillages (some of them accompanied by monetary awards) by open competition; if you wish to apply, write for details to John Stuart Colyer Esq. Q.C., 11 King's Bench Walk, Temple, London EC4. Apart from that, one of your law lecturers may be able to help. When a barrister comes to address your University or College law society, you can beard him on the subject. A solicitor may also be able to give you a recommendation. Oxford and Cambridge undergraduates receive the benefit of advice from special committees of old University men. Each Inn of Court has a Pupillage Committee which manages to fix up all suitable applicants in suitable places eventually. (The phrase "suitable applicants" refers only to ability and motivation.) Those who think that they may wish to practise in the North may avail themselves of advice kindly offered by Mr J.M. Shorrock, Hon. Sec., Northern Circuit Executive Committee, 2 Old Bank Street, Manchester M2 7PF.

If you fail to arrange pupillage you will naturally be very

---

[11] The Senate acts as agent for the sale of second-hand (and therefore well-ripened) robes and wigs, at about two-thirds the price of new. There is a waiting-list, so put your name down early.

disappointed, but should not feel aggrieved. Far more pupils are taken on than can hope to succeed in practice, and if you have not been able to impress any barrister sufficiently with your qualities to be taken on, it may perhaps be for the best that you are forced to look to a different career at this juncture. You may, for example, become a legal adviser to a firm (see later). Or you may transfer to the solicitors' branch.

The difficulties of the student in arranging pupillage make it rather theoretical to give advice on the assumption that he can pick and choose. If you have the opportunity of an introduction to a particular barrister, find out as much about him as you can. There are two dangers to be avoided, if you can avoid them, in the choice of chambers: reading with someone who is too busy, who cannot spare the time to give you instruction, except possibly over a snack lunch, and reading with someone who has not enough work to give you proper experience. The ideal person, if he can be found, is the young barrister in good practice who is rapidly rising and who may take you up with him. Someone, in other words, who is likely to take silk, but likely to take it at a time sufficiently far in the future to give you a chance of stepping into part of his practice as a junior. If your pupilmaster is now above doing the humbler type of work (in the county court or before magistrates) with which you will have to start in your own practice, he will arrange for you to accompany more junior members of chambers to these lower courts.

You may make your pupillage contract for six months in each of two different chambers. You may, for example, spend six months in London and six months with a local barrister if your intention is to join the local Bar. Some spend six months in Chancery chambers before turning to the common law side. An incidental advantage of splitting pupillage is that you thereby become known in two places instead of one. Wherever you spend your time, the most important thing to enquire about is the prospect of obtaining a seat after pupillage. If you do not get a seat in the chambers of which you are a pupil, you stand little chance elsewhere. The reason is that heads of chambers are not required to notify vacant tenancies to a central office, so that there can be fair competition for them; the tenancy is given to the person who happens to be on the spot and who is acceptable, or to a relative of the head of chambers, or otherwise by favour.

A pupil must do his level best to please his master (and the clerk) if he hopes to be invited to remain. He has the right, which he should exercise to the full, of reading his master's papers and accompanying him to court. He may be asked to take notes of the evidence. There is a temptation on both sides for the pupil to spend his time doing this, but it soon becomes rather profitless. The pupil spends his days far better drafting a pleading or writing an opinion and having his master criticise his work afterwards.

When listening to cases in court you should do so not passively, like the spectator of a play, but with active thought, as though you were yourself taking part; framing in your mind during the examination-in-chief the questions you would put to the witness if the cross-examination fell to you. If possible, the cases you attend should be those in which you have contrived to read the papers beforehand: the educational value of hearing them is then much greater. Always attend your master's conferences with solicitors if he allows you to do so.

By the way, barristers usually talk about cases by identifying themselves with their lay client. "I am a girl who was assaulted," etc.

If (as often happens) you find that your pupilmaster does not have enough work in the smaller courts and in administrative tribunals to give you adequate experience, ask him if he will arrange with another member of chambers to enable you to see more of these courts and tribunals.

Copy the dress of respected members of the Bar. A man should wear a dark suit and sober shirt, and a woman their equivalent.[12] I need hardly add that men should remember the importance of regular haircuts.

The Bar examinations should, of course, be got out of the way before pupillage commences, for you cannot do two things at once.

Pupillage in itself does not give experience in the art of advocacy, and you should therefore play your full part in the forensic exercises provided in the Inns of Court School and in the moots held at your Inn. If insufficient moots are organised, try to

---

[12] For further details see the Code of Conduct published by the Senate, Annex 11. A copy of this is given upon Call to all those intending to practise in England and Wales.

get a law teacher or barrister to judge a private one for yourself and friends.

To go back a little, there is much to be said for spending six months to a year (a small-minded regulation forbids any longer time) in a solicitor's office before pupillage. You could very well spend one of your Long Vacations in a solicitor's office (obviously, the Vacation immediately before your final year would be best), and it should not be difficult to arrange; the experience will be of great value whichever branch you intend to enter, and it could help you to make a wise choice. Work in a solicitor's office can give an understanding of the solicitor's difficulties and requirements which the ordinary barrister often lacks. If we had a sensible ordering of the legal profession everyone would start as a solicitor, moving to the Bar only when he felt ready to do so.

You may possibly have the chance of being marshal to a judge; if so, of course jump at it. There may be a circuit/county-court judge you know who would be willing to give you this experience.

When pupillage is over the young barrister may join a local Bar instead of practising in London. The Senate keeps a register of vacant places in chambers, both in London and in the provinces. You would be well advised to consider the local Bar, particularly (though not only) if you do not feel yourself to be of outstanding ability. The local Bar is less of a gamble; on the other hand, the most lucrative work is in London.

If the young aspirant survives all the obstacles and makes a start in practice he may still find himself with serious financial problems. On this it is worth quoting the comments of Lord Justice Lawton in a letter to The Times.

"A private income, a working wife, superb contacts or exceptional ability may help, but what really matters is a desire to be a barrister and nothing else.

I know. I had none of [the former] assets when I started at the Bar; but my 25 years in practice were the happiest in my life. I often wish I could live them over again, even though for the first four years I had to supplement my poor earnings by doing evening jobs."

A few will now find their position alleviated by obtaining a scholarship from their Inn of Court or a loan from funds administered by the Senate, but these cannot be counted on.

There is the possibility of "devilling" for fellow members of the Bar. This means giving them assistance in their cases, and even (with the client's consent) taking cases for them in court if owing to some clash of appointments they find themselves unable to appear. It is now obligatory to pay the devil a share of the fees (usually half) and the work therefore helps one's livelihood, as well as providing experience and (sometimes) bringing one to the notice of the professional client. But the possibilities of devilling must not be exaggerated. On the common law side only the busiest barristers have any devilling to give: they will themselves do all that they possibly can. On the Chancery side there is rather more, because of the amount of drafting work to be done. But drafting for a fellow-barrister, though desirable for experience, does not bring one into contact with the instructing solicitor, and so does not nurture one's own practice.

After three years' practice, you could make a comparatively painless change to the solicitors' branch, being exempted from articles, and also (at discretion) from some papers in the Final.

If the young barrister has any spare time in his early years he should use it to prolong his pupillage in fact if not in name. Perhaps his former master will allow him to continue to read his papers; or he may be prmitted to read the papers of another in his own chambrs with whom he is on friendly terms. There are many gaps in his legal knowledge that he now has an opportunity to make good, as he never will again. When his own practice begins he will find that his clerk has arranged conferences for him, and before the conference he will often know nothing of the questions that are likely to be put to him. If, for instance, he is on the common law side, the case that he is asked to consider may turn on the Landlord and Tenant Acts, the Rent Acts, the Consumer Protection Act, the Food and Drugs Act, the Town and Country Planning Acts, the Arbitration Act, tax law, separation, bankruptcy, conflict of laws, carriage of goods, insurance, and many other topics that he may never have studied at the University or for his Bar examinations He will not be expected, and will not need, to have every detail of all these subjects in his mind. But complete ignorance of their general structure will not raise him in the esteem of his professional clients.

If you have a social conscience you can satisfy it handsomely by taking part in your local legal advice centre or Citizens' Advice Bureau; and the same remark applies, of course, to solicitors. Some Bar students and pupil barristers offer their services in a Free Representation Unit for industrial tribunals; the office is at 3 Middle Temple Lane, London EC4Y 9AA (tel. 01-353 3697). Other barristers (as well as solicitors) take salaried employment in a community law centre, providing legal services for poorer people. A waiver is needed to permit working for clients without referral by a solicitor.

You may feel it worth while to spend a year abroad. Details are given below under Teaching, but it is worth mentioning here the training course in French law at the University of Aix/Marseille, for which scholarships have for some years been offered by the Cultural Service of the French Embassy, 22 Wilton Crescent, London SW1. Applications must be received by early January. The scholarships are open to young barristers and solicitors.

When your own practice starts it is of the utmost importance to give your cases the most meticulous attention of which you are capable, and particularly, before going into court, to familiarise youself with the various procedural contingencies. When you ask for damages on a continuing cause of action, do you know precisely the period for which you are claiming, so as to help the judge in framing his judgment? When you ask for costs, do you know the relevant Rule stating the power of the judge or master in this matter? It is quite wrong to expect to be prompted by the judge. In criminal matters you should know the sentencing powers of the court in case your client is convicted; not only may this help you in your plea in mitigation (if one is possible), but it is your duty to intervene if the judge by mistake exceeds his powers.[13] For magistrates' courts, familiarise yourself with *The Sentence of the Court,* the booklet published by the Government for magistrates; for the Crown Court read particularly D.A. Thomas, *The Principles of Sentencing,* 2nd ed. Take with you to court all the authorities that you may possibly require: leave them in the robing room if you think they will probably not be needed, but have them ready to back you up in case they are.

[13] *R.* v. *Dearden* [1978] Crim.L.R. 287.

Otherwise you may land your client in an unnecessary appeal.

Since most of the beginner's forensic work will be in county courts and magistrates' courts, he should make a special point of familarising himself with the procedure and powers of these courts. The Association of Magisterial Officers, in their evidence to the Royal Commission on Legal Services, spoke of a "woeful lack of knowledge with regard to the rules and procedures of magistrates' courts" by both solicitors and barristers, who were equally poor.

A few remarks on addressing your colleagues and your betters. Every barrister is entitled and expected to address other practising barristers of whatever eminence by their surnames. High Court judges and circuit judges are addressed by barristers out of court as "Judge" (not "Judge Smith"), a Law Lord as "Lord Smith," and other judges as "Lord Chancellor," "Lord Chief Justice" (or "Lord Chief"), "Lord Justice," "Master of the Rolls," "President," "Vice-Chancellor," "Common Sergeant," and "Recorder." These conventions are followed both in speech and in correspondence.[14] Members of the public, on the other hand, would speak to a judge as they would to any other knight or peer—Sir John, or Lord Smith. (All judges of the High Court and Court of Appeal are knights, if they are not peers.)

In court, address all judges from the High Court upwards (including both circuit judges and recorders when acting as High Court judges, and including also all judges sitting at the Central Criminal Court[15]) as "my Lord/Lady." Otherwise, circuit judges (and their deputies) and recorders and bankruptcy registrars are called "your Honour."[16] Masters are called "Master," magistrates are called "Sir/Madam" (or "your Worship"), and all other judicial officers (like registrars) are called "Sir/Madam."

FURTHER READING

A lively book of advice which all young barristers should read is Henry

[14] On the envelope, write "His [or, of course, Her] Honour Judge Smith" (circuit judge), or "The Hon. Mr/Mrs Justice Smith" (High Court judge), "The Rt. Hon. Lord Justice Smith," or "The Rt. Hon. the Lord Smith of Casterbridge," as the case may be.

[15] Including also the honorary recorders of Liverpool and Manchester.

[16] See Practice Direction, [1978] 1 W.L.R. 1435.

Cecil's *Brief to Counsel* (2nd ed., 1972). An even more informative book, which is at the same time a powerful condemnation of many practices (and non-practices) of the profession, is *The Bar on Trial,* edited by Robert Hazell (1978). At £1.95 (limp) it is a very good buy. All lawyers, solicitors as well as barristers, should read Michael Zander's *Legal Services for the Community* (1978), a scholarly and fair survey of the legal profession with many suggestions for improvement. Similarly salutary reading is provided by the Royal Commission on Legal Services in Chapter 22 of its Report (Cmnd. 7648) on "Quality of Service." Also on the critical side, see C.P. Harvey's frank and entertaining little book *The Advocate's Devil* (1958).

Of the many biographies and autobiographies of barristers giving some information about life at the Bar perhaps the most useful is Sir Harold Morris's *The Barrister* (1930). On advocacy, see Leo Page, *First Steps in Advocacy* (1943); also: Hilbery, *Duty and Art in Advocacy* (1946); J.E. Singleton, *Conduct at the Bar* (1933); F.J. Wrottesley, *Letters to a Young Barrister* (1930) and *The Examination of Witnesses* (3rd ed. 1961); Parry, *The Seven Lamps of Advocacy* (1923); R. Harris, *Hints on Advocacy* (18th ed., 1948); Lord Macmillan, *Law and Other Things* (1937) 171 *et seq.,* 200 *et seq.*; J.H. Munkman, *The Technique of Advocacy* (1951); Richard Du Cann, *The Art of the Advocate* (Pelican Books, 1964). Some notion of the nature and difficulty of cross-examination may be derived from E.W. Fordham's *Notable Cross-Examinations* (1950). Two excellent books giving an insight into procedure are David Barnard *The Civil Court in Action* (1977) and *The Criminal Court in Action* (1979). On drafting E.L. Piesse, *The Elements of Drafting,* (5th ed., 1976), is to be warmly commended. Finally, the lawyer practising in London will be helped by Andrew Goodman's *The Court Guide,* telling you how to reach the various courts and where to eat when you are appearing at them.

THE BAR AS A STEPPING STONE

In addition to the barristers in practice, a considerable number have used the Bar as a stepping stone or crutch leading them on to other things. There is, in fact, a glittering array of dignified and sometimes very lucrative offices open to members of the Bar. I shall proceed to describe some of them, prefacing the list only with the warning that for the more attractive of them there is, of course, considerable competition.

For the brilliantly successful or the politically fortunate there are the offices of Attorney-General and Solicitor-General and about 110 superior judgeships, the latter carrying very comfortable stipends, plus pensions. As consolation prizes there are many pensionable posts as circuit judges, recorders, chairmen of industrial tribunals, stipendiary magistrates, official referees, bankruptcy registrars, national insurance commissioners, and industrial injuries commissioners and deputy commissioners. Among miscellaneous posts are certain Parliamentary and Court of Protection appointments, and offices as Registrar of Companies, Masters and Registrars of the Supreme Court, and Clerk of the Crown Court. A list of most of the offices referred to in this paragraph, and others, will be found in the *Law Society's Handbook,* and in Halsbury's *Laws of England,* 4th ed., iii, 605–609. A barrister who applies for any office may reckon as part of his qualification period any time he has spent in practice or in employment as a solicitor.[17]

Other legal posts in government are discussed later in the chapter.

Many private concerns also employ a legal staff of barristers and solicitors. (It was recently calculated that these barristers probably number about 3,000 and solicitors between 1,000 and 2,000.) Banks, for instance, have executor and trustee departments. The work involves the legal processes of obtaining probate of wills and the winding up of a deceased person's affairs so that the wishes expressed in those wills may be carried out. This entails such transactions as the settlement of business contracts, the purchase and sale of stocks and shares, house property and lands, and provision for beneficiaries under wills and other trust instruments. It may mean managing an estate worth several millions of pounds. Then there are the legal departments of transport undertakings and big insurance companies, which deal principally with claims for damages, and the legal departments of large business forms and combines. The legal adviser helps to negotiate the firm's contracts (and may have to travel all over the world in order to do so), keeps it right on matters of company law and employment law, pilots takeovers, etc., and may, on a wider front, advise on what is proper conduct within a system of self-regulation adopted within the industry by means of a Code of Practice. For all these purposes he needs not only to be a good lawyer but to have business acumen and an intimate knowledge of the problems of the trade or industry in question. All the big newspapers employ a legal staff to read proofs in order to minimise the risk of libel

---

[17] Barristers (Qualification for Office) Act 1961.

actions, and also to watch the interests of the newspaper generally.

Salaries are substantial; a survey for the years 1978–1980 found that the middle remuneration bracket for lawyers in a wide variety of industries was £16,000–£18,000, which placed lawyers on a level with the average director. Thirty per cent. earned over £20,000. Barristers do better than solicitors, but both do better than lawyers in private practice. Many of these posts carry fringe benefits such as a company car, pension scheme, free medical insurance, and assistance with house purchase.

Appointments are not confined to those with professional qualifications or a knowledge of law; men and women not uncommonly read for the Bar or for an external University degree after appointment. But naturally a person who already has these qualifications starts with an advantage. After taking the Bar examination you may obtain employment in the legal department of a commercial firm under the aegis of an employed barrister as a "commercial pupil," and this will give you three months' exemption from pupilllage if you afterwards decide to take up practice at the Bar. You are, however, unlikely to want to change. Unless you are very strongly attracted to private practice you would be well advised to prefer one of these careers in salaried employment.

Information is given in a booklet published by the Bar Association for Commerce, Finance and Industry entitled *Barristers in Business:* address to 63 Great Cumberland Place, Bryanston Square, London W1H 7LJ (tel. 01-723 9556). Apply to the Secretary if you wish to become a commercial pupil.

SOLICITORS

The life of a successful solicitor is not so exacting as that of his opposite number at the Bar: the solicitor has his clerks and junior partners, assistant solicitors and legal executives to do some of his work for him. He misses the *camaraderie* of the Bar and the exhilaration of forensic battle in the exalted courts. Nor does his work lead to the same fame as does great success at the Bar; but some solicitors are as affluent as their opposite numbers at the Bar, and they achieve their wealth in a more relaxed way. (An able pupil of mine who became a successful solicitor was glad he did not become a barrister, who in his experience is driven too hard; the clerk piles too much work on him, he has no one to delegate to, and has virtually no assistance except of a secretarial kind; also, counsel in general common law practice has much travelling to do.) As between youngsters of the same ability, there is better assurance of reasonable success in the solicitors' branch. Not all solicitors have large incomes: the 1976 Remuneration Survey (given in evidence by the Law Society to the Royal Commission on Legal Services) showed that half of those working in private practice earned less than £7,050. The median earnings of all principals were £8,630, but of sole practitioners were £5,750, and of principals doing only contentious work were a disappointing £4,100. Legal aid fees have been improved substantially since then.

The type of work done by a solicitor is well known. On the property side he investigates title to land, prepares contracts of sale, conveyances and wills, obtains probate of wills, and frequently acts as executor and trustee. He interviews clients, advises them generally on their legal position, and writes letters. He pilots company promoters through the legal technicalities of forming companies. On difficult questions he takes the opinion of counsel, and he also prepares briefs for counsel in legal proceedings in which counsel are employed.

As in the United States, English lawyers are now distinctively class-structured. A few very large and affluent City firms have adapted themselves to act as the agents and advisers of commerce and industry; they have modern offices with every aid and convenience, and the partners specialise intensively. They may be asked, for example, to draft and help negotiate important commercial contracts of all kinds.[18] These firms may even have overseas branches. Next come medium-sized firms with about ten partners, specialising in some particular field of commerce or industry such as shipping or insurance or property development, and other smaller but still highly-specialised firms, all of them mainly in London. The great majority of solicitors continue in their traditional ways, making their staple living from

---

[18] You will not be examined on this subject, and will have no formal instruction in it; but read the excellent article by Bedell-Pearce in 2 *The Company Lawyer* 3.

conveyancing, probate, advising middle-class clients in minor disputes and business affairs, and litigation—though some firms prefer not to do the last if they can help it.

The qualities required of a country-town solicitor appear clearly enough from the foregoing description of his work. He should be able to interview all types of client in order to ascertain what their problem is. He should have a knowledge of human nature, practical wisdom, and the ability to dictate a good letter. Naturally he needs a working knowledge of property and company law and the law of procedure; and the better his knowledge, the better he is at his job. It is a great mistake to suppose that a solicitor can get along without having mastered the legal topics with which he is called upon to deal. However, the finer points of such subjects as tort can with relative safety be left to repose in his books of reference.

It is solicitors, not barristers, who conduct much the greater number of cases in the lesser courts—county courts and magistrates' courts. What I have written in relation to barristers as advocates applies equally to solicitors. However, a solicitor is unlikely to be able to concentrate on advocacy as a barrister can. He has to do much interviewing and paper work, and his advocacy is confined to the comparatively small cases. The training provided for solicitors now lags behind that of the Bar; it does not invariably include the instruction in advocacy, practical exercises and discussions of court cases now required for Bar students.

The spate of new legislation imposes a great strain upon the smaller firm. One client will have a problem under some recent Act relating to divorce or maintenance; another will need advice on capital gains tax, or redundancy payments, or VAT, or company law, or agricultural tenancies, or rent control; another will be enraged by a refusal of planning permission, or the threat of a motorway through his garden. Each of these subjects involves a highly intricate body of law, and it is not to be expected that any one man or even three or four men can master them all. At present, many solicitors simply fail to give adequate advice, and this is not because of any immediate fault on their part but because they are operating in units that are too small.

The constantly increasing complexity of the law is one reason, but by no means the only reason, why many solicitors in small practices are now dissatisfied with their position. Over the years, the solicitor has slowly lost the prestige he formerly held as family counseller and preserver of the family property. Lawyers are criticised for being slow to adapt to demands for new legal services, particularly services to the poor. (Although the charge has some basis, the lawyer is a professional, not a charity, so the failure to make proper provision is primarily a failure of government.) Again, many solicitors are incompetent, and leave important matters to unsupervised articled clerks or inadequately trained legal executives. The very work that solicitors are called to perform, which includes doing certain nasty things to people, cannot be expected to make them universally popular; so the profession can retain public respect only if it observes high ethical standards, which not all practitioners do. Many solicitors, in writing a letter for a client, will misrepresent the law, even though they are addressing themselves to a layman, and will lend themselves to various abuses and suppressions (not involving a breach of law) in order to obstruct a just claim.[19] The Law Society takes virtually no interest in these matters, or in the too frequent instances of gross negligence or dilatoriness by solicitors in dealing with their clients' affairs.

Blemishes like these upon the work of the profession obscure but do not efface the public services it renders. Competent solicitors are a blessing to their clients and a necessity for the economic life of the country. Unfortunately, firms have had to face discouraging difficulties in recent years. They have been hit by sharply rising expenses without corresponding rises in income. While the principals are required to confer the benefits of the various employment protection laws upon their employees, they themselves are deprived of any such security, and must pay the special tax for self-employed people masquerading as national insurance, in addition to the insurance premiums needed to provide for retirement or illness. Solicitors also complain of the expense of the practising certificate, the contribution to the compensation fund to recompense defrauded clients, the professional negligence indemnity premium, and the contribution to the Law Society advertisements for the profession. These disbursements do not worry the senior partner in a

[19] See the letter in 124 N.L.J. 471.

large firm who makes £40,000 or more a year net, but they fall heavily upon the less successful.

The most profitable part of the solicitor's work is conveyancing. But this depends in practice, even though not in theory, on the current aggregate value of property transactions; and the conveyancing monopoly is under attack from non-solicitor conveyancing firms (who use a solicitor only to draw up the conveyance itself). Again, implementation of the Pearson Report would put an end to many compensation claims handled by solicitors. The extension of the fixed penalty system that is now projected will reduce the number of small cases in magistrates' courts. A more important consideration is that the large increase in recruitment to the profession during the last few years means that new entrants (unless of top quality) are quite likely to fail to get started in private practice. The President of the Law Society calculated in 1980 that, with some 44,000 solicitors in practice, the number of young people actively trying to qualify was 15,000, and this at a time when work was stagnating.[20]

Those of my readers who are already in articles will know the technicalities of becoming a solicitor, and I can therefore address myself to those who are not yet in articles. The Law graduate who has gained full exemption proceeds at once to the Final; this requires attendance for nine months at one of the law schools recognised by the Law Society for this purpose. As with the Bar, many local authorities award grants for maintenance, but some do not, and the grants that are made are often inadequate. Two years' service under articles is required, which must be after passing the Final.

A non-graduate, or a graduate (Law or otherwise) who has not obtained full exemption because he lacks one or more of the "core" subjects in his degree, is required to take the new Common Professional Examination before the Final; and this again needs a year's attendance at a law school. However, exemption is granted in respect of particular subjects taken at University, and the requirement of attendance at the lecture course for the C.P.E. can be waived. The six core subjects are:

[20] See 77 Law Society's Gazette 981.

Constitutional and Administrative Law; Contract; Torts; Criminal Law; Land Law; and Trusts.

Finding a suitable firm for articles can present problems if you have no friends or relatives who are in a position to help. There is no system of open competition: the grant of articles, like kissing, goes by favour. The Law Society keeps a register for those seeking articles,[21] but many applicants fail to be placed in this way. Some local Law Societies (of solicitors in the area) will help. You can put an advertisement in the Law Society's Gazette or write to firms at random, but if this method produces an offer you will need to take all possible steps to sound opinions upon the standing of the firm. A bad firm can only teach you bad practices. Advice may be obtained from the Law Society or the teaching staff of your law school or your University Careers Service.

So tight is the position at present that many would-be solicitors have to take the gamble of completing the Final before they have fixed up articles. They then knock at solicitors' doors, presenting their credentials and asking if there is a vacancy for an articled clerk.

Under new Law Society regulations the articled clerk must be paid an "acceptable" salary, the intention being that this shall be at least equivalent to the undergraduate maintenance grant, grossed up to cover 52 weeks instead of 38 and further increased to take account of the income tax and national insurance contributions payable. The principal is required to give his clerk specified minimum training (or to enable him to receive it from others). If you are about to enter articles, make yourself familiar with the kind of training to which you are entitled,[22] though you should of course use tact in bringing any inadequacies to the attention of your principal.

Let me now assume that you are being considered by a prospective principal and are seeing him for the first time. A number of important questions need to be asked, with all the tact at your command; some of them may be best addressed to an articled clerk who is already with the firm. How often will you be

[21] There are two helpful directories of solicitors: see 145 Justice of the Peace Newspaper 668.
[22] See 77 Law Society's Gazette 170, 249. A useful summary of the proper training of an articled clerk will be found in 123 New Law Journal 901–902.

allowed to sit in with your principal or another solicitor? Will you have to do your own typing or will you be allowed to use the office typists? What courts will you be able to attend? If in local government, will you attend committee meetings?

How wide will be the experience you will receive in the firm? Before the new regulations were introduced it was found that most prospective solicitors gained some practical experience of: registered and unregistered conveyancing, landlord and tenant, matrimonial causes, probate and succession, family law, criminal law, accident claims, litigation generally and briefing counsel. Most of them never had experience of: town and country planning, administration of trusts, company law, partnership law, tax planning, book-keeping and accounts, commercial law, or (doubtless) advocacy. The law has become so complex that it cannot be expected that the solicitor will be proficient in everything, and the trend is towards the large firm with specialised partners. All the same, it is important that the trainee should have as broad a base as possible, particularly if he is not certain which field is likely to offer the best opening. For this reason, an all-round practice gives better training than a specialised one—but it may be well worth taking articles in a specialised firm if you are assured that they are looking out for a bright young man/woman like you to be a partner. Large firms generally move their protégés around from one department to another—a very satisfactory arrangement.

Will you have the opportunity of spending some time with London Agents, and if so what are the financial terms likely to be? What about holidays and paid sickness leave? Will you be paid while attending an examination course? If you can attend any practical exercises or advocacy training courses provided for those in articles (*e.g.* in London or Birmingham), do so.

It is probably too delicate to ask the principal the final question: How much of your time will you give to instructing me?—but you may be able to find out the probabilities from any other articled clerks in the firm.

Proposals have been made to replace the outmoded apprenticeship system by a proper training course, but they have foundered because no one is willing to put up the funds.

Among the skills that are in short supply are advocacy and probate, so procedure, evidence and wills are good subjects to choose when planning your academic course. On advocacy, the advice to solicitors is the same as to barristers (see also Chapter 11 on mooting). Remember the importance of neat and sober suiting when you are in court, or indeed out of it.

Newly qualified solicitors begin as salaried assistant solicitors. Getting a partnership is not easy, and the new partner who cannot provide capital is inevitably burdened with some form of payment for his share. One practice is to establish a retirement benefit scheme, whereby the younger partners, instead of paying an initial sum as their share of capital, contribute to the pensions of the senior partners as they go. Another plan is for the new partners to be admitted merely on undertaking to contribute their share of the partnership capital, and this may either be raised by borrowing from a bank or insurance company (with periodic repayments) or be left to be paid over a period of years by deduction from their share of the profits. Either way, the new recruit's earnings are greatly reduced, and some legal assistants continue in their salaried position because they cannot afford a partnership.

Instead of going into private practice, or after some years of practice, the solicitor may seek an appointment. The most favourable field is in the local government service, which will be described in the next section. In addition, solicitors are eligible for appointment to the legal departments of Government Departments as described in connection with the Bar, though not always to the head positions. In some cases, by law or practice, the chief appointments are confined to solicitors. Within the judicial system solicitors are appointed as masters and registrars of the Chancery Division, taxing masters, Official Solicitor, bankruptcy registrars, district registrars of the High Court, registrars of county courts,[23] stipendiary magistrates, recorders (and, by way of promotion, circuit judges), magistrates' clerks, and as various kinds of clerk in the Supreme Court, the last with opportunities of promotion (see later, under Civil Service). However, the better judicial and quasi-judicial appointments generally go to barristers. Then again, various public utility undertakings offer important positions to solicitors. Details of the foregoing can be seen in the *Law Society's*

[23] See 61 Law Society's Gazette 669.

Handbook, or in Halsbury's *Laws of England,* 3rd ed., xxxvi, 52–55. Current vacancies both in private practice (for legal executives,[24] assistants and partners) and in outside appointments are listed by the Law Society's Appointments Registry.

Solicitors may be appointed to positions in industry, and remarks made previously in relation to barristers apply equally to solicitors. Most legal departments in industry merely do the work that would ordinarily be entrusted to a solicitor; sometimes it is largely confined to routine conveyancing and the drawing of contracts, but a much wider field may be touched, including the formation of subsidiary companies, company finance, insurance and employers' liability, patents, trade marks—there is, in fact, hardly any limit to the economic activities upon which a large corporation may engage. In addition, all concerns need advice on labour law. Some corporations entrust their routine legal work to outside solicitors, but have legal advisers whose task is to give advice at high level within the industry; these advisers organise the legal work which is to be executed by the outside solicitors—perhaps in many countries. The position of legal adviser to a large and growing industry can be of high importance and interest.

In view of the difficulty of obtaining articles with a reasonable salary in private practice, the prospect of obtaining a salaried position and articles in the legal department of a company is attractive. The Royal Commission on Legal Services found that in 1976 the apprentice in commerce or industry received a considerably greater salary than that paid by private practitioners; also, the median salary of solicitors in this type of employment was substantially more than in private practice (£7,584 outside Greater London, as compared with £4,346 in private practice). On the other hand, the openings in companies' legal departments are much fewer than in private practice; and in any case you should not consider articles in commerce or industry unless you are keen to make this your career. You will only be taken on if you can convince your employer of this keenness. Articles in industry are not the best preparation for private practice, and unless you have a fairly fixed intention to

[24] Legal executives (the former managing clerks) have a legal qualification but have not been admitted as solicitors.

make your career in industry or commerce you may find it difficult to settle down even for only two or three years in the atmosphere of a company's legal department.

Another possibility worth considering is taking articles with the clerk of a magistrates' court with a view to this type of appointment.

Solicitors are frequently appointed not only in the legal departments but in the secretarial departments of large concerns; but a person who intends to go for a secretarial department would be better advised to obtain a secretarial rather than a legal qualification (to have both would, of course, be best of all). To these possibilities must be added miscellaneous positions not capable of concise description, in building societies, insurance companies, and so on.

A highly specialised profession, open to barristers and solicitors and indeed to those who are neither, is that of Parliamentary Agent, whose work lies in promoting and opposing Bills and Departmental Orders. A description of this work will be found in 7 The Lawyer 21.

FURTHER READING

Information on the technical details of becoming a solicitor can be obtained from the Secretary, Law Society's Hall, Chancery Lane, London WC2A 1PL. The Law Society publish and will supply free two good brochures: *Becoming a Solicitor* and *A Guide for Articled Clerks.* Descriptions of the work of a solicitor are given in a series of booklets published by the Solicitors' Law Stationery Society called *The Doorstep Series,* and in a highly entertaining book by G.A.L. Burgeon, *This Ever Diverse Pair* (1950). See also Michael Gilbert, *The Law* (1977), in the series *The Professions*; Harry Kirk, *Portrait of a Profession* (1976). Fictionalised accounts will be found in the various books by Julian Prescott, such as *Both Sides of the Case* (1958), and in an entertaining story by John Malcolm entitled *Let's Make it Legal* (1966). Other useful hints are given in H.O. Locke's *Advice to a Young Solicitor* (1946) and C.D. Wickenden's *The Modern Family Solicitor* (1975). Elementary advice on litigation is given in Leonard C. Lockwood's *Solicitor's Clerk in Court,* and, on conveyancing, in Edward Moeran's *Practical Conveyancing* (6th ed., 1974). In addition to the books on advocacy previously given, there is Sir David Napley's *The Technique of Persuasion* (2nd ed., 1975) and F.J.O. Coddington's *Advice on Advocacy to Solicitors* (2nd ed., 1954). Sir Thomas Lund has written a *Guide to the Professional Conduct and Etiquette of Solicitors* (1960). Words of wisdom for both solicitor and client on the lottery of litigation are contained in Michael Rosser, *Going tò Court? Second Thoughts* (1980). Colin Shuttleworth, *Check Lists for Solicitors* (3rd ed., 1979), will help you to bear in mind all the important points that normally arise in different types of transaction. An excellent check-list for criminal cases in magistrates' courts is given in 130 N.L.J. 1086.

LAWYERS IN THE CIVIL SERVICE

Most Government Departments make appointments from professional lawyers, and here, although practical experience is an important qualification, it is not always regarded as essential. Barristers and solicitors are appointed in about equal proportions. (Even when the head of the department is a barrister, he may be known as the department's solicitor.) The career is very rewarding in every sense. Pay in the professional grade of the civil service is better at starting than in the administrative grade, and it is only one step down at the top.

A list of the Departments concerned will be found in the *Law Society's Handbook* and in Halsbury. No examination is required; vacancies are advertised in the legal weeklies (*Law Society's Guardian Gazette, New Law Journal, Solicitor's Journal*, and in The Times. Since it is hard to change departments once you are in, choose the department in which you think you will be able to settle down. You can write to the Establishment Officer of the department of your choice and ask for an interview in expectation of the next vacancy. In this case you will probably join as temporary legal assistant with a view to establishment later. Alternatively, you may be immediately recruited as an established legal assistant (or senior legal assistant) through the Civil Service Commission, the address of which is Alencon Link, Basingstoke, Hants, RG21 1JB.

Pupillage or articles can be waived for candidates with outstanding examination results. In addition, a method of entry has been devised by which legal training is obtained after entry. Young men and women with honours degrees or postgraduate degrees can be appointed as "legal trainees" and be articled to solicitors in the Legal Service, normally after obtaining exemption from passing or obtaining exemption from the C.P.E. An appointment as Legal Assistant follows admission as a solicitor. Unfortunately, not many clerkships are offered, so competition is likely to be keen. Details can be obtained from the Civil Service Commission.

Those who have worked in the legal civil service report that it is much more interesting than appears at first sight. The work is not purely legal, and in no department is it narrowly specialist. There are opportunities for foreign travel, as adviser to international conferences, etc., in several Departments, including the Diplomatic Service. The Board of Inland Revenue has many problems wholly unrelated to tax law. A barrister who left the Inland Revenue for practice at the Bar summed up his opinion of the service in the following words: "I enjoyed it, they enjoyed me, and I would always consider returning if the Bar did not prove satisfying."

Most legal civil service posts do not require advocacy at any level. By a discreditable rule of the Bar, a member who is in paid employment (apart from the Attorney-General and Solicitor-General) cannot appear in court in his professional capacity. However, civil servants may appear in magistrates' courts as prosecutors without violating this restrictive practice. The legal staff of Customs and Excise, for example, carry on prosecutions for smuggling in magistrates' courts, and brief counsel for the higher courts.

The various public corporations (such as the National Coal Board, the Airways Corporations, the Railways Board, and the Development Corporations under the New Towns Act 1946) require some lawyers on their staffs, but there is no standard method of recruitment. Vacancies are generally advertised in The Times

There is no more important, exciting and intellectually rewarding work for a lawyer than that of drafting legislation. The post of Parliamentary Counsel is open to both barristers and solicitors, and candidates of adequate intellectual quality are in short supply. My little book will have performed a useful function if it persuades one or two of the best of its readers to take up this career. Vacancies are notified by the Civil Service Commission.[25]

---

[25] For the work of Parliamentary Counsel see Sir Harold Kent's entertaining autobiography, *In on the Act* (1979); Sir Granville Ram in (1951) 1 J.S.P.T.L. 422; Sir Noel Hutton in (1967) 64 Law Society's Gazette 293.

LOCAL GOVERNMENT

Local government offers a highly attractive field for the lawyer. Solicitors in local government take articled clerks, who are paid salaries, and local authorities are more generous than most private employers in giving paid study leave and assistance for the purchase of books. Lawyers have been conspicuously successful in obtaining the top job of chief executive (the former town clerk or county clerk). The valuable pension rights attaching to these posts must also be remembered.

The work of local authorities is wide-ranging; it includes public health in all its branches, education, housing and town planning, public utilities, transport, recreation and social services. It is good practice for a trainee to be given the opportunity to work in more than one department to broaden his experience.

The drawback of employment in central and local government, to some minds, is that so often you fail to see any outcome to your work. You may toil on a project enthusiastically for many years, only to find that it all comes to naught because of a political change of direction. To be a good government officer you must be able to put up with these frustrations. The price of all social improvement is effort, often wasted effort.

For advice and assistance on articles write to Mr R.A.Leyland, LL.B., Hon.Sec. of the Society of County Secretaries, The Castle, Winchester SO23 8UJ, or Mrs M. Mullins, Asst.Sec. of the Association of District Secretaries, Smokey Acre, Broadoak Hill, Dundry, Bristol BS18 8NB.

Nearly all lawyers in local government are solicitors, and it is better to qualify this way than at the Bar. If, however, you have started at the Bar, there is no reason why you should not apply for any local government post that tempts you. Pupillage is not required. You would be well advised to include Conveyancing in your Bar examination.

Solicitors are appointed as county prosecutors, and they can also be appointed as prosecutors for the Inland Revenue and Customs and Excise. The work is interesting, but promotional prospects are limited.

THE GENERAL CATEGORY OF THE CIVIL SERVICE

For the man or woman with a first-class academic brain the administrative posts in the Home Civil Service have great attraction, above all because they give the satisfaction of doing work of paramount social and national importance. There is the interest of being "in the know" when important governmental decisions are being made, and at the rank of Assistant Secretary there is real governmental power. Promotion, however, tends to be slow, since it is generally governed by the principle of "Buggins's turn"; one reaches the top or near-top only at about the age of 55, when one is not far off retirement.

The qualities looked for in a higher civil servant are: intelligence; fluency of mouth and pen, particularly in producing a persuasive argument and in composing a good ministerial speech; the capacity to induce other people to carry out a policy that perhaps they do not much wish to carry out; a political "nose"; the ability (in a Department or a local or regional office) to organise those beneath him or her; and capacity for hard work (many of those at the top work extremely hard).

The civil service is organised into three groups of staff—the General Category, the Science Category and the Professional and Technology Category. The last, as it affects lawyers, has already been dealt with, and we are now considering the General Category, where the prospects at the top levels are better than in the others. All civil servants, however, have the very valuable privilege of an index-linked pension.

A graduate may join the General Category either as an Administrative Trainee or as an Executive Officer. Selection is by qualifying tests (meant to assess general ability) and interviews.[26] An alternative mode of entry is available for the Tax Inspectorate. If you are undecided whether to apply, you may visit a Government Department during vacation in order to see what goes on, your reasonable expenses being refunded.

The mode of entry described above covers not only the administrative class of the Home Civil Service, but also certain

[26] The technique of the Civil Service Selection Board interview is explained in booklets called *Appointments in Administration* and *CSSB: A Guide to the Civil Service Selection Board*, both available free from the Civil Service Commission.

clerkships in the House of Commons, the administrative class of the Northern Ireland Civil Service, and the diplomatic service. There is a shortage of suitable recruits in the diplomatic service, which offers varied experience abroad and a good career structure.

Administrative trainees obtain a salary on a par with that obtainable from industry; they enjoy incremental salary scales which ensure progress even during periods of pay restraint, together with near-certain promotion within the administrative grade to under-secretary level. Small wonder that industry feels itself to suffer unfairly in the competition for talent.

Intending candidates should obtain further information as soon as possible from the Secretary, Civil Service Commission, Alencon Link, Basingstoke, Hants, RG21 1JB (tel. 0256-68551).

FURTHER READING

A good impression of the work of the higher civil service is conveyed in John Carswell's witty book, *The Civil Servant and his World* (1966). See also the volumes in the *Whitehall Series* (published by Putnams), each devoted to a different Government Department, and Frank Dunnill's provocative book: *The Civil Service: Some Human Aspects* (1956).

The classic account of departmental incompetence and extravagance is Leslie Chapman, *Your Disobedient Servant* (1979). Peter Kellner and Lord Crowther Hunt, *The Civil Servants* (1980) contains entertaining material, but it is somewhat slanted and over-simplified.

BUSINESS MANAGEMENT

Large industrial and business concerns provide many places for Arts graduates—an expression which for this purpose includes law graduates. One advantage is that salaries are paid even during training; and a career in the world of manufacture and commerce is attractive to those who want to do something "real," to take part in the basic process of creating wealth, to tackle a variety of problems and jobs and to have a chance to organise and administer, and perhaps to travel. The general impression of investigators is that the great majority of the graduates, in spite of certain difficulties, enjoy their work. At the same time, the vast output of Arts graduates from the Universities, coupled with high unemployment, means that competition for vacancies is acute.

If your ambition takes this line, there are certain basic truths that you will have to recognise. First, your company is out to make money, to provide goods and services at a profit, for otherwise it cannot survive. This does not mean that you should stay in a firm that stoops to fraud or illegality; but idealistic notions have to face an economic assessment. Secondly, whatever knowledge you have acquired before, you are now at the starting-post of your career and have to serve an apprenticeship. This means being ready and anxious to learn, approaching problems with an open mind, and being sensitive to the feelings of others. Success in business requires a knowledge of human nature and an acceptable personality. Seize every opportunity for formal training that is open to you. Do not be afraid to ask questions, particularly, perhaps, questions as to why things are done in the way they are—though you should for a long time be very restrained in any suggestions you make for improvement.

Some of this advice was put better and more fully by Mr A.D. Bonham-Carter.

"I would say to every ambitious and able young man who is choosing to make his career in industry: first, you must realise that the way to the top is something which has to be worked out with your employer, and although you have to fight your way up in the face of keen competition your employer is not one of your competitors but is just as keen that you should reach the top as you are. Secondly, you will best get there by squeezing all you can out of every position you hold and out of the experience of every man you serve or meet: pick their brains, study their successes and their failures; never be afraid to ask questions or put new ideas, but do not get upset or angry if they are not accepted at first, and do not assume that the other man's judgment is wrong. Maybe it is, but it is just as likely that your idea was not quite right. Finally, look after your health—if you are really going to the top enormous demands are going to be made on your time and strength and you cannot afford to be careless."

TEACHING

I need say very little about this, because the kind of life led by a law teacher is well known to the student, and if he aspires to it himself he will not lack advisers. Owing to present stringencies a University teaching post will be hard to come by, but there may be an opportunity to teach in one of the Polytechnics or Technical Colleges, where Law is taught at every level from "O" level to degree courses.

Ideally, a person seeking to become a law teacher at top level should not only be outstandingly able but also have some practical experience of the profession and some published or approved writings to demonstrate his ability in research. But few applicants have all these points to recommend them; so most law teachers are appointed without having had practical experience. If you are such an appointee, it is highly desirable that you should acquire at least some brief experience by being given leave of absence or by a period of teaching part-time.[27]

The usual way of preparing oneself for a teaching appointment (or for promotion) is by research work. This activity can be profitably combined with a visit to another University, preferably abroad. Consult the *Grants Register* (published biennially) and *Study Abroad* (published by UNESCO). They may be found in your Careers Adviser's office, or in the larger public libraries. The United States, in particular, offers varied opportunities: for details of American Law Schools offering postgraduate degrees and an informative booklet *Postgraduate Study in the United States,* write to the United States-United Kingdom Educational Commission, Student Adviser's Office, 6 Porter Street, London W1M 2HR. This office will also supply details of the numerous scholarships and fellowships available; some are offered by the Commission itself. The list includes Fulbright awards, which do not necessarily cover tuition, but Universities are generally ready to allow tuition waivers to Fulbright scholars. The following is a supplementary list of bodies offering awards.

American Council of Learned Societies (American Studies Research Fellowships), 800 Third Avenue, New York, N.Y. 10022, U.S.A.

University of California School of Law (Fellowships): address Graduate Assistant, Room 327, Boalt Hall, U.C., Berkeley, Calif. 94720, U.S.A.

Columbia University School of Law, New York, N.Y. 10027, U.S.A. (teaching associateships, funded in connection with graduate degree studies; write to Executive Secretary, Committee on Graduate Instruction).

University of Chicago, Chicago, Ill., U.S.A., awards British Commonwealth Fellowships (apply to the Secretary of the British Common-

---

[27] See Professor R.M. Goode in 129 N.L.J. 1117 for an excellent statement of the reasons why academics should have practical experience.

wealth Program) and Bigelow Teaching Fellowships (apply to Dean of Law School).

University of Illinois, College of Law, Champaign, Ill. 61820, U.S.A. (Graduate Fellowships).

Northwestern University School of Law, 357 East Chicago Avenue, Chicago, Ill. 60611 (Fellowships, and Lectureship for Legal Writing Program: address to Chairman of the Graduate Committee).

Rutgers University School of Law, 15 Washington Street, Newark, N.J. 07102, U.S.A. (Teaching and Research Associates).

Tulane University School of Law, New Orleans, La. 70118, U.S.A. (graduate Fellowships and visiting research scholars).

University of Virginia Law School, Charlottesville, Va. 22901, U.S.A. (Fellowships for graduate study; address to Secretary of the Graduate Committee).

Yale Law School, New Haven, Conn. 06520, U.S.A. (graduate work and visiting research scholars).

Except where otherwise stated, address the Dean of the Law School. State your position, achievements, proposals for U.S. study (research, reading for degree), and whether you would like to teach. If you are contemplating an academic career, say so. Make your inquiries well in advance, otherwise you may be caught by closing dates.

Commonwealth scholarships and fellowships are tenable at Universities in Australia, New Zealand, Canada, Ghana, Hong Kong, India, Jamaica, Malaysia, Nigeria, Sierra Leone and Sri Lanka; write to the Secretary, Association of Commonwealth Universities, 36 Gordon Square, London WC1H 0PF. The Association publishes two handbooks: *Scholarships Guide for Commonwealth Postgraduate Students* and *Awards for Commonwealth University Academic Staff.* In Canada, McGill University and the University of Montreal offer courses in comparative law. Research scholarships are offered by the Research School of Social Sciences, Australian National University, Box 4, G.P.O., Canberra, A.C.T., Australia. One of these scholarships might well give you the opportunity to take a teaching post in the country concerned.

With our association with Europe, it is vital that some lawyers should interest thmselves in the law of the EEC and improve their contacts with European lawyers. A booklet *Scholarships Abroad* is available (price £1 post free) from the British Council, 65 Davies Street, London W1Y 2AA, and details of foreign Universities are given in *The World of Learning,* published annually. There is also a flow the other way: law teachers from "new" Commonwealth countries may apply for research Fellowships to the University of London Institute of Advanced Legal Studies, 17 Russell Square, London WC1B 5DR. Irrespective of the place of study, senior workers may apply for Leverhulme Research Fellowships and grants, particulars of which may be obtained from the Secretary, 15–19 New Fetter Lane, London EC4A 1NR. The British Academy, Burlington House, London W1V 0NS, awards grants and a Fellowship for research. The Social Sciences Research Council, 1 Temple Avenue, London EC4Y 0BD, awards studentships for research in socio-legal topics. Oxford also makes awards in this field: write to the Director, Centre for Socio-Legal Studies, Wolfson College, Oxford OX2 6UD. Lists of other awards in this and other countries are compiled by the Association of Commonwealth Universities (address above).

International law is especially favoured. The University of Cambridge offers Humanitarian Trust Studentships in this subject (write to the Secretary, Faculty Board of Law, The Old Syndics Building, Cambridge CB2 1RX). The British Institute of International and Comparative Law, 17 Russell Square, London WC1B 5DR, offers Research Fellowships to students from overseas. The Hague Academy of International Law offers a course of study and scholarships (write to the Secretariat of the Academy, 2517 KJ, The Hague, Palais de la Prix, Holland). The Directorate of Human Rights, Council of Europe, Strasbourg offers Fellowships for study in the field of human rights.

In addition to posts in the ordinary teaching institutions there are lectureships, tutorships and examinerships offered at the Inns of Court School of Law, and tutorships, assistant tutorships, and examinerships at the Law Society's College of Law. Vacancies in the Inns of Court lectureships (which are part-time) are advertised in the legal papers and in The Times; they are also announced on the notice boards in the Inns. Vacancies in the Law Society's teaching staff are advertised in the Law Society's Guardian Gazette.

There are many teaching opportunities overseas, where you will be paid more highly than in the United Kingdom. Certainly go to a teaching post in Canada or Australia or elsewhere if you are unmarried and can easily return later on to look for your first post here; or go intending to make a new life in a new country; but do not go, severing your connections with the United Kingdom, intending to make this a step to advancement in this country. It is very difficult to transfer to a teaching post in this country from one overseas, because the appointments committee will rarely appoint without interview, and will not be able to pay travel expenses for candidates who are abroad.

If you wish to work in a University and believe that your law degree may not be strong enough, consider taking a course in librarianship. Every law school has a library, and it is difficult to find people who have the double qualification.

ACCOUNTANCY

Few law students go in for accountancy, even though a knowledge of law is useful both for the examinations and for practice. Accountants have become advisers to industry, and many accountants are to be found on the Boards of large public companies. An important part of their work is giving advice on tax matters; yet they often fail to understand taxing statute because they are unfamiliar with the language and with the legal background of the statute. It should be obvious, therefore, that a law degree combined with a qualification is accountancy is a great advantage.

THE SOCIAL SERVICES

You may be interested in a job in the probation and after-care service, or other department of social work. Most social workers have no recognised qualification. The usual qualification of those who have one is a two-year postgraduate course. Graduates in sociology can take the course in one year, but Law graduates are not generally allowed this privilege.[28] Alternatively, would you be interested in the Graduate Entry Scheme in the police force?

APPLYING FOR JOBS

If you are asked to name referees when applying for a job, always seek the permission of the person concerned before giving his name; and if he agrees to act he may appreciate

[28] See David Carson in 127 New Law Journal 776.

receiving a copy of your application, so as to refresh his memory on the details of your career.

A few points on the technique of being interviewed. Before the interview, make sure that you know the details of your own career, and can explain anything requiring explanation, such as the reason why you left your previous job. Find out what you can about the firm offering the job. (Your University Careers Service can probably help). How big is it; what does it make or do; does it operate abroad? And what does the job entail? At the interview, remember that you are a salesman for yourself. Do not answer all questions with a mere Yes or No even if they admit of such answers. If you have to answer No, try to follow it with something positive. Some of the questions are likely to be on your past career as evidenced by your letter of application; so be ready to add explanations when you are given an opening on any item. Explain why you continued your studies for longer than usual; why you changed your course, or your university or college; why you took the vacation job. Be quick to mention what the experience brought you. Decide beforehand what are your best points and try to indicate them; make them as specific as possible. What motivates you? What attracts you about the job? What is there in your background or qualifications that make it seem specially suitable for you? Keep your voice up, and your head up. Look the interviewer in the eye (as you should always do when people are talking to you); and if you can manage a smile now and then, to show what a pleasant person you are to work with, so much the better (A psychological study of non-verbal behaviour in interviews showed that successful outcomes were associated with smiling, eye contact and head nodding by the candidate!)

Towards the close of the interview you will probably be invited to ask questions yourself. Consider beforehand precisely what you want to know. Do not commence with enquiries about the salary, holidays and prospects; it gives a better impression to start with questions about the work itself. How has the vacancy arisen? Is training provided for? What will be your relationship to others in the department? Can you meet them before joining? What are the working conditions and fringe benefits? What are the prospects of promotion, and who decides upon promotion?

If you are willing to go abroad, you can lead into this by asking if the firm is opening up abroad.

I can say things in print that might naturally give offence (or at least cause distress) if I were speaking to you personally. In print my remarks are obviously indiscriminate. I should not have chosen in a personal conversation to mention the manner of slurred vowels and meaningless noises, as I did on p.166. Now here are some words of wisdom, after the manner of Polonius, on the delicate matter of your appearance. It is accepted that students can dress comfortably if inelegantly in jeans and pullovers, or in garb expressing a more extravagant fancy. What I want to say is that by the time you are thinking of a career you should be prepared to relinquish these carefree ways. Your acceptance and progress in any walk of life depends upon the judgment of an older generation (to which you will yourself shortly belong), and they will value conspicuous cleanliness, neatness and absence of undue ostentation in dress and hair style. Neither the Sex Discrimination Act nor the Race Relations Act prohibits discrimination on the ground of dress, and, to most members of selection committees, "dress" means approved European business or professional dress. So, if you are a man, buy a single-breasted suit, dark blue or dark grey, of conservative cut. Avoid wide lapels, buttons on pockets, fancy trimmings. Take a friend with you when you buy the suit, to assure you that the collar fits snugly. If there is any suspicion of the suit not fitting well, have it altered; see particularly that it is not too small. Women, similarly, should dress conservatively, without sexual display, in a way that betokens quiet efficiency rather than fashion. Remain a conformist when you start your job. It is a folly to let your appearance handicap your career.

On a less personal subject, why not learn to type? Admittedly, you may be given a secretary to whom you can dictate, and this is a great convenience; but often you will find that the draft you want in a hurry is still in her notebook or on her tape. Anyway, it is much easier to compose a difficult draft by typing it yourself than by dictating it. You can learn to type by touch in only one day, as I did. I bought an instruction book with a chart of the keyboard showing the proper fingering, and I tied an apron round my neck and over the keyboard so that I could not see the keys. (This is essential). Then I practised the exercises for one day. After that I could remove the apron without having the temptation to peep, and I knew all the finger-stretches and could type by touch. It is far and away the best day's work I ever did. I grievously lacked accuracy at first, but that improved with practice.

GENERALLY

The student should not neglect his University or College Careers Service, which can often give him valuable assistance. Solicitors can obtain help from the Law Society's Appointments Officer. Anyone looking out for a public appointment should keep his eye regularly on the Public Appointments column of The Times. There is a useful annual publication by the Cornmarket Press called *Directory of Opportunities for Graduates,* which not only provides details of the major employers but gives valuable advice. Read, particularly, the advice there given on the wording of your application.

If you have some fluency in a foreign tongue, try to keep it up. If the language is French, consider studying your law at a University offering a mixed English and French law course (King's College, London, and the Universities of Birmingham, Kent and Leicester); part of your time will be spent in a French University, and you emerge with a double qualification. A similar course with the additional option of a German qualification is available at the University of Exeter. Other Universities and Polytechnics offer mixed courses in Law and Languages. See *A Second Survey of Legal Education in the U.K.*—Supplement No. 2, obtainable from the Institute of Advanced Legal Studies, University of London (price £2). See also pp.199 and 220 above. Solicitors with an international legal practice (who are to be found not only in London but in some other large cities) will give preference to recruits with linguistic ability. Some City Firms have branches in Europe and elsewhere where English solicitors are employed. Recruitment to international legal bodies such as the staffs of the EEC Court and Commission requires proficiency not only in law but in languages.

CHAPTER 14

GENERAL READING

A lawyer without history or literature is a mechanic, a mere working mason; if he possesses some knowledge of these, he may venture to call himself an architect.

—Scott, *Guy Mannering.*

No one wants to read law all the time; but some of the hours not spent on serious legal reading may be devoted with profit and pleasure to lighter literature touching upon the law, and to works that set the background in which the lawyer lives. The following, which is hardly more than a list, may be of assistance not merely to the beginner at law but to the practitioner in his leisure moments. What is offered is a collection of titles that may come the reader's way at intervals during his life, and that are worth reading if they do. Not all the books included are in print.

DRAMA

The number of legal references in Shakespeare has given rise to a theory that he was a trained lawyer. This thesis would be more attractive if the internal evidence had not also been used to assign him to a number of other walks in life.

> The bard play-writing in his room,
> The bard a humble clerk,
> The bard, a lawyer, parson, groom,
> The bard, deer-stalking after dark,
> The bard a tradesman—and a Jew—
> The bard a botanist—a beak—
> The bard a skilled musician, too—
> A sheriff and a surgeon, eke![1]

---

[1] W.S. Gilbert, *The Bab Ballads.*

In fact, modern research has shown that there are as many references to legal concepts among the lesser Elizabethan dramatists as in Shakespeare, and that there is no reason to suppose that Shakespeare possessed any unusual knowledge. Much the best discussion of the plays from the legal point of view is G.W. Keeton, *Shakespeare's Legal and Political Background* (1967). See also the very learned study by Professor O. Hood Phillips, *Shakespeare and the Lawyers* (1972). A specialised work comes from America, entitled *The Law of Property in Shakespeare and the Elizabethan Drama*, by Paul S. Clarkson and Clyde T. Warren (1942). It need hardly be added that, as any commentator will allow, the plays themselves are worth a shelf-full of commentaries; commentaries are for those who know the plays. There is endless fascination in picking out the legal allusions in Shakespeare without the help of commentaries.

Among dramatists of the present century, three of Galsworthy's plays have a direct interest for lawyers—*The Silver Box, Justice* and *Loyalties*, the last involving a strict application of professional etiquette. A performance of *Justice* was witnessed in 1911 by Mr Winston Churchill, then Home Secretary, and he was so moved by it that he made a long-overdue reform in prison administration by drastically curtailing the period of solitary confinement.[2] It is of interest to note that Galsworthy was called to the Bar in 1890; but he never practised.

FICTION

Dickens started life as (among other things) a lawyer's clerk and court reporter, and most of his novels contain legal characters or legal references. The famous trial scene in *Pickwick* (written when the author was only 24) shows the working of the system of advocacy in a common law court at its worst. We have moved far since those days, not least because, since 1851, the parties to the suit have been allowed to testify on their own behalf. Students of the reports may like to know that Dickens's Mr Justice

---

[2] He reduced it to one month for all but recidivists. Such a reform had been advocated by a Departmental Committee as long before as 1895. See S. and B. Webb, *English Prisons under Local Government* (1922) 223, n.1.

Stareleigh was modelled upon the real Mr Justice Gaselee, while
Serjeant Buzfuz was Serjeant Bompas.[3]

Less widely read but even more engrossing for the lawyer is
the description of the appallingly inefficient proceedings of the
Court of Chancery in *Bleak House*. Space forbids extended
discussion of Dickens's works, but a good commentary is
Holdsworth's *Charles Dickens as a Legal Historian* (1929).[4]

An earlier writer, Henry Fielding, must occupy a special place
in the esteem of the lawyer and the law-abiding citizen, for it was
he who, with his blind half-brother, sitting as London magistrates, founded the Bow Street Runners, the ancestors of our
present professional police.[5] Most of his novels were written
when, for want of any other source of income, he was practising
at the Bar[6]; but his *Tom Jones* deserves to be read for its own
sake, and not merely for the incidental legal allusion.

Thackeray entered the Middle Temple (though he did not get
much further), and his experience there is pictured in Chapter 29
of *Pendennis*.

The name of Samuel Warren is no longer known to the general
public. He was a snob and often a bore, but withal quite a sound
lawyer, and his legal novel, *Ten Thousand a Year*, is assured of
immortality within his own profession. It is somewhat over-long,
and may be commenced without loss at Chapter 7. The plot
involves an action in ejectment which succeeded because the
judge refused to admit in evidence a deed on which there
appeared an erasure (Chapter 13). The refusal was based on the
ancient rule that a material alteration in a document after
execution renders it void. Unfortunately Warren is guilty of bad
law in this particular: the rule is that there is a presumption in the
case of a deed or other document *inter vivos* that any alteration

---

[3] For a legal study see Percy Fitzgerald, *Bardell* v. *Pickwick* (1902). It is
pointed out in (1923) 1 Can. Bar Rev. 631 that in *Brooke* v. *Pickwick*
(1827) 4 Bing. 753, 130 E.R. 753, the defendant was the coach
proprietor of Bath from whom Dickens took the name of his hero, and
one of the judges was Gaselee J. The legal purlieus of London as they
survive since Dickens's time are described in 120 New Law Journal
492.

[4] See also T.A. Fyfe, *Charles Dickens and the Law* (1910): Sir Gerald
Hurst, *Lincoln's Inn Essays* (1949) 109.

[5] Anthony Babington, *A House in Bow Street* (1969).

[6] See Pat Rogers, *Henry Fielding: a Biography* (1979).

appearing in it was made before execution; and on the facts supposed in the novel there was no evidence to rebut this presumption. Also, the rule avoiding deeds for material alteration does not apply to deeds of conveyance,[7] as the deed in Warren's novel was. It is said that the character of "Mr Sterling" was intended to represent Pollock C.B.; Mr Subtle was Scarlett, Mr Quicksilver was Brougham, Mr Crystal and Mr Lynx were Cresswell and Wightman, Mr Chaffanbrass was Serjeant Ballantine, Sir Charles Westenholme was Lord Lyndhurst, Lord Widdrington was Lord Tenterden, and Mr Justice Grayley was Bayley J.[8] To Warren and other legal writers of the nineteenth century belongs the credit of inventing the detective novel.[9]

Galsworthy's *Forsyte Saga* has a solicitor as one of the principal characters, a libel action conducted on somewhat irregular lines,[10] and a will that neglects the Thellusson Act. Someone brought the latter mistake to the author's attention, and in the sequel, entitled *On Forsyte 'Change*, the point is admitted but ingeniously evaded.[11]

Outside the field of English law there are the works of Sir Walter Scott and Honoré de Balzac—both lawyers, and both prolific in legal allusion. Scott combined novel writing with the practice of a busy Scottish advocate and judicial duties. His more boyish romances do not appeal to all; but the reader may like to know that two novels with a strong legal flavour are *Guy Mannering* and *Redgauntlet*. Scott's best novel, *The Heart of Midlothian*, is also set against a legal background, and most of the main story is historically authentic. Students of Scots law will find instruction in *Sir Walter Scott and Scots Law*, by David Marshall (1932). R.L. Stevenson became qualified as a Scottish advocate, though he never practised. His unfinished *Weir of Hermiston* gives an arresting picture of a coarse and cruel Scottish judge, Lord Braxfield (in the story called Lord Hermiston).[12]

---

[7] *Bolton* v. *Bishop of Carlisle* (1793) 2 H.Bl. 260 at 263–264.
[8] See J.B. Atlay in Cornhill, October, 1907.
[9] 139 J.P.N. 572, 605.
[10] See 5 Can. Bar Rev. 500.
[11] (1931) 50 Law Notes 68.
[12] The number of novelists with legal connections is surprising, and it may be of interest to add a note on two others. Charles Reade was a

It is not only the lawyers, real or nominal, who have written novels with a legal angle. Trollope is best known for his descriptions of ecclesiastical life in the *Barchester* series; but lawyers will remember him for his account of their own profession in *Orley Farm*.[13] Emily Brontë's *Wuthering Heights* shows an accurate knowledge of the law of entails fifty years before her own time.[14] George Eliot's *Felix Holt* has an ambitious legal plot turning on a base fee—though the legal reader will want to know why the owner in possession of a base fee, with constant legal advice, did not take steps to bar the remainder.[15]

Modern novelists deserve a paragraph to themselves. Judge Gordon Clark wrote detective novels under the pseudonym of "Cyril Hare," and the plot of several of them turns on a point of law. Thus his *Tragedy at Law* involves an unobtrusive subsection (now repealed) of an Act of 1934; it is of interest for its detail of circuit life. *That Yew Tree's Shade* requires for the solution of the mystery a rule of law stated in Chapter 7 of the present book. *When the Wind Blows* is inspired by a bad old rule of the law of marriage. English law is steadily becoming more rational, and the rule in question was abolished in 1960. All these novels were reprinted as Penguins. Another former county court judge, H.C. Leon, wrote under the pen-name of "Henry Cecil." My own favourite is his first book *Full Circle*; but he wrote many other

---

barrister and read in chambers (though he never practised); but although he wrote novels bearing upon the law they are disappointing. His only worthwhile novel *(The Cloister and the Hearth)* is non-legal. Wilkie Collins, another nominal barrister, is notable as one of the forerunners of the modern detective novelists. His novel *No Name* (reprinted in 1980) has a plot depending in part on rules of law: see Sladen in 77 Law Society's Gazette 1123.

[13] Those who wish to pursue the legal errors (which do not spoil the tale) will find them unsparingly attacked by Sir Francis Newbolt, K.C., in (1924) 95 Nineteenth Century 227, reprinted in his *Out of Court* (1925). Trollope's views on the ethics of advocacy are discussed in E.B.V. Christian's *Leaves of the Lower Branch* (1909), 65–66. See also Henry S. Drinker, *The Lawyers of Anthony Trollope*; Hugh Cockerall in 127 N.L.J. 1252.

[14] See C. P.S[anger], *The Structure of Wuthering Heights* (Hogarth Essays, 1926).

[15] Earlier, Jane Austin had got into trouble on a similar point in *Pride and Prejudice*. See 124 N.L.J. 375, 466.

humorous best-sellers about judges and lawyers. Lawyers currently writing detective novels include Michael Gilbert and Michael Underwood.

From the many biographies of lawyers one should perhaps put first the lives of two great reformers: C.H.S. Fifoot's *Lord Mansfield* (1936) and Mary L. Mack's *Jeremy Bentham* (Vol. 1, 1962). The achievement of Sir Samuel Romilly can best be read in Sir Leon Radzinowicz's monumental *History of English Criminal Law*, Vol. 1, Part V. Romilly and Bentham figure, with Beccaria, in Coleman Phillipson's *Three Criminal Law Reformers* (1923). Mention may also be made of Lord Birkenhead's *Fourteen English Judges* (1926), and Catherine Drinker Bowen's biography of Coke C.J. called *The Lion and the Throne*.

The interest in these works is largely historical, and many readers will be more attracted by biographies of successful lawyers living nearer to our own time. The apex of success is traditionally the Woolsack, and the careers of those who have reached it are given by R.F.V. Heuston in scholarly detail in his *Lives of the Lord Chancellors, 1885–1940* (1964). However, the way lawyers function is of more importance than their biographical details, and a fascinating insight into the House of Lords in action is given by Robert Stevens in his *Law and Politics: The House of Lords as a Judicial Body 1800-1976* (1979). Edward Marjoribanks's *Life of Sir Edward Marshall Hall* (1929)[16] may be recommended for its portrayal of the last of the flamboyant advocates, and the same writer's *Life of Lord Carson* (1932) is fit to take its place among the best modern biography.[17] Derek Walker-Smith's *Lord Reading and his Cases* (1934) and H. Montgomery Hyde's *Norman Birkett* (1964) are also worth reading.

There is a plethora of autobiography. The late Lord Justice

---

[16] Reprinted in condensed form by Pelican Books.

[17] The author had written the first of what were intended to be two volumes when he died, and his work was then published. It was later completed in a further two volumes by I. Colvin; but those who have only Marjoribanks's volume will find that it gives a satisfying account in itself.

MacKinnon, in his book *On Circuit* (1940), said that most books of legal reminiscence are bad; and he named only two exceptions, in which I hesitate to follow him.[18] My own list of the best legal autobiographies would include one by a successful advocate of the last century, one by a judge who made his name on the criminal side, and one by a country solicitor. The first of these is *Some Experiences of a Barrister's Life*, by William Ballantine (1882)—better known as Serjeant Ballantine's *Experiences*. Its gossipy pages are crowded with Victorian personalities who are still alive to students of the law reports. Ballantine was retained on behalf of Orton, the false claimant in the Tichborne case, and his book gives shrewd advice on advocacy. Two generations on comes Sir Travers Humphreys (Humphreys J.), *Criminal Days* (1946). This is an autobiography full of good stories, with reflections upon the criminal law. Reginald Hine's *Confessions of an Un-Common Attorney* (1945) is a revelation of the interest that can be won from life by a country solicitor who observes his fellow creatures and is an antiquarian and *littérateur* to boot. Lord Denning's *The Family Story* (1981) is the personal testament of our best-known, most popular, most idiosyncratic, oldest, most energetic, and in some ways most reform-minded judge. Not one of these is a "must" book, though each is good in its own class.

Finally, it is convenient to mention here the remarkable *Pollock-Holmes Letters* (2 vols., 1942), the correspondence of two men who became the *doyens* of English and American law, carried on over a period of 58 years. This may well be read with Mark deWolfe Howe's two-volume biography, *Justice Oliver Wendell Holmes* (1957, 1963).

TRIALS

The historian, the devotee of detective fiction, the student of advocacy, and the novelist in search of a plot, should not ignore the very full collection of trials that may be found in some

---

[18] The two exceptions made by MacKinnon L.J. were *Pie-Powder*, by "A Circuit Tramp" (J. Alderson Foote, K.C.) (1911), and *As I Went on My Way*, by Arthur J. Ashton, K.C. (1924). The former is little more than a collection of anecdotes (chiefly humorous), though the anecdotes have merit.

libraries. Cases of historical interest are reported at length in the 34 volumes of Howell's *State Trials*, such, for example, as Coke's virulent prosecution of Sir Walter Raleigh (vol. 2, p.1). A selection from these trials was published in three volumes by J.W. Willis-Bund. Other series are the Notable British Trials Series, the Famous Trials Series, and the Old Bailey Trials Series; all these give a full transcript of the cases, so that each step in the evidence can be studied. The series presently running is called Celebrated Trials. There are also occasional publications, such as *The Trial of Lady Chatterley (R. v. Penguin Books Ltd.)*, edited by C.H. Rolph (1961).

Perhaps the most remarkable of the nineteenth-century *causes célèbres* was that of *The Tichborne Claimant*; Douglas Woodruffe's book under that title is noteworthy. Illustrations of the technique of famous advocates are given in Edgar Lustgarten's *Defender's Triumph* (1951). There is also an inexpensive series of Famous Trials in Penguins, each volume containing condensed accounts of a number of trials.

As a matter of interest it may be recorded that R.L. Stevenson's *Kidnapped* is based in part on the famous Appin murder case—*R. v. Stewart* (1752) 19 Howell's State Trials 1. This is itself the subject of a study by Sir William MacArthur *(The Appin Murder*, 1960). The *Annesley Case*, retold in the Notable English Trials Series (a series that later became Notable British Trials), supplied material for parts of three novels.[19] Another novelist who use these Trials was Nathaniel Hawthorne.[20]

ESSAYS

It would be possible to compile an anthology of essays bearing upon the law, beginning with Bacon's essay "Of Judicature," and passing through Selden's *Table Talk*, Lamb's "Old Benchers

---

[19] Tobias Smollett's *Peregrine Pickle,* Chap. 98; Scott's *Guy Mannering* and Charles Reade's *The Wandering Heir*. See David Marshall, *Sir Walter Scott and Scots Law*, 48-57.

[20] See Alfred S. Reid, *The Yellow Ruff and the Scarlet Letter* (University of Florida Press, 1955).

of the Inner Temple,"[21] Bagehot's "Lord Brougham,"[22] Haz-
litt's portrait of Eldon,[23] and several by Maitland, to modern
examples such as John Buchan's "The Judicial Temperament"
(in his *Homilies and Recreations)*, Lord Justice MacKinnon's
Murder in the Temple (1935), Theo. Matthew's *For Lawyers and
Others* (1937), and Lord Macmillan's *Law and Other Things*
(1937). (John Buchan, be it noted, started at the Bar and wrote a
book on the taxation of foreign income). Some of the best legal
essays are to be found in no other place than the law reports, in
the judgments of such men as Mansfield, Bowen, Macnaghten
and Sumner. The speech of Lord Macnaghten in *Gluckstein* v.
Barnes [1900] A.C. at 255 is a brilliant example of pungent wit,
which was thought worthy of inclusion in the *Oxford Book of
English Prose;* and Atkin L.J.'s judgment in *Balfour* v. *Balfour*
[1919] 2 K.B. 571 also deserves honourable mention. Mr Louis
Blom-Cooper has published his own selections of best legal
writing under the titles *The Law as Literature* (1961) and *The
Language of the Law* (1965).

HUMOUR

Collections of anecdotes are usually poor things, but exceptions
are Sir Robert Megarry's *Miscellany-at-Law* (1955), and *A
Second Miscellany-at-Law* (1973), both including many speci-
mens of judicial wit and wisdom. The best book of humorous
reminiscence comes from Ireland: it is Maurice Healey's *The Old
Munster Circuit* (1939). W.S. Gilbert's libretto to *Trial by Jury* is
a joy to read: but then, Gilbert was by training a lawyer! The
Complete Forensic Fables by "O" (Theo. Matthew) is well
known. Sir Alan Herbert's even more famous *Misleading Cases*
are collected together under the title *Uncommon Law* (1935)
with its sequels *Codd's Last Case* (1952) and *Bardot, M.P.?*

---

[21] Included among the *Essays of Elia* and republished with notes by
    MacKinnon L.J. in a limited edition (1927), and again in the same
    writer's *Inner Temple Papers* (1948).
[22] Republished in *Collected Works*, ed. N. St. John-Stevas (London,
    1968) iii, 159.
[23] Included in his essays entitled *The Spirit of the Age*, first printed in
    1825.

HISTORY

Legal histories are generally outside the scope of this chapter, but three are so clearly entitled to rank as literature that mention may be made of them. They are Maine's *Ancient Law* (which should be read in Pollock's edition), Maitland's *Constitutional History*, and Holmes's *The Common Law*. E.S. Turner, *Roads to Ruin* (Pelican Books, 1966) is an entertaining history of the lamentations that greeted attempts to pass obvious reforms.

Lawyers and the Courts, by Brian Abel-Smith and Robert Stevens (1967), covers the engrossing history of the legal profession to the year 1965, omitting none of our blemishes and indeed giving a general picture of selfishness, chicanery and corruption. This and its companion volume, *In Search of Justice* (1968), should diminish our professional self-esteem. But the last work should not be read without the counterblast from E.J. Cohn in his review in (1969) 32 M.L.R. 336.

THE CONSTITUTION

Every lawyer will take delight in Sir Alan Herbert's *The Ayes Have It* (1937)—an account of the passage of the Matrimonial Causes Act—and *The Point of Parliament* (1946). If you feel that your knowledge of the working of government is deficient, read S.A. de Smith's vastly informative book, *Constitutional and Administrative Law*, which is available in paperback.

Sir Geoffrey Vickers's *The Art of Judgment* (University Paperbacks) is a classic on policy-making not only in government but in industry.

JURISPRUDENCE, LOGIC, PHILOSOPHY AND ECONOMICS

Selection becomes more difficult when one turns to the theoretical treatment of the law. Much has been written on this, but not of a character to appeal to the general reader. A simple and readable account of juridical thinking is Lon L. Fuller's *Anatomy of the Law* (Pelican). Judge Jerome Frank's *Law and the Modern Mind* (reprinted 1951) is a pungent and provocative book, with which may be coupled Thurman Arnold's *The Folklore of Capitalism* (1937). A classic by a great American judge is Cardozo's *Nature of the Judicial Process* (1921).[24] All four of these books are American. Sir Carleton Allen's *Law in the Making* and Julius Stone's *Legal System and Lawyers' Reasonings* are heavier going, but every lawyer should read them.

From time to time judges and even Law Lords tell us that logic is not compulsive in legal reasoning. In this they merely betray a lack of understanding of what logic is. A good simple account is Anthony Flew's *Thinking about Thinking* (Fontana 1975). Other popular expositions of practical logic are R.H. Thouless's *Straight and Crooked Thinking* (1930, later published in paperback) and E.R. Emmet's *The Use of Reason* (1960), Chapter 9.

Nineteenth-century Liberalism and economic *laissez-faire* have moulded the outlook of lawyers more than they themselves realise. In their application to constitutional law the classic is, of course, Dicey's *Law of the Constitution* (10th ed. by E.C.S. Wade, 1961); on the wider aspects there is the same writer's *Law and Opinion in England during the Nineteenth Century* (reissued as a paperback in 1962). A continuation volume, *Law and Opinion in England in the 20th Century,* was produced by a group effort under the editorship of Morris Ginsberg in 1959. It has become the fashion to decry Dicey's Rule of Law as well as Adam Smith's economics: before finally subscribing to the current opinion the student should read Professor Hayek's defence of these doctrines in his book *The Constitution of Liberty* (1960), followed by his important trilogy on *Law, Legislation and Liberty* (1973–). This is an attack upon Socialism, written by a distinguished economist but employing chiefly political arguments which all can understand, whether they agree with them or not. Lord Robbins's powerful dissent from Hayek can be read in his *Politics and Economics* (1963). We must not leave the philosophy of Liberalism without mentioning J.S. Mill's famous essay "On Liberty."[25] This is not only a classic but

---

[24] Now available in a collected edition including other works of the author: *Selected Writings of Benjamin Nathan Cardozo*, ed. Margaret E. Hall (New York, 1947).

[25] Reprinted in Fontana Philosophy Classics (paperback) together with the same writer's "Utilitarianism" and "Essay on Bentham," ed. by Mary Warnock.

one that can still be read with keen enjoyment. H.L.A. Hart's *Law, Liberty and Morality* is in the same tradition.

If you are going to practise at the Bar or as a solicitor you must be able to understand a balance-sheet. *How to Read a Balance Sheet* (I.L.O., Geneva, 1966) is a programmed book; you learn by answering questions.

CRIMINOLOGY AND PENOLOGY

All those concerned with the administration of the criminal law should make some effort to keep abreast of the work done by criminologists and penologists. Such knowledge is needed not only by the judge or magistrate in the interests of society but by the defending advocate in the interests of his client. When the defendant has pleaded or has been found guilty the question of punishment or treatment arises, and with the width of choice now open it is most important for the defendant that his advocate should know the possibilities and be able to make proper representations on his behalf. Further, it may be said to be the professional duty of every lawyer to educate himself in these topics in order that he may help to spread enlightenment among the lay community.

Nigel Walker's *Punishment, Danger and Stigma* (1980) discusses the theoretical background to sentencing. If someone propounds the half-truth that punishment does not deter, Chapter 4 of this book will enable you to answer him effectively. Problems of sentencing are discussed in the same author's *Sentencing in a Rational Society* (Pelican, 1972), and Sir Rupert Cross's *The English Sentencing System* (2nd ed. by Andrew Ashworth).

INDEX